W. Howard Russell

Canada ; Its Defenses, Condition, and Resources

W. Howard Russell

Canada ; Its Defenses, Condition, and Resources

ISBN/EAN: 9783337120290

Printed in Europe, USA, Canada, Australia, Japan

Cover: Foto ©Suzi / pixelio.de

More available books at **www.hansebooks.com**

CANADA;

ITS DEFENCES, CONDITION, AND RESOURCES.

BEING

A THIRD AND CONCLUDING VOLUME OF "MY DIARY, NORTH AND SOUTH."

BY

W. HOWARD RUSSELL, LL.D.,

LONDON:
BRADBURY AND EVANS, 11, BOUVERIE STREET.
1865.
[*The Right of Translation is reserved.*]

PREFACE.

I BEGAN to write this book by way of sequel to "My Diary North and South," with the intention of describing Canada as I saw it at the close of my visit to North America, but the subject grew upon me as I went on, and at last I discarded much personal detail, and set to work with the view of calling attention to the capabilities of the vast regions belonging to the British Crown on the American Continent, and of pointing out the magnificent heritage which is open to our redundant population. But the subject was too great for the compass of one volume, because connected with it, too intimately to be over-looked, were the questions of the defence and of the future of countries, which the establishment of a Monarchical principle on an imperfect basis, and their dependence on the Crown, exposed to the hostility of a great Republic. I was, therefore, obliged to contract my own experiences, small as they were, and to omit many topics included in the original scope of my writing. The book was nearly finished when suddenly, as it seemed, the whole of the Provinces, yielding to a common sentiment of danger, sent their delegates to consider the policy and possibility of a great Confederation, which had been strongly recommended in the pages already written. The idea of such a Confederation was an old one; but the prompt resolve to carry it into practical effect, and the words spoken and acts done in consequence, rendered it necessary to cancel the work of many hours, as much of what I had written would have been anticipated by what has been printed. There are many dangers inherent in the nature of the proposed Confederation: there are many obstacles to its harmonious and successful working; but on the whole some such scheme appears to be the only practical mode of saving the British Provinces from the aggression of the North American Republicans.

What is to become of the existing Governments of Provinces? How regulate the contentions which may arise between Provincial Parliaments and Provincial Ministers and Provincial Governors by the action of the Federal Parliament and of the representative of the Crown at the seat of Government? The difficulties we foresee may never come to pass, and others far greater, of which we have no foresight, may arise; but for all this the Confederation presents the only means now available, as far as we can perceive, for securing to the Provinces present independence and a future political life distinct from the turbulent existence of the United States. A glance at the map will reveal the extent of the Empire which rests upon the Lakes with one arm on the Atlantic and the other on the Pacific, whilst its face is wrapped in a mantle of eternal snow; but it tells us no more. No reasoning man can maintain that the people whom a few years will behold as numerous as the inhabitants of these islands, will be content to live permanently under the system of the Colonial Office. That system is probably the only one our Constitution permits us to adopt; but it is nevertheless the policy, if not the duty, of this State to foster the youth and early life of the colonies we have founded, and to protect them, as far as may be, from the evils which shall come upon them in consequence of their present connection with Great Britain. Despised, neglected, and abandoned, the Provinces would feel less irritation against their conquerors than against their betrayers, and England might regret with unavailing sorrow the indifference which left her without a foot of land or a friend in the New World. Generosity not inconsistent with justice may yet lay the foundations of an enduring alliance where once there was only cold fealty and unsympathising command. A powerful State may arise whose greatest citizens shall be proud to receive such honours as the Monarch of England can bestow, whose people shall vie with us in the friendly contests of commerce, and stand side by side with us in battle. And when the inevitable hour of separation comes, the parting will not then be in anger. A Constitutional Republic, in which Monarchy would have been possible but for the prudence of the mother-country, may exist without any hatred of Monarchy or of England; and the people, born with equal rights to pursue liberty and happiness, would love the land from which flowed the sources of so many substantial blessings.

I hope that my apprehensions may prove ill-founded, and that the dangers to which our North American possessions now, and England herself and the peace of the world hereafter, are in my opinion exposed, may be for ever averted.

WILLIAM HOWARD RUSSELL.

TEMPLE, *January*, 1865.

CONTENTS.

CHAPTER I.

Introductory—Canada and the Mason and Slidell case—Threats of annexation—Defence of Canada—Reasons for visiting the British Provinces—Illness at New York—Hostility displayed there—Monotony of New York—Hotel life—"Birds of a feather"—Nationality absorbed—Start for Canada—Railway Companions—Public credulity—A victory in the papers—History of "A Big Fight"—General Pumpkin and Jefferson Brick 1

CHAPTER II.

To the Station—Stars and Stripes—Crowd at Station—Train impeded by Snow—Classic ground—"Manhattan"—"Yonkers"—Fellow-travellers and their ways—"Beauties of the Hudson"—West Point : their education, &c.—Large Towns on the banks of the Hudson—Arrive at East Albany—Delavan House—Beds at a premium—Aspect of Albany not impressive—Sights—The Legislature 17

CHAPTER III.

Unpleasant journey to Niagara—Mr. Seward—The Union and its dangers—Pass Buffalo—Arrival at Niagara—A "Touter"—Bad weather—The Road—Climate compared—Desolate appearance of houses—The St. Lawrence viewed from above—One hundred years ago—Canada the great object of the Americans—The Welland Canal—Effect of the Falls from a distance—Gradual approach—Less volume of water in winter—Different effect and dangers in winter—Icicles—Behind the Cataract—Photographs and Bazaar—Visit the "Lions" generally—Brock—American and Canadian sides contrasted—Goat Island—A whisper heard—Mills and Manufactories 28

CHAPTER IV.

Leave Niagara—Suspension Bridge—In British territory—Hamilton City—Buildings—Proceed eastward—Toronto—Dine at Mess—Pay visits—Public edifices—Sleighs—Amusement of the boys—*Camaraderie* in the army—Kindly feeling displayed—Journey resumed towards Quebec—Intense cold—Snow landscape—Morning in the train—Hunger and lesser troubles—Kingston, its rise and military position—Harbour, dockyards—Its connection with the Prince of Wales' Tour—The Upper St. Lawrence—Canada as to Defence 53

CHAPTER V.

Arrive at Cornwall—The St. Lawrence—Gossip on India—Aspect of the country—Montreal—The St. Lawrence Hall Hotel—Story of a Guardsman—Burnside—Dinner—Refuse a banquet—Flags—Climate—*Salon-à-manger*—Contrast of Americans and English—Sleighs—The "Driving Club"—The Victoria Bridge—Uneasy feeling—Monument to Irish emigrants—Irish character—Montreal and New York—The Rink—Sir F. Williams—Influence of the Northerners 71

CHAPTER VI.

Visit the "lions" of Montreal—The 47th Regiment—The city open to attack—Quays, public buildings—French colonisation—Rise of Montreal—Stone—A French-Anglicised city—Loyalty of Canadians—Arrival of Troops—Facings—British and American Army compared—Experience needed by latter—Slavery 87

CHAPTER VII.

First view of Quebec—Passage of the St. Lawrence—Novel and rather alarming situation—Russell's Hotel—The Falls of Montmorency, and the "Cone"—Aspect of the city—The Point—"Tarbogginiag"

CONTENTS. xi

PAGE

Description of the "Cone"—Audacity of one of my companions
—A Canadian dinner—Call on the Governor—Visit the Citadel—
Its position—Capabilities for defence—View from parapet—The
armoury—Old muskets—Red-tape thoughtfulness—French and
English occupation of Quebec—Strength of Quebec . . . 100

CHAPTER VIII.

Lower Canada and Ancient France—Soldiers in Garrison at Quebec—
Canadian Volunteers—The Governor-General Viscount Monck—
Uniform in the United States—A Sleighing Party—Dinner and
Calico Ball 121

CHAPTER IX.

Canadian view of the American Struggle—English Officers in the
States—My own position in the States and in Canada—The Ursulines in Quebec—General Montcalm—French Canadians—Imperial
honours—Celts and Saxons—Salmon fishing—Early Government of
Canada—Past and future 128

CHAPTER X.

Canadian Hospitality—Muffins—Departure for the States—Desertions
—Montreal again—Southerners in Montreal—Drill and Snow Shoes
—Winter Campaigning—Snow Drifts—Military Discontent . . 148

CHAPTER XI.

Extent of Canada—The Lakes—Canadian Wealth—Early History—
La Salle—Border Conflicts—Early Expeditions—Invasions from
New England—Louisburgh and Ticonderoga—The Colonial In-
surrection—Partition of Canada—Progress of Upper Canada—
France and Canada—The American Invasion—Winter Campaign—
New Orleans and Plattsburgh—Peace of Ghent—Political Con-
troversies—Winter Communication—Sentiments of Hon. Joseph
Howe—General view of Imperial and Colonial relations . . 158

CHAPTER XII.

The Militia—American Intentions—Instability of the Volunteer Principle—The Drilling of Militia—The Commission of 1862—The Duke
of Newcastle's Views—Militia Schemes—Volunteer Force—Apathy
of the French Canadians—The first Summons 200

CONTENTS.

CHAPTER XIII.

Possible dangers—The future danger—Open to attack—Canals and railways—Probable lines of invasion—Lines of attack and defence—London—Toronto—Defences of Kingston—Defences of Quebec . 222

CHAPTER XIV.

Rapid Increase of Population—Mineral Wealth—Cereals—Imports and Exports—Climate—Agriculture—A Settler's Life—Reciprocity Treaty—Report of the Committee of the Executive Council—Mr. Galt—Senator Douglas—A Zollverein—Terms of the Convention—Free Trade, and what is meant by it—Mr. Galt's opinion on the subject—Canadian Imports and Exports 241

CHAPTER XV.

Reciprocal Rights—American ideas of Reciprocity—The Ad Valorem System—Commercial Improvements—Trade with America—The Ottawa Route—The Saskatchewan—Fertility of the country—Water communication—The Maritime Provinces—Area and Population . 259

CHAPTER XVI.

The "Ashburton Capitulation"—Boundaries of Quebec—Arbitration in 1831—Lord Ashburton's Mission—The questions in dispute—"The Sea" v. "The Atlantic"—American Diplomatists—Franklin's Red Line—Compromise—The Maps—Maine—Damage to Canada—Mr. Webster's Defence—His Opinion of the Road—Value of the Heights—Our Share of Equivalents—Strategic value of Rouse's Point—Mr. Webster on the Invasion of Canada—Vermont—New Hampshire 283

CHAPTER XVII.

The Acadian Confederation—Union is Strength—The Provinces—New Brunswick—The Temperature—Trade of St. John—Climate and agriculture of Nova Scotia—Newfoundland—Prince Edward Island—The Red River District—Assiniboia—The Red River Valley—Minnesota and the West—The Hudson's Bay Company—Their Territory—The North-West Regions—Climate of Winnipeg Basin—The area of Winnipeg Basin—Finances of the Confederation—Imports, exports, and tonnage—Proposed Federal Constitution—Lessons from the American struggle 310

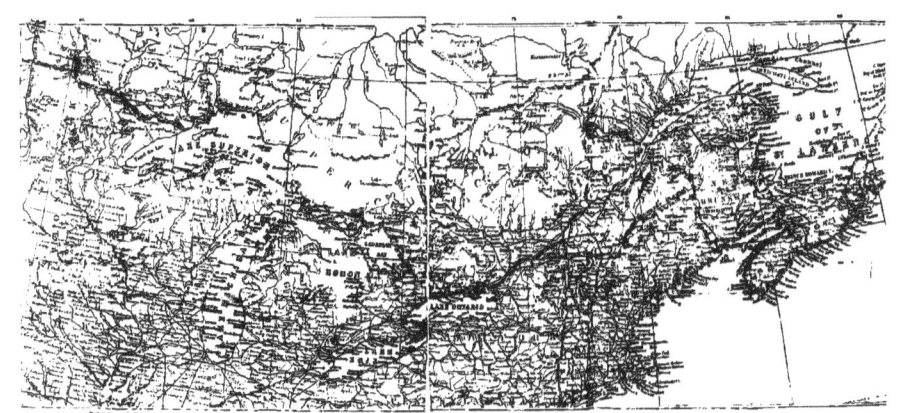

CANADA:
ITS DEFENCES, CONDITION, AND RESOURCES.

CHAPTER I.

Introductory—Canada and the Mason and Slidell case—Threats of annexation—Defence of Canada—Reasons for visiting the British Provinces—Illness at New York—Hostility displayed there—Monotony of New York—Hotel life—"Birds of a feather"—Nationality absorbed—Start for Canada—Railway Companions—Public credulity—A victory in the papers—History of "A Big Fight"—General Pumpkin and Jefferson Brick.

I DO not pretend to offer any new observations on the climate, soil, or capabilities of Canada, nor can I venture to call these pages a "work" on that great province. I have nothing novel to advance in the hope of attracting an immigration to its widespread territories, and any statistical facts and figures I may use are accessible to all interested in the commerce or in the past, present, and future of the land.

Nor do I write with any particular theory in view, or with any crotchet on the subject of colonies, outlying provinces, and dependencies, and their value or detriment to the dominant commercial and imperial power.

My actual acquaintance with the country and the people is only such as I acquired in a few weeks' travelling in the depth of winter; and such sort of knowledge as I gathered would certainly afford no great excuse in itself for intruding my remarks or opinions on the public when so many excellent books on Canada already exist.

But it happened that my visit took place at a very remarkable period of Canadian and American history, and at a time, too, when certain doctrines, broached not for the first time, but urged with more than usual ability, as to the relations between what for convenience I call the mother-country and her colonies, were exciting great attention across the Atlantic.

When I left Washington in the winter, a great crisis had been peacefully but not willingly averted by a concession on the part of the Federal Government to what the sentiment of the American people considered an exhibition of brute force. The first year of the war had closed over the Federals in gloom. Their arms were not wielded with credit at home—if credit ever can attach to arms wielded in a civil war—and the foreign power which it had been their wont to treat with something as near akin to disrespect as diplomatic decency would permit, aroused by an act which outraged the laws of nations and provoked the censure of every European power with business on the waters,. had made preparations which could only imply that she would have recourse to hostility if her demands for satisfaction were refused.

It was under these circumstances that England obtained the reparation for which she sought, and in the eyes of Americans filched a triumph over their flag and took an insolent advantage over their weakened power "to do as they pleased." General McClellan, playing the part of Fabius, perhaps because he knew not how to play any other part, had fallen sick and was nigh at death's door in the malarious winter at Washington. The great Union army, like a hybernating eel in the mud, lay motionless, between the Potomac and the clever imposture of the Confederate lines and wooden batteries at Manassas.

But haughty and hopeful as ever, in tone if not in heart, the Americans raved about vengeance for their own just concessions. They boasted that the seizure of Canada would be one of the measures of retaliation to which they intended promptly to resort, as the indemnity to their injured vanity and as compensation for the surrender of Messrs. Mason and Slidell.

Meanwhile the small force of British troops stationed in Canada was reinforced by the speedy dispatch of some picked regiments from England, which did not raise it much beyond its regular strength, and tardy steps were taken to organise an efficient militia in the province. The volunteer movement had extended its influence across the ocean, and a commendable activity all over the British Colonies and Canada falsified the complacent statements of the American papers that the people were not loyal to the Crown nor careful of the connection, which, it was alleged, they would gladly substitute for the protection of the standard of the Northern Republic.

All these necessary precautions against the consequences of the refusal of the American Government to yield the passengers taken from under our flag, were watched angrily and jealously in the States. The British reinforcements were ridiculed; their tedious passages, their cheerless marches, were jeeringly chronicled.

Whole ships were reported to have gone down with living cargoes. Those who landed were represented as being borne on sleighs by sufferance routes, which would be impracticable in war. The Canadians were abused—and so were the Provincialists. The volunteers were assailed with the weapons which the American press knows so well how to use.

But that was false policy. It gave a stimulus to the loyal feeling of the subjects of the Crown. The Canadian press retorted, and, exulting in the triumph of the Home Government over the Republican Administration, uttered the taunts which Americans least brook to hear.

It was assumed that the task of vengeance and conquest would be light. I received letters in which it was maintained that Canada could not be defended, and that she was not worth defending; others merely urged that if the Canadians would not take a prominent part in aid of imperial measures for their protection, they must be handed over to the invading Americans; that their country cost more than it was worth, and that it was a mistake to keep any connection with the wrong side of the ledger, no matter what the results of rupturing it might be.

Americans told me "General Scott declares the Canadian frontier is not capable of defence." True, Americans had told me some months ago that General Scott, now *mis en retraite* in New York, after a hasty return from Europe—not, as was asserted, with diplomatic authority or with the view of invading Canada, but to save his pension in case of foreign war—would be in Richmond about July 22nd or 24th, 1861. I heard some views of the same kind from our own officers, who expressed doubts respecting the possibility of a successful resistance to American invasion.

Now if that were so, it struck me that the troops we had in the country could prove but of little use, and that at the same time the relative condition of strength between the United States and Great Britain had undergone a vital change in face of the very agencies which ought to have established more solidly the results obtained in the last trial of force and resources between them on Canadian ground. It was worth while trying to ascertain the truth and to resolve these questions.

The United States, dreading a foreign war which might interfere with their invasion of the Southern States, had ungraciously made a concession, in revenge for making which their press declared they would on the first convenient occasion make war on the Power they had offended, in a country which they had invaded with all their united power—when Great Britain, steamless and remote, was engaged in European conflicts and destitute of maritime allies—only to meet with defeat, or with success of a nature to prove their incompetency to conquer.

Was the power of this distracted republic, contending furiously with rebellious members, then, become so great? If so, with what motive was Great Britain hurrying across the sea the élite of her troops—too few to save these vast domains, too many to lose, and far too many to return as paroled prisoners? Why try to defend on such terms what was worthless and indefensible? Canada, if not susceptible of defence, would be certainly unsuitable as a base for offensive operations against the States. Obviously the matter stood thus: that the military question depended on the temper and spirit of the people themselves.

The whole force of the Canadians, sustained by Great Britain, might, apparently, defy all the offensive power of the United States; and I desired to ascertain in what condition were their temper and defences.

At this time British officers were endeavouring to prepare the possessions of the Crown against threatened invasion. The Americans on their side were busy fortifying some important points on the lakes.

General Totten, an officer of the United States Engineers, well known for his ability, was understood to be engaged on a very elaborate plan of works along the frontier. Colonel Gordon, whose name will be for ever associated with the left attack at the siege of Sebastopol, aided by an experienced staff, was employed on our side, studying the capabilities of the frontier, and maturing a plan for the consideration of the Government in case of an American war.

There were reasons, too, of a personal character for my visiting Canada. I had a fever, which was contracted at Washington and laid me prostrate at New York. It was of the low typhoid type, which proved fatal to so many in the Federal army at the same time, and its effects made me weaker for the time than I ever remember to have been. There was no promise whatever of military operations, and I read every day of the arrival of friends and acquaintances in Canada, whose faces it would be pleasant to see, after the endurance of so many hostile glances and such public exhibition of illw-ill.

I do not wish to dwell on private annoyances, but as an instance of the feeling displayed towards me in New

York I may mention one circumstance. On my arrival in 1861 I was elected an honorary member of the club which derives its name from the state or city, and was indebted to its members for many acts of courtesy and for more than one entertainment. Returning to the city from Washington early this year, I was invited to dine at the same club by one or two of my friends. Certain members, as I afterwards heard, took umbrage at my presence, and fastened a quarrel on my entertainers. A day or two subsequently the people of New York were called on, by the notorious journalist who had honoured me with his animosity ever since I refused the dishonour of his acquaintance, to express their indignation at the conduct of the club; and the members received a characteristic reprimand for their presumption in letting me into the club, from which they had kept their censor and his clientelle carefully out. My offence was rank; and public opinion—or what is called so—perhaps was in favour of the ostracism at that moment; for, as far as I know, the people must have believed I was the sole cause of the Federal defeat and flight at Bull Run.

There was some novelty in the idea of starting for Canada in the midst of the bitter winter wind and the dazzling snow; but I would have gone to Nova Zembla at the time to have escaped the monotony of New York, which the effects of recent illness rendered more irksome.

New York is among cities, what one of the lower order of molluscous animals, with a single intestinal canal, is to a creature of a higher development, with various organs, and full of veins and arteries. Up and down the Broadway passes the stream of life to and from the heart in Wall-street. In the narrow space from water to water on either side of this dry canal there is comparatively little animation, and nothing at all to reward the researches of a stranger.

Johnson's remark about Fleet-street would apply with truth to the gawky thoroughfare of the Atlantic Tyre. In the Broadway or its "west-end" extensions are to be found all the hotels, which are the ganglia of the feverish nervous system so incessantly agitated by the operations of the journalistic insects living in secret cysts nigh at hand. All day the great tideway is rolling in, headed by a noisy crest of little boys, with extras under their arms, and heralded by a confused surfy murmur of voices telling "lies" for cents, and enunciating "Another Great Union Victory!" in one great bore; or it is rushing out again with a dismal leaden current, laden with doubts and fears, as the news of some disaster breaks through the locks of government reservoirs and floods the press.

In my hotel, where I was fain to seclude myself in my illness, and to follow the very un-American practice of living in a suite of private rooms, there was but little conflict of opinion on any great event, real or fictitious, which turned up from day to day. The guests and visitors were well-nigh all of one way of thinking. They were of the old conservative party, so oddly denominated Democrats, who believed in States Rights: in the right of states to create and maintain their domestic institutions—to secede, if they pleased, from the Union—to resist the attempts of the General Government of the other states to coerce them by force of arms.

Some of these gentlemen were satisfied the South

would not be coerced; some hoped the South would resist successfully. None, I fear, were "loyal" to President Lincoln and Mr. Seward, and I am sure none would have said so much for either of them or their friends as I would.

The majority principle forces people who hold similar views to meet together, and to select the same hotels to live in. This is unfortunate for a stranger who desires to hear the views of both sides. In the New York, from the highly artistic and skilful operator who flashed out cocktails at the bar, up to the highest authority, there was no man who would like to say that he was on good terms with Mr. Sumner, or that he did not think Mr. Seward the representative of evil principles. The rule was proved by the exceptions: two I suspect there were—stout Irish waiters, who did not approve of the attempts to destroy "our glorious Union," but who did not find the atmosphere of the place quite favourable to the free expression of the opinion they mildly hinted at to myself.

The sameness of ideas, of expressions, of faces, became unbearable. I could tell quite well by the look of men's faces what news they had heard, and what they were saying or going to say about it. Here were crafty politicals and practical men of business, and persons of a philosophical and reflective temperament, as well as the foolish, the mere pleasure-hunters, and the unthinking mass of an hotel world, all looking forward to a near to-morrow to end the woes of the state, always waiting for a "decisive" battle or "an indignant uprising of the people" to drive the Republicans out of power and office.

Not one of them could or would see that the contest,

when terminated, would give birth to others—that the vast bodies of diverse interests, prejudices, hatreds, and wrongs set in motion by war over so enormous a surface, where they had been kept suspended and inert by the powers of compromise, could never be reconsolidated and restored to the same state as before, and that it would be the work of time, the labour of many years, ere they could settle to rest in any shape whatever.

I am told respectable Americans do not use the word "Britisher," but I am bound to say I heard Americans who looked very respectable using the word at the time of which I speak, when there was still irritation on both sides in consequence of the surrender of Mason and Slidell—in the minds of the friends of the South, because they were balked in their anticipation of a foreign war; in the Federal mind, because, after much threatening and menaces, they had seen the captives surrendered to the British by the President, or, more properly speaking, by Mr. Seward.

Hence it was, perhaps, that Canada was always mentioned in such a tone of contempt, as though the speakers sought to relieve their feelings by abuse of a British dependency.

"Goin' to Canada!" exclaimed the faithful Milesian who had been my attendant—in fact, my substitute for a nurse. "Lord help us! *That's* a poor place, anyhow. I thought you'd be contint wid the snow we've got here. It's plinty, anyhow. But Canada!" The man had never been there in his life, but he spoke as if it were beyond the bounds of civilisation. He had served in a British regiment for many years; many of his brothers had been, I think he told me, in the service, but now they were all in the States, and to his notion thriving like himself.

In no country on earth is an old nationality so soon absorbed as in America. I am inclined to think the regard professed for England by American literary men is sentimental, and is produced by education and study rather than by any feeling transmitted in families or by society.

The emigrant, it is remarked, speedily forgets—in the hurry of his new life the ways of the old slip out of his memory. One day I said to my man, as a regiment of volunteers was marching down Broadway, "Those fellows are not quite as well set up as the 41st, Pat." "Well, indeed, and that's thrue; but they'd fight as well I b'lieve, and better maybe, if they'd the officers, poor craychures! Anyhow," continued he with great gravity, "they can't be flogged for nothin' or for anything." "Were you ever flogged?" "No, sirir—not a lash ever touched my back, but I've known fine sogers spiled by it." It is likely enough that he had never thought on the subject till he came to the States—a short time before and he would have resented deeply the idea that any regiment on earth could stand before Her Majesty's 41st.

It was now near the end of January, and as a gleam of fine weather might thaw the glorious Union army of the Potomac, and induce them to advance on the inglorious army of the Confederacy, I resolved to make the best of my way northwards forthwith.

My companions were a young British officer, distinguished in the Crimea, in India, and in China, who represented a borough in Parliament, and had come out to see the great contest which was raging in the United States; and an English gentleman, who happened to be at New York, and was anxious to have a look at Niagara, even in its winter dress.

On the 27th January we were all packed to start by the 5.30 P.M. train by Albany to Niagara, and thence to Toronto. The landlord made me up a small assortment of provisions, as in snow-time trains are not always certain of anything but irregularity. I was regarded as one who was about to make myself needlessly miserable when he might continue in much happiness. "You had better stay, sir, for a few days. I have certain intelligence, let me whisper you, that the Abolitionists will be whipped at the end of this week, and old Abe driven out of Washington."

The little boys still shout out, "Another great Union victory." The last, by-the-bye, was of General Thomas, at Somerset, which has gradually sublimed into uncertainty, though he handled his men well, and is not bad at a despatch.

The credulity of the American mind is beyond belief. *Populus vult decipi*—and certainly its wishes are complied with to the fullest extent. The process of a Union victory, from its birth in the first telegram down to its dissolution in the last despatch, is curious enough.

Out comes an extra of the *New York Herald*— "Glorious Union Victory off Little Bear Creek, Mo.! —Five Thousand Rebels Disposed of!—Grand Skedaddle!—General Pumpkin's Brilliant Charge!—He Out-Murats Murat!—Sanguinary Encounters!—Cassius Mudd's Invincibles!—Doom of the Confederacy!—Jeff Davis gone to Texas!" and so on, with a display of large type, in double-headed lines, and a profusion of notes of admiration.

There is excitement in the bar-rooms. The Democrats look down-hearted. The War Christians are jubilant. Fiery eyes devour the columns, which contain but an elaboration of the heading—swelled perhaps with a biographical sketch of Brigadier-General Cyrus Washington Pumpkin, "who was educated at West Point, where he graduated with Generals Beauregard and McDowell, and eventually subsided into pork-packing at Cincinnati, where he was captain of a fine company till the war broke out, when he tendered his sword," &c. Cassius Mudd's biography is of course reprinted for the twentieth time, and there is a list of the names of all the officers in the regiments near the presumed scene of action.

Then comes the action :—"An intelligent gentleman has just arrived at Chicago, and has seen Dr. Bray, to whom he has given full particulars of the fight. It was commenced by Lieutenant Epaminondas Bellows ("son of our respected fellow-citizen, the President of the Bellowstown and Bellona Railway"—here follows a biography of Bellows), who was out scouting with ten more of our boys when they fell into an ambuscade, which opened on them with masked batteries, uttering unearthly yells. With Spartan courage the little band returned the fire, and kept the Seceshers, who were at least 500 strong, at bay till their ammunition was exhausted. Bellows, his form dilated with patriotism, his mellow tones ringing above the storm of battle, was urged to fly by a tempter, whose name we suppress. The heroic youth struck the cowardly traitor to the earth, and indignantly invited the enemy to come on.

They did so at last. The lieutenant, resisting desperately, then fell, and our men carried his body to the camp, to the skirts of which they were followed by the Secesh cavalry and four guns. Our loss was only two more— the enemy are calculated to have lost 85. The farmers at Munchausen say they were busy all day carrying away their dead in carts.

" On reaching the camp, General Pumpkin thought it right to drive back the dastardly polluters of our country's flag. He disposed his troops in platoons, according to the celebrated disposition made by Miltiades at Marathon, covering his wings with squadrons of artillery in columns of sub-divisions, with a reserve of cavalry in echelon; but he improved upon the idea by adding the combination of solid squares and skirmishers in the third line, by which Alexander the Great decided the Battle of Granicus.

" In this order, then, the Union troops advanced till they came to Little Bear Creek. Here, to their great astonishment, they found the enemy under General Jefferson Brick in person (Brick will be remembered by many here as the intelligent clerk in our advertisement department, but he was deeply tainted with Secesh sentiments, and on the unfurling of our flag manifested them in such a manner that we were obliged to dispense with his services). The infamous destroyer of his country's happiness had posted his men so that we could not see them. They were at least three to one—mustering some 7,000, with guns, caissons, baggage waggons, and standards in proportion—and were arranged in an obtuse angle, of which the smaller end was composed of a mass of veterans, in the order adopted by Napoleon with the Old Guard at Waterloo:

the larger, consisting of the Whoop-owl Bushwackers and the Squash River Legion in potence, threatened us with destruction if we advanced on the other wing, whilst we were equally exposed to danger if we remained where we were.

"General Pumpkin's conduct is, at this most critical moment, generally described as being worthy of the best days of Roman story. He simply gave the word 'Charge.' 'What, General?' exclaimed our informant. 'Charge! Sir,' said the general, with a sternness which permitted no further question. With a yell our gallant fellows dashed at the enemy, but the water was too deep in the creek, and they retired with terrific loss. The enemy then dashed at them in turn. They drove our right for three miles; we drove their left for three-and-a-quarter miles. Their centre drove our left, and our right drove their centre again. They took five of our guns; we took six of theirs and a bread-cart.

"Night put an end to this dreadful struggle, in which American troops set an example to the war-seamed soldiers of antiquity. Next morning General Pumpkin pushed across to Pugstown, and occupied it in force. Union sentiment is rife all through Missouri. We demand that General Pumpkin be at once placed at the head of the Army of the Potomac."

Now all this—in no degree exaggerated—and the like of which I have read over and over again, affords infinite comfort or causes great depression to New York for an hour or so, coupled with an "editorial," in which the energy and enterprise of the Scarron are duly eulogised, old Greeley's hat and breeches and umbrella handled with charming wit and eloquence, and the inevitable flight of the Richmond Government to Texas clearly demonstrated. Next day some little doubt is expressed as to the exact locality of the fight—" Pumpkin's force was at Big Bear, 180 miles west of the place indicated. We doubt not, however, the account is substantially correct, and that the Secesh forces have been pretty badly whipped."

Next day the casualties are reduced from 200 killed and 310 wounded to 96 killed and none wounded; and scrutinising eyes notice a statement, in small type, that the "father of Lieutenant Bellows has written to us to state his son was not engaged on the occasion in question, but was at home on furlough." And by the time " Another Great Union Victory !" is ready, the fact oozes out, but is by no means considered worth a thought, that General Pumpkin has had an encounter with the Confederates in which he suffered a defeat, and that he has gone into winter quarters.

I do not suppose for a moment that these deceitful agencies are exercised only in the North, but am persuaded, from what I know, that the Southern people are at least as anxious for news, and as liable to be led away by suppressions of truth or distorted narratives, as those of the Free States. If we had had a telegraphic system and a newspaper press during the Wars of the Roses, or the struggle of 1645, it is probable our partisans, on both sides, would have been as open to imposture; but I do not think they would have continued long in the faith that the ever-detected impostor was still worthy of credence.

CHAPTER II.

To the Station—Stars and Stripes—Crowd at Station—Train impeded by Snow—Classic ground—"Manhattan"—"Yonkers"—Fellow-travellers and their ways—"Beauties of the Hudson"—West Point: their education, &c.—Large Towns on the banks of the Hudson—Arrive at East Albany—Delavan House—Beds at a premium—Aspect of Albany not impressive—Sights—The Legislature.

As we drove over the execrable snow-heaps to the station, the streets seemed to me unusually dreary. The vast Union flags which flapped in the cold air, now dulled and dim, showed but their great bars of blood, and the stars had faded out into darkness.

Apropos of the stripes and stars, I may say I never could meet any one in the States able to account for the insignia, though it has been suggested that they are an amplification of the heraldic bearing of George Washington. Strange indeed if the family blazon of an English squire should have become the flaunting flag of the Great Republic, which with all its faults has done so much for the world, and may yet, purged of its vanity, arrogance, and aggressive tendency, do so much more for mankind! Not excepting our own, it is the most widely-spread flag on the seas; for whilst it floats by the side of the British ensign in every haunt of our commerce, it has almost undisputed possession of vast tracts of sea in the Pacific and South Atlantic.

At last we got to the end of our very unpleasant journey, and approached the York and Albany Terminus, over an alpine concrete of snow-heaps, snow-holes, and street-rails. At the station my coach-driver affectionately seized my hand, and bade me good-bye with a cordiality which might have arisen from the sensitiveness of touch in his palm as much as from personal affection. The terminus was crowded with citizens (eating apples, lemon-drops, and gingerbread-nuts, and reading newspapers) and a few men in soldier's uniform, going north—only one or two of what one calls in Europe gentlemen or ladies, but all well dressed and well behaved, if they would only spare the hissing stoves and the feelings of prejudiced foreigners.

The train, with more punctuality than we usually observe in such matters, started to the minute, but only went ten yards or so, and then halted for nearly half an hour—no one knew why, and no one seemed to care, except a gentleman who was going, he said, to get his friend, "the Honourable Something Raymond, to do something for him at Albany," and was rather in a hurry. When the engine renewed the active exercise of its powers, the pace was slow and the motion was jerking and uneven, owing to snow on the rails, and the obstacles increased as the train left the shelter of the low long-stretching suburb which clings to it, and is dragged, as it were, out of the city with it along the bank of the Hudson. But even 181st and 182nd streets abandoned their attempts to keep up with the rail; and all that could be seen of civilisation were sundry chimneys and walls and uncouth dark masses of wood or brick rising above the snow. The lights in the wooden stations shone out frostily through the dimmed windows as we struggled on.

We were passing through at night what is to Americans classic ground, in spite of odd names: for here is "Manhattan" (associated in my mind for ever with a man who, unfortunately for himself and me, had a wooden leg, as he planted the iron ferule of that insensible member on the only weak point of my weaker foot)—and next is "Yonkers," where a lady once lived with whom Washington was once in love, and several "fights" took place all around, in which the Americans were more often beaten than victorious;—"Dobb's Ferry" "Tarrytown" (poor André! let those who wish to know all that can be known of the "spy" read Mr. Sargent's life of him, published in Philadelphia), which is "nigh on toe Sleepy Hollow," where Mr. Diedrich Knickerbocker had such a remarkable interview with the ancient Hollander;—"Sing Sing," where many gentlemen, not so well known to fame, have interviews of a less agreeable character with modern American authorities. We are passing, too, by Sunnyside, where Washington Irving lived. I would rather have seen him than all the remarkable politicians in the States— old Faneuil, or Bunker's Hill, or all the wonders of the great nation; though I am told he was unbearably prosy and sleepy of late days.

Cold and colder it becomes as we creep on, and slower creaks the train with its motley freight. The men round the stoves "fire up" till the iron glows and gives out the heated air to those who can stand it, and an unsavoury odour, as of baked second-hand clothing, and a hissing noise to those beyond the torrid circle. The slamming of the door never ceases. Sometimes it is a conductor, sometimes it is not. But no matter who makes the disturbance, he has a right to do so. No one can sleep on account of that abominable noise, even if he could court slumber in a seat which is provided with a rim to hurt his back if he reclines, and a ridge to smite his face if he leans forward. Apples and water and somebody's lemon-drops are in demand; and vendors of vegetable ivory furtively deposit specimens of ingenious manufacture but inscrutable purpose in the lap of the unoffending stranger, who in his sleepy state often falls a victim to these artifices, and finds himself called on to pay several dollars for quaint products of the carver, which he has unduly detained in his unconsciousness.

The train arrives at Poughkeepsie, seventy-five miles from New York, an hour and a half late. We hear that, instead of reaching Albany at 10.30 or 11 P.M., we shall not be in till 1 or 1.30 A.M., and will "lose communications;" therefore we eat in desperation at refreshment-rooms large oysters boiled in milk out of small basins. In the night once more. We have passed West Point long since, and an enthusiastic child of nature, who has been pointing out to me the "beauties of the Hudson," which is flowing down under its mail of ice close to our left, has gone to sleep among the fire-worshippers at the stove.

Now, the fact is, that scenery under snow is, I may safely affirm, very like beauty under a mask, or a fine figure in a waterproof blanket. The hills were mere snow-mounds, and the lines of all objects were fluffy and indistinct; and I was glad my eulogistic friend slept at last. West Point I longed to see; for though its success in turning out great generals has as yet not been very remarkable, I had met too many excellent specimens of its handiwork in making good officers and pleasant gentlemen not to feel a desire to have purview of the institution. Had I not heard a live general sing "Benny Haven, ho!"—had I not seen Mordecai sitting at the gate of Pelissier in vain, and McClellan and Delafield engaged in a geological inquiry on the remains of the siege of Sebastopol? Above all, does not West Point promise to become something like a military academy, in a country such as America is likely to be after the war?

It is a mistake rather common in England, and in Europe, to suppose that a majority, or even a minority, of the American generals are civilians. With very few exceptions indeed, they have either been some time at West Point, or have graduated there. In a country which has no established lines to mark the difference of classes, which nevertheless exists there as elsewhere, there is a positive social elevation acquired by any man who has graduated at West Point; and if he has taken a high degree, he is regarded in his State as a man of mark, whose services must be secured for the military organisation and public service in the militia or volunteers.

There is no country in the world where so many civilians have received their education in military academies without any view to a military career. There are of course many "generals" and "colonels" of States troops who have had no professional training, but not nearly so many as might be imagined.

But the great defect under which American officers laboured until this unhappy war broke out, was the purely empirical and theoretical state of their knowledge. They had no practical experience. The best of them had only such knowledge as they could have gleaned in the Mexican war. A man whose head was full of Jomini was sent off to command a detachment in a frontier fort, and to watch marauding Indians, for long years of his life, and never saw a regiment in the field. As to working the three arms together creditably in the field, I doubt if there is an officer in the whole army who could do it anything like so well as the Duke of Cambridge, or as an Aldershot or Curragh brigadier.

It would be hard for any Englishman to be indifferent to the advantages of military training in a country where every village around could have told tales of the helpless, hopeless blundering which characterised the operations of the British generals hereabouts in the War of Independence. Reflecting thus, too, I felt less inclined to wonder at the mistakes made by the Federals, and by the Confederates. Had the British generals proved more lucky and skilful, should we now have been passing the towns which cluster on the banks of the Hudson, or would "monarchy" have impeded the march of life, commerce, and civilisation out here?

Towns of 5,000, 10,000, 20,000, and even of 30,000 inhabitants rise on the margin of the fine river, which in summer presents, I am assured, a scene of charming variety and animation, and in autumn is fringed by the most beautiful of all beautiful American landscapes, surcharged with the glorious colours of that lovely season. Through the darkness by the bright starlight we could see the steamboats locked fast in the ice, like knights in proof, awaiting the signal to set them free for the charge. But, ah me! how weary it was!—how horrible the stoves! At last and at last the train stopped, and finally deposited us at three o'clock in the morning on the left bank of the Hudson, at East Albany.

The city proper lies on the opposite shore of the river; and I got, as I was directed, into a long low box called the omnibus, which was soon crowded with passengers. In a few minutes we were off. Then I was made aware that the 'bus was a sleigh, and that it was on runners and ——— Just at that moment the machine made a headlong plunge, like a ship going down by the bows at sea, and in an instant more had pierced the depths of darkness, and with a crashing scrunching bump touched the bottom. "We're on the river now, I guess," quoth one. And so it was. We had shot down the bank, which must be higher than one would like to leap, even on snow, and were now rolling, squeaking, and jerking over the frozen river, amid the groans and shrieks and grumbling protests of the ice, which seemed in some places to give way as if it were going to let us down bodily, and in others to rise up in strong ridges to baffle the horses' efforts. Then, after a most disagreeable drive, which seemed half-an-hour long—and about thrice as long as it really was, I suppose—a prodigious effort of horse muscle and whipping, and of manual labour, accomplished the ascent of the other bank, and the vehicle passed through the deserted streets of Albany—the capital of the great State of New York—to the Delavan House, which was open to receive but not to entertain us. A rush of citizens was made to "the office" of the hotel. More citizens followed out of fast-arriving vehicles from the train—for there was no means of getting on till the forenoon—and all went perforce to the Delavan House.

The hotel office consisted of a counter with a raised desk, enclosing a man with a gold chain, a diamond stuck in the front of a dress shirt—not as pin to a scarf or as a stud, but as a diamond *per se*, after the fashion of those people and of railway conductors in the land—his hat cocked over one eye, a toothpick even at that hour in his mouth, a black dress suit of clothes, a dyed moustache and beard *à la* Rowdy Americain, and an air of sovereign contempt for his customers. The crowd pressed around and hurled volleys of questions—"Can we have beds, sir?" &c. But the man of Delavan House replied not. To all their entreaties he returned not a word. But he did take out a great book and spread it on the counter, and putting a pen in the ink he handed it to the citizen nearest, who signed himself and his State, and asked meekly "if he could have a bed at once, as he was so" &c. To him the man of Delavan House deigned no reply. The pen was handed to another, who signed, and so on—the arbiter of our destinies watching each inscription with the air of an attorney's clerk who takes signatures to an attestation.

There were at least fifty people to sign before me, and I heard from a waiter there were only ten beds—which on the most ample allowance would only accommodate some thirty people—vacant. Were the Britishers to be beaten? Never! Leaving our luggage, we dashed out into the snow. And lo! a house nigh at hand, with lights and open doors. A black waiter sallied out at the tramp of feet in the hall. He told us, "De rooms all tuk, sar." He was told to be less indiscreet

THE STATE CAPITOL. 25

in his assertions, and all the time of colloquy the invading Celts and Saxons pushed onwards and upwards to the first landing. Here were doors standing open. We entered one. Three small rooms—beds empty! no luggage! This will do. "Massa, dis room's all ——" "You be quiet!" And the luggage was dragged over by our own right hands, eventually aided by the Ethiop.

I had the satisfaction, as I was gliding away with my hat-box, to hear the man of Delavan House reading the book of fate, and selecting his victims at his grim pleasure. In fact, the house on which we had stumbled was a sort of succursal to the hotel; and the proprietor, afraid of offending so mighty a potentate, was shocked at the idea of letting in any one without his leave. What became of the victims I know not, but I do know that the beds—though we went to them supperless—of the humble hostelry were very grateful.

I went to bed about 4 A.M., with the fixed intention of getting up early and visiting the capitol, when I could have seen with these eyes the glories of the Hon. — Raymond as Speaker in the State Hall, and have heard something more of the interesting proceedings against a New York alderman, who accused senators and representatives of being accessible as Danaë to the golden shower, and even to greenbacks.

No man can see the real merits of a city in snow. I shall repeat the remark no more; therefore if I say I don't like a place, let the snow bear the blame: but Albany did not impress me when I did get up, and the sight of the State Capitol at the top of a steep street was so utterly depressing, that I abandoned my resolve, and sought less classic ground. What have not these Greeks to answer for in this new land?

There was a comforting contrast to the hideous domes and mock porticoes, and generally to the ugliness of the public buildings, in the solid unpretentious look of the old Dutch-built houses of private citizens. Though there is an aspect of decadence about Albany, it seems more, far more respectable and gentlemanly than its smug, smirking, meretricious but overwhelming rival, New York.

I was informed by an American that it was called after the second name in the title of James the Second, before he ascended the throne. "Bad as the Stuarts were to you, they were a great deal better for the colonies," said he, "than your Hanover House, and perhaps if you hadn't changed them you might not have lost us." It was curious to hear an American saying a good word for the luckless house, though I am by no means of the opinion that England could ever have ruled colonies which were saturated with the principles of self-government.

It was too cold at such a season as this for philosophical research in a sleigh, and too slippery for sauntering; and we were whirled out of the State capital without seeing much of it, except church steeples, and some decent streets, and the ice-bound river studded with hard-set steamers.

There are, however, in summer time, as I hear, and can well imagine, many fine sights to be seen. There is the Fall of Cohoes, where the Mohawk River, a stream of greater body than the Thames at Richmond, leaps full seventy feet down into a gulf, whence it collects itself to pursue its course to the Hudson. There are Shaker settlements, and many communities of "isms" and astounding congregations of "ists;" and there are clean Dutch streets, and Dutch tenures and customs to this day. With the tenures, however, the rule of the majority has made rough work; and the lords *in capite*, or padroons, have suffered pauperisation by the simple process of nonpayment of their rents.

The Legislature is now in solemn conclave. They are investigating charges implied in the speech of a New York alderman, who declared he could get any measure passed he liked, by paying the members—of course extra-officially, because the payment, *per se*, could only be an agreeable addition to their income. The Speaker is Mr Raymond, of the *New York Times*, who, in spite of or perhaps in consequence of the opposition of the *Caledonian Cleon*, his rival, was elected to that high office. It was in course of conversation with an American gentleman respecting the election, that I learned there was no more certain way of succeeding in any contest in the State, than to obtain the abuse of the organ under that person's control. Be it senator, mayor, or common-councilman, the candidate he favours is lost, for all respectable people instinctively vote against him.

CHAPTER III.

Unpleasant journey to Niagara—Mr. Seward—The Union and its dangers—Pass Buffalo—Arrival at Niagara—A 'Touter'—Bad weather—The Road—Climate compared—Desolate appearance of houses—The St. Lawrence viewed from above—One hundred years ago—Canada the great object of the Americans—The Welland Canal—Effect of the Falls from a distance—Gradual approach—Less volume of water in winter—Different effect and dangers in winter—Icicles—Behind the Cataract—Photographs and Bazaar—Visit the "Lions" generally—Brock—American and Canadian sides contrasted—Goat Island—A whisper heard—Mills and Manufactories.

It was past noon ere the train once more began its contest with the snow—now conquering, now stubbornly resisted, and brought to a standstill:—the pace exceedingly slow, the scenery that of undulating white tablecloths, the society dull.

The journey to Niagara was as unpleasant as very bad travelling and absence of anything to see could make it. The train contained many soldiers or volunteers going back to their people, who discussed the conduct of the war with earnestness and acuteness; but though we were so far north, I could not hear any of them very anxious about the negro.

Well-dressed men and women got in and out at all the stations, nor did I see persons in the whole line of the cars who seemed to have rubbed elbows with adversity. Shenectady! Utica! Syracuse! Auburn! Here be comminglings!—the Indian, the Phœno-Numidian, the Greek-Sicilian, the Anglo-Irish, all reviving here in fair towns, full of wealth, commerce, and life.

The last-named is, I believe, the birthplace, and is certainly what auctioneers call the residential abode, of Mr. Seward. I remember his Excellency relating how, after the Battle of Bull Run—when he was threatened by certain people from Baltimore with hanging, as the reward of his misdeeds in plunging the country into civil war—he resolved to visit his fellow-citizens and neighbours, to ascertain whether there was any change of feeling amongst them. He was received with every demonstration of kindness and respect, and then, said he, "I felt my head was quite safe on my shoulders." It is but just to say, Mr. Seward altogether disclaims the intention of seizing on Canada, which has been attributed to him in England; although he certainly is of opinion, that the province cannot continue long to be a dependency of the English Crown. How long does he think California will be content to receive orders from a government at Washington?

The danger which menaces the Union will become far greater after the success of the Unionists than it was during the war, because the extinction of the principle of States Rights will naturally tend to centralise the power of the Federal Government. They cannot restore that which they have pulled down. In virtue of their own principles, they must maintain a strict watch and supreme control over the State Governments and Legislatures. Endless disputes and jealousies will arise. The Democrats, at once the wealthiest and the ablest party in each State, will take every opportunity of opposing the centralised Government; and although the Republicans may raise armies to fight for the Union, they will not be able to prevent the slow and certain action of the State Legislatures, which will tend to detach the States more and more from any federation in which their interests are not engaged, and to form them into groups, bound together by community of commerce, manufacture, feeling, and destiny.

Canada must of course accept its fate with the rest; but Englishmen, at least, will not yield it to the menaces or violence of the Northern Americans, as long as the people of the province prefer being our fellow-subjects to an incorporation in the Great Republic, or any section of it that may be desirous of the abstraction.

I fear we mostly look at Mr. Seward's conduct and language from a point which causes erroneous inferences. It should be remembered that he is an American minister—that he has not only the interests but the passions and prejudices of the American people to consult, and that, like Lord Palmerston, he is not the minister of any country but his own. His son, the Under-secretary of State, is the proprietor and editor of a journal here, which is conducted with the moderation and tact to be expected from the amiable character of the gentleman alluded to.

There was little to be seen of the towns at which we halted, and our journey was continued from one to the other monotonously enough. The weary creeping of the train, the foul atmosphere, the delays, however inevitable and unavoidable, rather spoiled one's interest in the black smoky-looking cities on the white plains through which we passed; and night found us still "scrooging on," and occasionally stopping and digging out. Thus we passed by Rochester and the Genessee Falls, which seem extensively used up in mill-working, and arrived at Buffalo (278 miles) a little before midnight. There we branched off to Niagara, which is 22 miles further on.

Up to this time we had been minded to go to the Clifton House, which is on the Canadian side of the river, though it is kept by Americans, and of which we had agreeable memories in the summer, when it was the headquarters of many pleasant Southerners. There were only three or four men in our car, one of whom was, even under such hopeless circumstances, doing a little touting for an hotel at the American side. After a while he threw a fly over us and landed the whole basket. All the large hotels, he said, were shut up on both sides of the Falls, but he could take us to a very nice quiet and comfortable place, where we would meet with every attention, and it was the only house we would find open. This exposition left us no choice.

We surrendered ourselves therefore to the tout, who was a very different being from the type of his class in England: a tall, pleasant-faced man, with a keen eye and bronzed face, ending in an American Vandyke beard, a fur collar round his neck, a heavy travelling coat—from which peered out the ruffles of a white shirt and a glittering watch-chain—rings on his fingers, and unexceptionable shoeing. He smoked his cigar with an air, and talked as if he were conferring a favour. "And I tell you what! I'll show you all over the Falls to-morrow. Yes, sir!" Why, we were under eternal obligations to such a guide, and internally thanking our stars for the treasure-trove at once accepted him.

At the gloomy deserted station we were now shot out, on a sheet of slippery deep snow, an hour after midnight. We followed our guide to an hostelry of the humbler sort, where the attention was not at first very marked or the comfort at all decided. The night was very dark, and a thaw had set in under the influence of a warm rain. The thunder of the Falls could not be heard through the thick air, but when we were in the house a quiet little quivering rattle of the window-panes spoke of its influence. The bar-room was closed—in the tawdry foul-odoured eating-room swung a feeble lamp: it was quite unreasonable to suppose any one could be hungry at such an hour, and we went to bed with the nourishment supplied by an anticipation of feasting on scenery. All through the night the door and window-frames kept up the drum-like roll to the grand music far away.

We woke up early. What evil fortune! Rain! fog! thaw!—the snow melting fast in the dark air. But were we not "bound" to see the Falls? So after breakfast, and ample supplies of coarse food, we started in a vehicle driven by the trapper of the night before. He turned out to be a very intelligent, shrewd American, who had knocked about a good deal in the States, and knew men and manners in a larger field than Ulysses ever wandered over.

The aspect of the American city in winter time is decidedly quite the reverse of attractive, but there was a far larger fixed population than we expected to have seen, and the fame of our arrival had gone abroad, so that there was a small assemblage round the stove in the bar-room and in the passage to see us start. I don't mean to see us in particular, but to stare at any three strangers who turned up so suspiciously and unexpectedly at this season. The walls of the room in the hotel were covered with placards, offering large bounties and liberal inducements to recruits for the local regiment of volunteers; and I was told that a great number of men had gone for the war after the season had concluded—but Abolition is by no means popular in Niagara.

It was resolved that we should drive round to the British side by the Suspension Bridge, a couple of miles below, as the best way of inducting my companions into the wonders of the Falls; and I prepared myself for a great surprise in the difference between the character of the scene in winter and in summer.

For some time the road runs on a low level below the river bank, and does not permit of a sight of the cataract. The wooden huts of the Irish squatters looked more squalid and miserable than they were when I saw them last year—wonderful combinations of old plank, tarpaulin, tinplate, and stove pipes. "It's wonderful the settlement doesn't catch fire!" "But it does catch fire. It's burned down often enough. Nobody cares: and the Irish grin, and build it up again, and beat a few of the niggers, whom they accuse of having blazed 'em up. They've a purty hard time of it now, I think."

There are too many free negroes and too many Irish located in the immediate neighbourhood of the American town, to cause the doctrines of the Abolitionists to be received with much favour by the American population; and the Irish of course are opposed to free negroes, where they are attracted by papermills, hotel service, bricklaying, plastering, housebuilding, and the like—the Americans monopolising the higher branches of labour and money-making, including the guide business.

At a bend in the road we caught a glimpse of the Falls, and I was concerned to observe they appeared diminished in form, in beauty, and in effect. The cataract appeared of an ochreish hue, like bog-water, as patches of it came into sight through breaks in the thick screen of trees which line the banks. The effect was partly due to the rain, perhaps, but was certainly developed by the white setting of snow through which it rushed. The expression on my friends' faces indicated that they considered Niagara an imposition. "The Falls are like one of our great statesmen," quoth the guide, "just now. There's nothing particular about them when you first catch a view of them; but when you get close and know them better, then the power comes out, and you feel small as potatoes."

As we splashed on through the snow, I began to consider the disadvantages to which the poor emigrant who chooses a land exposed to the rigours of a six months' winter, must be exposed; and I wondered in myself that the early settlers did not fly, if they had a chance, when they first experienced the effects of bitter cold. But I recollected how much better were soil, climate, and communications than they are in the sunny South, where, for seven months, the heat is far more intolerable than the cold of Canada—where the fever revels, where noxious reptiles and insects vex human life, and the blood is poisoned by malaria, and where wheat refuses to grow, and bread is a foreign product.

Even in Illinois the winter is, as a rule, as severe as it is in Canada, the heat as great in summer—water is scarce, roads bad. It is better to be a dweller on the banks of the St. Lawrence than a resident in the Valley of the Mississippi, even if a tithe of its fabled future should ever come to pass. There is no reason why the Canadas should be regarded with less favour than the Western States, although the winters are long enough: in the prairie there is a want of wholesome water in summer, and a scarcity of fuel for cold weather, which tend to restore the balance in favour of the provinces.

The country, which I remembered so riant and rich, now was cold and desolate. At the station, near the beautiful Suspension Bridge—which one cannot praise too much, and which I hope may last for ever, though it does not look like it—the houses had closed windows, and half of them seemed empty, but the German proprietors no doubt could have been found in the lagerbeer saloons and billiard-rooms. The toll-takers and revenue officers on the bridge showed the usual apathy of their genus. No novelty moves them. Had the King of Oude appeared with all his court on elephants, they would have merely been puzzled how to assess the animals. They were not in the least disconcerted at a group of travellers visiting the St. Lawrence in winter time.

The sight of the St. Lawrence as we crossed over, roaring and foaming more than a hundred feet below us, and rushing between the precipitous banks on which the bridge rests, gave one a sort of "*frisson:*" it looked like some stream of the Inferno—the waters, black and cold, lashed into pyramids of white foam, and seeming by their very violence to impede their own escape. Some distance below the bridge, indeed, they rise up in a visible ridge, crested with high plumes of tossing spray; but it is related as a fact that the steamer "Maid of the Mist," which was wont to ply as a ferry-boat below the Falls, was let down this awful sluice by a daring captain, who sought to save her from the grip of certain legal functionaries, and that she got through with the loss of her chimney, after a fierce contest with the waters, in which she was whirled round and buffeted almost to foundering. At that moment the men on board would no doubt have surrendered to the feeblest of bailiffs for the chance of smooth water.

About one hundred years ago, the spot where we now stood was the scene of continual struggles between the Red man, still strong enough to strike a blow for his heritage, and the British. It was on the 14th September, 1764, that the Indians routed a detachment at Niagara, and killed and wounded upwards of two hundred men; and their organisation seemed so formidable that Amherst was glad to make a treaty with the tribes through the instrumentality of Sir W. Johnston. The colonists then left on us the main burden of any difficulty arising from their great cupidity and indifference to the rights of the natives. In ten years afterwards they were engaged in preparing for the grand revolt which gave birth to the United States and to the greatest development of self-government ever seen in the world.

As they were setting about the work of wresting

the New World from the grasp of the monarchical system, Cook was exploring the shores of the other vast continent in the Southern Sea, where the spirit of British institutions, with the widest extension of constitutional liberty, may yet successfully vindicate the attachment of a great Anglo-Saxon race to the Crown.

There are many in America who think the colonies would never have revolted if the French had retained possession of Canada, and, indeed, it is likely enough the Anglo-Saxons would have held to the connection if the Latin race had been sitting upon them northwards; but the political accidents and the military results which expelled the fleur-de-lys from Canada, doubtless created an unnatural bond of union between the absolutist Court of St. Germains and the precursors of Anacharsis Clootz in the colonies. To the seer there might have been something ominous in the coalition.

The men who were battling for the divine right of kings in Europe could scarce fight for the divine right of man in America without danger. The kiss which was imprinted at Versailles on Franklin's cheek, by the lips of a royal lady, must have had the smack of the guillotine in it.

Anyway, we must allow, the French-Canadians, who stood by us shoulder to shoulder and beat back the American battalions, whose power to invade was mainly derived from foreign support, showed they had a surprising instinct for true liberty. No doubt they would have fought at least as stoutly, had the arrogant colonists been aided by red-coats, for the sake of the white banner and the fleur-de-lys; but in the time of trouble and danger they stood loyally by the Crown and connection of England, and their services in that day should not be lightly forgotten.

It is above all things noteworthy, perhaps, that the Americans in all their wars with the mother-country have sought to strike swift hard blows in Canada, and that hitherto, with every advantage and after considerable successes, they have been driven, weather-beaten back, and bootless home. It was actually on the land shaken by the roar of these falling floods that battles have been fought, and that the air has listened in doubt to the voice of cannon mingling with the eternal chorus of the cataract.

There are here two points at which Canada lies open to the invader. The first lies above the Rapids—the latter is below them, where the St. Lawrence flows into the lake. Three considerable actions and various small engagements have taken place on the Canadian side of the river, all of which were characterised by great obstinacy and much bloodshed. Let us consider them, and see what can or ought to be done in order to guard the tempting bank which offers such an excellent base of operations for future hostile occupation.

An inspection of the map will show the Welland Canal, running from Port Maitland, Dunnville, and Port Colborne, on Lake Erie, to Lake Ontario at Port Dalhousie. The command of this canal would be of the very greatest importance to an invading army, as it would establish a communication inside the Falls of Niagara; but it would be very difficult to obtain such a command so as to prevent the destruction of the canal in case of necessity. It is obvious, however, that the line of it should be defended, and that garrisons should be stationed to hold points inside the line, such as Erie and Chippewa, to render it unsafe for the enemy to move down inside them. At Fort Erie there is a very insignificant work, but, with that exception, the line of the Welland Canal may be considered as perfectly open and defenceless—not by any means as utterly indefensible.

The river is not broad enough to prevent the dwellers on the banks from indulging in hostilities if they pleased; but no practical advantage would be gained in a campaign by any operation which did not settle the fate of the Welland Canal. The locks will permit vessels 142 feet long, with 26 feet beam, and drawing 10 feet of water, to pass between Erie and Ontario; and from the latter lake to the sea, or *vice versâ*, they can pass by the St. Lawrence Canal, drawing one foot less water. It would be above all things important to prevent an enemy getting possession of this Welland Canal. It would not suffice for us to destroy it by injuring a lock or the like, as such an act would militate against our own lines of communication, —more important to us, who have an inferior power of transport on the lakes, than it would be to the Americans.

In addition to a well-devised system of field-works, it is desirable that permanent fortifications should be constructed to cover the termini of the canal and the feeder above Port Maitland. At present, the defensive means of Fort Erie, at the entrance of the river above the Rapids, are very poor, and quite inadequate to resist modern artillery. However, this subject will be best discussed when I come to speak of the general defence of Canada.

This yawning gap is barrier enough between the two countries should they ever, unhappily, become belligerent, but the banks can be commanded by either; and in case of war the bridge would no doubt be sacrificed by one or other, as well as the grander structure at Montreal would be, without some special covenant.

When still a mile and a half away, a whirling pillar of a leaden gray colour, with wreaths of a lighter silvery hue playing round it, which rose to the height of several hundred feet in the air, indicated the position of the Falls. The vapour was more solid and gloomy-looking than the cloudlike mantle which shrouds the cataract oftentimes in the summer. I doubt if there is a very satisfactory solution of its existence at all. Of course the cloud is caused by particles of water thrown up into the atmosphere by the violent impact of the water on the surface, and by the spray thrown off in the descent of the torrent; but why those particles remain floating about, instead of falling at once like rain, is beyond my poor comprehension. Sure enough, a certain portion does descend like a thick Scotch mist: why not all? As one of my companions, with much gravity and an air of profound wisdom, remarked last summer, "It's probable electricity has something to do with it!" Can any one say more?

Assuredly, this ever-rolling mighty cloud draping and overhanging the Falls adds much to their weird and wonderful beauty. Its variety of form is infinite, changing with every current of air, and altering from day to day in height and volume; but I never looked at it without fancying I could trace in the outlines the indistinct shape of a woman, with flowing hair and drooping arms, veiled in drapery—now crouching on the very surface of the flood, again towering along and tossing up her hands to heaven, or sinking down and bending low to the edge of the cataract as though to drink its waters. With the aid of an active fancy, one might deem it to be the guardian spirit of the wondrous place.

The wind was unfavourable, and the noise of the cataract was not heard in all its majestic violence; but as we came nearer, we looked at each other and said nothing. It grew on us like the tumult of an approaching battle.

There is this in the noise of the Falls: produced by a monotonous and invariable cause, it nevertheless varies incessantly in tone and expression. As you listen, the thunder peals loudly, then dies away into a hoarse grumble, rolls on again as if swelled by minor storms, clangs in the ear, and after a while, like a river of sound welling over and irrepressible, drowns the sense in one vast rush of inexpressible grandeur—then melts away till you are almost startled at the silence and look up to see the Falls, like a green mountain-side streaked with fresh snowdrifts, slide and shimmer over the precipice.

It may well be conceived with what awe and superstitious dread honest Jesuit Hennepin, following his Indian guides through the gloom of the forest primæval, gazed on the dreadful flood, which had then no garniture of trimmed banks, cleared fields, snug hotels, and cockney gazabos to alleviate the natural terror with which man must gaze on a spectacle which conjures up such solemn images of death, time, and eternity.

No words can describe the Falls; and Church's picture, very truthful and wonderful as to form, cannot convey an idea of the life of the scene—of the motion and noise and shifting colour which abound there in sky and water. I doubt, indeed, if any man can describe his own sensations very accurately, for they undergo constant change; and for my own part I would say that the effect increases daily, and that one leaves the scene with more vivid impressions of its grandeur and beauty than is produced by the first coup-d'œil.

A gradual approach does not at all diminish the power of the cataract, and the mind is rather unduly excited by the aspect of the Styx-like flood—black, foam-crested, and of great volume, with every indication of profound depth—which hurries on so swiftly and so furiously below the road on which you are travelling, between banks cut down through grim, dark rock, so sheer that the tops of the upper trees which take root in the strata can be nearly touched by the traveller's stick. The idea that the whole of the great river beneath you has just leaped over a barrier of rock prepares one's conception for the greatness of the cataract itself.

In summer time there were wild ducks flying about, and terns darted up and down the stream. Now it was deserted and desolate, looking of more inky hue in contrast with the snow. Close to the boiling cataract the fishermen's tiny barks might then be seen rocking up and down, or the angler sought the bass which loves those turbulent depths; but no such signs of human life and industry are visible in winter.

Before Niagara was, odd creatures enough lived about here, which can now be detected fossilised in the magnesian limestone. How many myriads of years it has been eating away its dear heart and gnawing the rock let Sir Charles Lyell or Sir Roderick Murchison calculate; but I am persuaded that since I saw it some months ago there has been a change in the aspect of the Horseshoe Fall, and that it has become more deeply curved. The residents, however, though admitting the occurrence of changes, say they are very slow, and that no very rapid alteration has taken place since the fall of a great part of Table Rock some years ago: but masses of stone may be washed away every day without their knowing it.

One very natural consequence of a visit in the winter was undeniable—that the Falls were visibly less: they did not extend so far, and they rolled with diminished volume. The water did not look so pure, and incredible icicles and hanging glaciers obscured the outlines of the rocks and even intruded on the water-course; whilst the trees above, laden with snow, stood up like inverted icicles again, and rendered it difficult to define the boundary between earth, air, and water.

A noiseless drive brought us to the village. Clifton House was deserted—the windows closed, the doors fastened. No gay groups disported on the promenade; but the bird-stuffer's, the Jew's museum, the photographer's shed, the Prince's triumphal arch, were still extant; and the bazaars, where they sell views, seashells, Indian beadwork and feathers, moccasins, stuffed birds, and the like, were open and anxious for customers. Our party was a godsend; but the worthy Israelite, who has collected such an odd museum here—one, under all the circumstances, most creditable to his industry and perseverance as well as liberality—said that travellers came pretty often in fine winter weather to look at the cataract. We walked in our moccasins to the Table Rock, and thence to the verge of the Falls, and gazed in silence on the struggling fury of the terrible Rapids, which seem as if they wrestled with each other like strong men contending against death, and fighting to the last till the fatal leap must be made.

The hateful little wooden staircases, which like black slugs crawl up the precipice from the foot of the Falls, caught the eyes of my companions; and when they were informed that they could go down in safety and get some way behind the Fall itself, the place was invested with a new charm, and ice, rheumatism, and the like, were set at defiance. I knew what it was in summer, and the winter journey did not seem very tempting; but there was no alternative, and the party returned to the museum to prepare for the descent.

Whilst we were waiting for our waterproof dresses to go under the Falls, we had an opportunity of surveying the changes produced by winter, and I was the more persuaded that the effect is not so favourable as that of summer. The islands are covered with snow—that which divides the sweep of the cataract looking unusually large; the volume of water, diminished in the front, is also deprived of much of its impressive force by a decrease in the sound produced by its fall. The edges of the bank, covered with glistening slabs of ice, were not tempting to the foot, and could not be approached with the confidence with which they are trod by one of steady nerves when the actual brink is visible.

There were some peculiarities, however, worthy of note; and in a brighter day, possibly the effect of the light on the vast ranges of icicles, and on the fantastic shapes into which the snow is cut on the rocks at the margin of the waters, might be very beautiful. These rocks now looked like a flock of polar bears, twined in fantastic attitudes, or extended singly and in groups by the brink as if watching for their prey. Above them rose the bank, now smooth and polished, with a fringe of icicles—some large as church steeples; above them, again, the lines of the pine-trees, draped in white, and looking like church steeples too. At one side, near Table Rock, the icicles were enormous, and now and then one fell with a hissing noise, and was dashed on the rock into a thousand gliding ice arrows, or plunged into the gulf.

By this time our toilette-room was ready, and each man, taking off his overcoat, was encased in a tarpaulin suit with a sou-wester. In this guise we descended the spiral staircase, which is carried in a perpendicular wooden column down the face of the bank near Table Rock, or what remains of it, to the rugged margin, formed of boulders now more slippery than glass.

Our guide, a strapping specimen of negro or mulatto, in thick solid ungainly boots, planted his splay feet on them with certainty, and led us by the treacherous path down towards the verge of the torrent, which now seemed as though it were rushing from the very heavens. On our left boiled the dreadful caldron from which the gushing bubbles, as if overjoyed to escape, leaped up, and with glad effervescence rushed from the abyss which plummet never sounded. On our right towered the sheer precipice of rock, now overhanging us, and garnished with rows of giant teeth-like icicles.

After a slow cautious advance along this doubtful path, we perceived that the thin edge of the cataract towards which we were advancing shot out from the rock, and left a space between its inner surface and a black shining wall which it was quite possible to enter. There was no wind, the day was dull and raw, but the downright rush of the water created a whirling current of air close to it which almost whisked away the breath; and a vapour of snow, fine sleet, and watery particles careered round the entrance to the recess, which no water kelpie would be venturesome or lonesome enough to select, except in the height of the season.

On we thus went, more and more slowly and cautiously, over the polished ice and rock, till at last we had fairly got behind the cataract, and enjoyed the pleasure of seeing the solid wall of water falling, falling, falling, with the grand monotony of eternity, so nigh that one fancied he could almost touch it with his hand. When last I was here, it was possible to have got as far as a ledge called Termination Rock; but the ice had accumulated to such an extent that the guide declared the attempt to do so would be impracticable or dangerous, and indeed where we stood was not particularly safe at the moment. As I was in the cave, gazing at the downpoured ruin of waters with a sense of security as great as that of a trout in a mill-race, an icicle from the cliff above cracked on the rocks outside, and threw its fragments inside the passage. I own the desire I had to get on still further and pierce in behind the cataract, where its volume was denser, was greater than the gratification I derived from getting so far. But we had reached our ultima thule, and, with many a lingering look, retraced our steps—now and then halting to contend the better with the gusts from the falls, which threaten to sweep one from the ledge. If the foot once slipped, I cannot conceive a death more rapid: life would die out with the thought, " I am in the abyss ! " ere a cry could escape.

Whilst returning, another icicle fell near at hand; therefore it is my humble opinion that going to Termination Rock in winter is not safe except in hard frost, the safer plan being not to go at all. And yet no one has ever been swept or has slipped in, I believe, and so there is a new sensation to be had very easily. The path on our return seemed worse than it was on our going—a very small slippery ridge indeed between us and the gulf; but danger there can be but little. As we emerged from the wooden pillar we submitted to a photographer for our portraits in waterproof.

Poor man! In summer he has a harvest, perhaps; in winter he gleans his corn with toil and sorrow, making scenes for stereoscopes. I am not aware that we omitted anything proper to be done ; for we purchased feather fans—the griffs did—and beadwork and other "mementoes of the Falls," which are certainly not selected for any apposite quality. As if the Falls needed a bunch of feathers and beads to keep them in remembrance! Well, many a time has a lock of hair, a withered flower, the feeblest little atom of substantial matter, been given as memento ere now, and done its office well.

As I passed by Clifton House on my return to the American side, I observed a solitary figure in a blue overcoat and brass buttons, pacing rapidly up and down under cover of the verandah. Who on earth could it be? It can't be—yes it is—it is, indeed, our excellent guardian of British customs rights and revenues—good Mr. ——. The kindly old Scotchman stares in surprise when he hears his name from an unknown passer-by, but in a moment he remembers our brief acquaintance in summer time. Every one who knows him would, I am sure, be glad, with me, to hear that some better post were got for Mr. —— in his old age than that of watching smugglers on the waters of the St. Lawrence, below Niagara.

After a brief interview, we proceeded on our way, and continued our explorations. Due honour was paid to the Rapids, Bath Island, Goat Island, the Cave of the Winds, Prospect Tower, and all the water lions of the place, though rain and sleet fell at intervals all the time when there was no snow.

When the Prince was here he laid the last stone of the obelisk which marks the place where Brock was killed, in the successful action against the Americans at Queenstown in 1812. The present monument to that general is certainly in as good taste as most British designs of the sort, and seems but little open to the censure I have heard directed against it. Its predecessor was so atrociously bad, that some gentleman of fine feelings in art, who was probably an American and a Canadian patriot as well, blew it up some years ago.

There are not wanting at the present time many men in Canada of the same stuff as Brock and his men. It is astonishing to find the easy and universal conviction prevailing in the minds of Americans, contrary to their experience, that the conquest of Canada would be one of the most natural and facile feats in the world.

Except in their first war, when they displayed energy and skill in the attack on Quebec, the active operations of the Republicans in Canada were not marked by any military excellence, notwithstanding the very hard fights which took place, but they showed themselves most formidable opponents when they were attacked in position.

The Canadian side of the Falls boasts of charming scenery. Even in the snow, the neat cottages and houses—the plantations, gardens, and shrubberies—evince a degree of taste and comfort which were not so observable on the American side, notwithstanding the superior activity of the population.

Our observations on our return to the right bank of the river confirmed my impression concerning the diminished volume and effect of the cataract. The ice, formed by spray, hung over the torrent, which, always more broken and less ponderous than that on the other side, is in summer very beautiful, by reason of the immense variety of form and colour in the jets and cascades, and of the ease with which you can stand, as it were, amid the very waters of Niagara.

The town half populated; the monster hotel closed; the swimming-baths, in which one could take a plunge into the active rapids safely enclosed in a perforated room, now fastened up for winter,—presented a great contrast to the noise and bustle of the American Niagara in the season. This is the time when the Indians enable the shopkeepers to accumulate their stores of bead and feather work; and a few squaws, dressed in a curious compromise between the garments of the civilised female and the simpler robes of the "untutored savage," flitted through the snow from one dealer to another with their work. In some houses they are regularly employed all day, and come in from their village in the morning and go home at night when their work is done.

The view of the Rapids from the upper end of Goat Island is not, to my mind, as fine as that obtained from the island on the British side higher up. The sight of that tortured flood, loaded with its charging lines of "sea horses,"—its surging glistening foam-heaps streaking the wide expanse which rolled towards us from a dull leaden horizon,—was inexpressibly grand and gloomy, and struck me more forcibly than the aspect of the Rapids had done in August, when I beheld them in a setting of rich green landscape and forest.

On the whole, I would much rather, were I going to Niagara for the first time, select the Canadian side for my first view. It would be well never to look at the Falls, if that were possible, till the traveller could open his eyes from the remnant of the Table Rock on the Great Horseshoe; but curiosity will probably defeat any purpose of that kind. Still, the Horseshoe is grand enough to grow on the spectator day after day, even if there be some disappointment in the first aspect. The noise, though it shake the earth and air, is not of the violent overwhelming character which might have been expected from its effect on window-panes and shutters. As the voice of a man can be heard in the din of battle by those around him, so can even the low tones of a clear speaker be distinguished most readily close to the brink of a cataract, the roar of which at times is very audible, nevertheless, from twelve to fifteen miles away.

The only drawback to a sojourn on the Canadian side is, perhaps, the feeling of irritation or unrest produced by the ceaseless jar and tumult of the Falls, which become well nigh unbearable at night, and vex one's slumbers with unquiet dreams, in which water plays a powerful part. The American side is not so much affected in that way. The Horseshoe presents by far the greatest mass of water; its rush is grander—the terrible fathomless gulf into which it falls is more awe-inspiring than anything on the American side; but the latter offers to the visitor greater variety of colour—I had nigh said of substance—in the water. At its first tremendous blow on the seething surface of the basin, the column of water seems to make a great cavern, into which it plunges bodily, only to come up in myriad millions of foaming particles, very small, bright, and distinct, like minute, highly-polished shot. These gradually expand and melt into each other after a wild dance in the caldron, which boils and bubbles with its awful hell-broth for ever. In the centre of the Horseshoe, which is really more the form of two sides of an obtuse-angled triangle, the water, being of great depth—at least thirty feet where it falls over the precipice—is of an azure green, which contrasts well with the yellow, white, and light emerald colours of the shallower and more broken portions nearer the sides.

It would be considered rather presumptuous in any one to think of improving upon Niagara, but I cannot help thinking that the effect would be increased immensely if the island which divides the cataract into the Horseshoe and the American Falls, and the rock which juts up in the latter and subdivides it unequally, were removed or did not exist; then the river, in one grand front of over one thousand yards, would make its leap *en masse*. The American Falls are destitute of the beauty given by the curve of the leap to the Horseshoe; they descend perpendicularly, and are lost in a sea of foam, not in an abyss of water, but in the wild confusion of the vast rocks which are piled up below. But they are still beautiful exceedingly, and there is more variety of scene in the islands, in the passage over the bridges to Goat Island and to the stone tower, which has been built amid the very waters of the cataract, so that one can stand on the outside gallery and look down upon the Falls beneath.

Goat Island is happily intersected with good drives and walks, laid out with sufficiently fair taste through the natural forest, and seats are placed at intervals for the accommodation of visitors. It is no disparagement to the manner in which the grounds have been ornamented to say that a good English landscape gardener would convert the island into the gem of the world. The ornamentation need not be overdone; it should be congruous and in keeping with the Falls, which nature has embellished with such infinity of colouring. As it is, the island is much visited. Strange enough, the softest whispered vows can be heard amid the thunder of Niagara, and it is believed that many marriages owe their happy inspiration to inadvertent walking and talking in these secluded yet much-haunted groves. Sawmills, papermills, and manufactories delight the utilitarian as he gazes on the Rapids which have so long been wasting their precious water-power, and it is not unlikely that a thriving town may grow up to distressing dimensions on the American side of the stream, at all events.

CHAPTER IV.

Leave Niagara—Suspension Bridge—In British territory—Hamilton City—Buildings—Proceed eastward—Toronto—Dine at Mess—Pay visits—Public edifices—Sleighs—Amusement of the boys—*Camaraderie* in the army—Kindly feeling displayed—Journey resumed towards Quebec—Intense cold—Snow landscape—Morning in the train—Hunger and lesser troubles—Kingston, its rise and military position—Harbour, dockyards—Its connection with the Prince of Wales' Tour—The Upper St. Lawrence—Canada as to defence.

We left the Falls with regret—the "city of the Falls" without any painful emotion. The people at the hotel were perfectly civil and obliging, though they bore no particular goodwill, perhaps, to one whom they had been taught to regard as the bitter enemy and traducer of their country and their cause.

Our guide seemed to pity us for our folly in going to such a place as Canada, when we could, if we liked, stay in an American hotel in the States. He assured us it was "only fit for Irish, Frenchmen, and free niggers." The true American of this type is perhaps the most prejudiced man in the world, not even excepting the old type of the British farmer, or men of the Sibthorp epoch. His conviction of his immense superiority is founded on the readiness with which others flock to serve him. By their service he becomes a sort of aristocrat in regard to all immigrants, and can live without having recourse to any menial office or duty. I presume our hairy friend never brushed his boots in his life, and would sooner wear them dirty for ever than stoop to the unwonted task. At last came our time to depart.

Our sleighs glided smoothly down to the railway station at the Clifton, where the train was waiting to take us over the Suspension Bridge. That structure is, I fear, too beautiful to last. It requires a good deal of coolness and custom to look down from it on the fearful flood of the river rolling below, and mark the vibration as a heavy train passes over it. Then, too, there is the influence of cold on iron to be considered, the effects of tension, and the like: all have been duly provided for; and yet the bridge looks very light and very graceful, and let us hope it may be very strong and very lasting.

In five minutes we were in British territory. The first palpable and outward sign of the fact was an examination of our luggage by the customs officers at a station a few miles from the frontier, during which, or by which, one of the party lost a hat and its guardian box. The examination was rendered as little irksome as possible by the civility of the officials; and it made me quite happy to see the crowns on their brass buttons, degraded British subject as I was. One burly fellow congratulated me on "escaping alive out of the hands of the Yankees—he would not have given a cent for my life for the last six months."

Our journey was not so much impeded by snow as we expected. It is forty-three miles from Niagara to the rising city of Hamilton, and we were little more than one hour and a quarter in doing the distance. All

I am aware of is that on our way we passed through
vast snow-fields, by the mineral waters of St. Catherine's,
the frozen canal, and that we caught glimpses on our
right of the blue expanse of Lake Ontario.

The first sight of Hamilton caused a rapid change in
my mind respecting the condition of Canada, and a most
agreeable feeling of surprise. It was evident the Americans were not justified in their affected depreciation of
the provinces, if they contained such towns as these.
Despite the unfavourable circumstances under which it
was visited, the city presented an appearance of comfort
and prosperity which even a democratic people might
envy, and which scarcely justified the corporation in
refusing, as I hear they do, to rely on local sources for
liquidation of certain claims against them.

Fine-looking streets, a forest of spires, important
public buildings, did no discredit to the old standard
which floated over the Custom-house near the station.
And yet it was not possible to help remarking that the
passengers in the train were reading American not
Canadian newspapers. They were enjoying the fruits
of American piracy in their more serious studies. The
literary thefts of the sanctimonious Harpers, who play
for ever on the moods and tenses of the verb to steal—
were in the hands of all the people who were reading
books.

Not alone the British flag did we see at Hamilton, but the British soldier; for at the doorway
of the hotel were two well-known faces. A battalion of the Rifle Brigade was expected every
moment, and two officers had been sent on to provide
for their reception, as there were no barracks to receive
the force, and they were hunting up house-owners to

let their premises on the instant. It may be imagined that house-owners take a favourable view for themselves of the value of property thus suddenly in request; and the officers were proportionately indignant with those griping Canadians, as if they would have met different treatment from English colonists anywhere.

Hamilton is a city of some 20,000 inhabitants. It is on a bay (Burlington), which runs in at the west of Lake Ontario north of the peninsula formed by the lake, by the St. Lawrence, by Lake Erie, and by the river falling into Erie at Maitland. It is on the rail between the west from Detroit and London, the southeast from the States, and the east from Toronto, Montreal, and Quebec. In event of war it is exposed to an attack by any American gunboat from the harbours on the south shore of Lake Ontario, and yet, to the best of my belief, it is utterly destitute of defence, and has not even a martello tower for its protection.

The name is not fifty years old, and twenty years ago Hamilton had less than 4000 inhabitants. Its growth bears no comparison with that of some American cities, but it is still very remarkable, and its wealth, importance, and defencelessness are quite sufficient to make it an object of attack. The houses are built of stone. Banks, hotels, manufactories, churches—well constructed and handsome—give proof of the prosperity of the community; and the residence there of Sir Alan MacNab, who lived somewhere in the vicinity in a bran new mediæval castle, should be some guarantee for their loyalty. Indeed, I was told that in no place had the Prince a more gratifying or enthusiastic reception.

But men without discipline, organisation, or defensive works can do but little against gunboats. It is true that Hamilton would not be of much service to the enemy, as it would not command the communications; but its possession by them would be very embarrassing, and its destruction, for lack of means to defend it, would be very discreditable. The population ought to yield at least 4000 able-bodied men for local service; and a casemated work, armed with powerful guns, could keep a mere mischief-seeking gunboat at proper distance, and save the place from destruction or injury.

Our halt at Hamilton was brief, and soon we were on our way eastwards once more, skirting the shores of the lake, fenced in by a monotonous line of snow-laden fir trees and palings. The people who got in and out at the stations were of a different race from the Americans—stouter and ruddier of hue, and many of them spoke with a Scotch or Irish accent, the former predominating. They did not talk much about anything but the weather, and did not give themselves concern about anything except the winter and its prospects, having made up their minds long ago that there was to be no fight between England and the United States.

Just as it became dusk we reached Toronto, having accomplished the thirty-eight miles in two hours, but late as it was we could make out the picturesque outlines of a large city. Close to the station a line of sleighs, and a mass of well-dressed people drawn up by the margin of a sheet of ice, on which a skated crowd were whirling about, gave an air of gaiety to the place.

A sharp smart sleigh drive, and we were at the comfortable hotel, called Rossin House, where an invitation from the officers of Her Majesty's 30th to dinner was awaiting us. They were quartered in a substantial old-fashioned barrack on the shore of lake Ontario, some distance outside the city. The barracks are surrounded by an earthen parapet, provided with traverses and embrasures, and there is a very quaint and fantastic earthen redoubt on the beach, but any ordinary vessel of war could lay the whole establishment in ruins with perfect impunity in half-an-hour.

The mess table was surrounded by an unusual number of old Crimean officers, and I was glad to find the fears I had entertained that the inducements offered by the Americans to soldiers to desert, had not as yet given any considerable increase to the tendency in that direction, which causes such anxiety to regimental officers stationed near the frontier. Whilst I remained at Toronto, I dined daily at the same hospitable board.

A snapping fierce wind, laden with icy arrows, set in the day after our arrival. In the afternoon, however, I sleighed out and visited the bishop, one of the most lively, agreeable men conceivable, of the age of ninety or thereabouts; Mr. Brown, who is one of the powers of the State, and the editor and owner of the ablest paper in West Canada; the mayor, and other Torontians of eminence.

The city is so very surprising in the extent and excellence of its public edifices, that I was fain to write to an American friend at New York to come up and admire what had been done in architecture under a monarchy, if he wished to appreciate the horrible state of that branch of the fine arts under his democracy. Churches, cathedrals, market, post office, colleges, schools, mechanics' institute, rise in imperial dignity over the city; but there was a visible deterioration in the beer and billiard saloons, and the drinking exchanges. The shops are large, and well furnished with goods, and trade even now is brisk enough, considering the time of the year. All this is within an enemy's grasp, and more than this, the command of the railway east and west.

In this winter time the streets are filled with sleighs, and the air is gay with the caroling of their bells. Some of these vehicles are exceedingly elegant in form and finish, and are provided with very expensive furs, not only for the use of the occupants, but for mere display. The horses are small spirited animals, of no great pretension to beauty or breeding. The people in the streets were well-dressed, comfortable-looking, well-to-do—not so tall as the people in New York, but stouter and more sturdy-looking. Their winter brings no discomfort; for fuel is abundant and not dear, and when the wind is not blowing high, the weather is very agreeable.

Here, again, I observed that the young people have a curious custom of going about with small sleighs, which are, to the best of my belief, called "tarboggins," though I did not see them indulge in the practice by which the youth of New York vex and fret the drivers of all vehicles in sleighing-time. I have been amused by observing the urchins in the Empire City prowling about with these primitive sleighs, watching for an opportunity to exercise their talents. Fortunate it is for the British coachman that the youth of these islands are not acquainted with this pleasing mode of locomotion. Our omnibuses, having a conductor behind, would be better defended than the American vehicles, which have no such protection; but the four-wheeled cabs would fall a helpless prey into their hands.

The sport is carried on in this wise: the youths take their tarboggin or sleigh—a flat piece of board four feet long, with or without runners, will do; through a hole at one end is attached a piece of cord. The boys watch their opportunity, and when a vehicle passes, noiselessly on the snow they run out, slip the cord over the iron or any projection of the carriage behind, and, holding the end fast, throw themselves down on their sleigh, which is dragged along by the vehicle; and if cabby should arise in his wrath, in an instant the end of the cord is let go, and the young navigator, starting to his feet, runs off with his instrument of torture in search of a new victim. It adds much to this entertainment for one boy to catch hold of the leg or the sleigh of another boy, so that a string of four or five youths may be seen in full enjoyment of the recreation. Bless them! If I had not seen them following this sport, I should have fairly doubted if there were any boys in the United States.

If there was not all the cordiality which could be desired between the natives and the military, no fault could be found with the full measure of hospitality dealt out to their own countrymen by the officers of the garrison. Removed from the stiffness of home stations, the genial, kindly character of our young soldiers expatiates, in despite of middling cookery and colonial wines, and keeps open house for friends on foreign service. When sleighing for the day is over, and the skating party has come to an end, it is hard indeed for poor Jones to think of anything more than his dinner; but if he made the most of his opportunities, he might write a book in the solitude of his barrack, as those famous prisoners have done whose brains have conceived and brought forth such brilliant works in the darkness of the Tower.

The snows are well nigh as binding and environing for a third of the year in bad seasons, and no doubt something would come of it all, but that the officer has his duties to attend to, and cannot escape from Private 1000's stoppages, grievances, or failings. Now, it is no easy matter indeed for British officers to be very great friends in the same regiment. Of course you will find Pylades and Orestes there, but you may be sure if you do they are men who have no clashing interests, no contest of purses, no conflicting views about leave or steps. It is to me quite wonderful, all things considered, how bravely the natural kindliness of our officers contends against a system which, with all its advantages, creates a source of rivalry and jealousy not known in other services.

In a promotion-by-seniority service there can of course be no feeling against a man on the part of his juniors because he happens to be older; but no one can well brook the greater fortune which depends on the command of money,—though he may be willing to seize on it, if he can, by the same means,—in the case of his own juniors. I do not speak without some small knowledge when I say that there is a much larger amount of *camaraderie* in our service than ought to be found in it, but that there is much less than exists in some other armies. The French officer is jealous of the man promoted by merit, for the declaration of that superiority is a tacit censure on himself, and he is also prone to take umbrage at the good fortune of the *immortels* of the *État major;* but he has little ground for antipathy to any of his own set, as regards social position or military rank in the corps.

Our strong love of field-sports also tends to create small difficulties when at home, from which spring other causes of estrangement. One man, for instance, wants to get to the spring-meeting when another is burning for the spring-fishing—shooting-leaves and hunting-leaves clash together, though in no army in the world is there such a liberal system of furlough as in our own. These causes do not operate in Canada, where there is now, in fact, but little sport of any kind within easy distances. Moose shooting in snow is slow work, and for other game the sportsman must wander far and wide. But when the table is set, and the full tide of conversation flows, what a cheery group of warriors, young and old, may be seen in Canadian quarters! They have had sleighing parties and skating adventures, and altogether have got over the day somehow, and are prepared to look pleasantly on the world, albeit the snow is two feet deep over it.

As to the position afforded by the buildings in these particular old barracks in Toronto, no more uncomfortable place could well be imagined in face of an enemy. The defences are so ludicrous, that a Chinese engineer would despise them. Certainly, we have no right to laugh at Americans, or to hold their works *in petto*, if we take one glance at the fortifications of Toronto; and yet, as will be seen, it is a place of the very greatest importance.

My stay here would have been longer, perhaps, but that I was informed of a very kindly intention on the part of the people which I did not desire to have carried out, at all events under the existing circumstances—being in hopes that a future opportunity would occur of proving that I was not indifferent to the good feeling and very flattering sentiments of the gentlemen who had commenced the movement towards myself; and so, in the sure hope that I would be back in Toronto ere I left America, I bade my good friends good-bye, never, as it proves, in all likelihood, to see them again, and, in the midst of a snow-fall, resumed my journey with my companions towards Quebec.

After undergoing a year of obloquy, ill-looks, slander, and popular disfavour in a great country, it was very pleasant to meet with such marks of goodwill and kindness from one's countrymen and fellow-subjects on the same continent; and it was quite as gratifying to know that such feelings were entertained by them, as it would have been to receive the outward token of their existence, which alone would have contented my friends.

The evening on which I left Toronto was intensely cold. Never for a moment had the snow and frost relented, and a wind of piercing keenness swept up the frozen dust in thick clouds, which penetrated every chink. The railway officials did their best for us, and the stove in the carriage was poked up to excessive energy; but the heat of these calorifiers is worse than cold itself.

Our way lay through a snow-field bordered by snow-hills, or by the stiff cones of snow-covered firs. Our fellow-passengers were big men in fur-coats and thick boots, who were given to silence and sleep. Slowly the train creaked through the soft barrier which so gently yet stiffly, opposed the tramp of the iron horse. The landscape was simply nothing to see. It looked as if one were going for ever through a vast array of newly-washed sheets spread over the whole country. Darkness fell suddenly out of the skies on the whiteness, but still could not darken it. The whiteness shone through the depths of night, and flashed out in streaks of dazzling light, as the flare of the engine-fires and of the lamps shot out over the surface. And so it came to pass that at last we went to sleep, gathering up rug and greatcoat and wrapper into vast mounds, from which issued many a *spiritus asper* and susurrous sounds for the livelong night.

On waking up it seemed as though day had just dawned, but the watch said it was nearly eight o'clock. A cold white light, filled with rime, battled through the frost on the windows of the carriage, which was spread over the glass like beautiful damascened white tablecloths. Scraping away a lovely trellis pattern with my nail, I opened a space of clear transparent ocean in the ice-sea, and was rewarded for my pains by a view of a cloud of snow which had been falling all night, and now rested deep on the ground, and turned the pines and firs bounding the line of rail into ragged white tumuli.

The train still creaked and bumped now and then over the snow, squeaked, puffed, and grated, and at last came to a standstill, again went on, and again halted. At last we reached a station. Seven hours behind time! A sensation of hunger by no means slight fell upon us. Frost is an appetizer of undoubted merit. We had neglected laying in a *viaticum*. More prudent and accustomed travellers produced flasks and brown-paper parcels, and all the wonderful things which Americans consume on the voyage. Let me not be fastidious, however; for after a time I envied men who were discussing pleasantly fragments of unseemly cakes, spice-nuts, and brandy-balls for breakfast.

My companions prowled up and down the horrid car, reeking with the stove-drawn odours of many bodies during the night—they sought food like young lions. Pah! what an atmosphere it was!—all windows closed by reason of cold intense outside, the hateful stoves, one in the centre of the car, and one at each end, heated almost to redness, surrounded by men who crowded up, and chewed tobacco, and smote the iron surface with hissing burnt-sienna-coloured jets!—frowsty, fusty, and muggy exceedingly. There was a deposit of train-oil,—a hot humanised dew all over us. And water, there was none to wash with. So I applied a handful of snow gathered on the carriage platform to my face and hands in lieu thereof, and got back to my seat just as A——n returned from some distant part of the train with hands full of apples. They were delicious, and with three or four of them, and a few cigars, we managed to construct a charming breakfast.

It was so dark when the train reached Kingston, that we could see nothing more than the outlines of the station. I was exceedingly anxious to visit a place of so much importance historically, commercially, and strategically, and fully intended to remain there for some days on my return to Toronto; but the Fates ordained that it was not to be, and all my personal knowledge of Kingston was derived from that glimpse in the dark of the railway terminus, and certain steeples and spires rising above the snow. But the position of the city confers upon it a very high place on the list of military posts for the defence of Canada, and some considerations connected with it will be discussed hereafter.

Politically Kingston has become a dead body since 1844, when its short-lived career as the capital and seat of government was cut short. The military genius of the French occupants in early days, in seizing on the best positions for the defence and maintenance of their conquest, is shown still, by the fact that our forts occupy the sites of those which were originally constructed by them. More than a hundred years before there was any trace of a city at Kingston, or any building save the wigwam of the Indian or the log-huts of the soldiery, the Count de Frontenac built a fort in communication with the great system, from the St. Lawrence to the Ohio, of the French strongholds, which was destined to extend to the Mississippi, and to enclose the troublesome English Colonies within stringent limits. When this fort was captured by Colonel Bradstreet in 1756, the French had only established a kind of military colony and a very insignificant trading-post round the fort. In little more than twenty years subsequently, the present town was founded; and in the war with America the place became of very great consequence.

It is a fact curious enough, and worthy of some consideration, that the great war in the middle of the last century, which ended in the loss to France of her hopes of Indian influence and of empire, and in the seizure of her American Colonies by Great Britain, should have, according to the best of American statesmen and philosophical reasoners, led also to the establishment of the United States, and the foundation of the greatest Republic the world has ever seen.

Kingston commands the entrance to the Rideau Canal, one of the principal means of communication between Lake Ontario and the interior of the country, forming an admirable connection between the Ottawa River and Lake Ontario: it is, in fact, the most important means of inland intercourse, because the difficulties in the way of an enemy are very considerable, either in a direct attack upon Kingston, if properly fortified, or in a flank movement against it from the interior.

The canal is brought into working order with the Grand Trunk Railway; so that if the Americans, our only possible enemy, were to make demonstrations against our frontier and our lines, with a view of intercepting our supplies and internal relations between the east and west of the province, it would be easy to disembark men and munitions at Kingston Mills and forward them by railway. Kingston, again, is an excellent point of observation, and with proper defences and aggressive resources, ought to command Lake Ontario and the entrance from the St. Lawrence. An adequate force stationed there, with a proper flotilla, could effectually keep in check any hostile demonstration from Cape Vincent, Sacket's Harbour, or the other posts from Oswego to the western extremity of Lake Ontario.

The harbour is said to be excellent; there is a dockyard, which could be rendered capable of doing most of the work required for our light gunboats: and with the additions pointed out and urged by our engineer officers to the existing fortifications, Kingston could be made a position of as much military strength as it undoubtedly now is of strategical importance.

Between Toronto and Kingston there are, however, Port Hope, Coburg, and Belville on the line of railway, all of which present facilities for the landing of an enemy: at any one of these points a hostile occupation would cut the regular communications at once; and indeed it is very much to be regretted, in a military point of view, that engineering, commercial, or other considerations caused the makers of the Grand Trunk Railway to run the line close to the shores of a great inland sea, the opposite side of which belongs to a foreign country which has from time to time announced (if not through the lips of statesmen, by the popular voice) that the conquest of Canada is a fixed principle in its policy.

The Americans, whether by accident or design, have constructed the New York Central, which runs along the south coast, at a distance of many miles from Lake Ontario, but cross-lines connect it with the principal ports upon the lake, from Buffalo to Sandusky; their line runs tolerably close to the shore of Lake Erie higher up, but there is no position on that lake which has to fear the aggression of such a force as could be collected at Kingston.

Perhaps to the generality of people in England, Kingston was first made known by the unpleasant incidence which compelled the Prince of Wales to pass it unvisited, or rather to remain on board the steamer. No doubt the Orangemen are now very sorry for what they did, and, in fact, feel that they were led by the fanaticism or the desire for notoriety of some small local leaders to make themselves very ridiculous and offensive. The zeal of these Defenders of the Faith was no doubt stimulated by the presence of a large number of Irish Roman Catholics, who are at least as violent as their opponents.

The French-Canadians, with just as much fidelity to their faith, do not enter into the violent polemical, political, and miscalled religious controversies which led to such an unseemly result at Kingston; and certainly, it is much to be regretted that the peculiar influence of American institutions, which checks any attempt of religious parties to disturb the public peace or social relations for their own purposes and for the gratification of pride or lust of power, cannot be extended to the provinces and to the British Possessions, where they work such prodigious mischief.

From Kingston the line winds along the shore of the great lake-like river, studded with a thousand islands. Here, again, the Americans would possess considerable advantage in case of war, as their main-line is far inland, but branch-lines from it lead to Cape Vincent and Ogdensburgh, at right-angles to our line of communication. The American water-boundary, I believe, passes outside a considerable number of the more important islands; but the power which possesses naval supremacy on Lake Ontario will probably find the means of commanding the Upper St. Lawrence, no matter which belligerent establishes himself on the islands.

The Canadians with whom I conversed in the train declared they were quite ready to defend their country in case of invasion, but did not understand, they said, being taken away to distant points to fight for the homes of others. It seemed quite clear to them that the United States would only invade Canada to humiliate and weaken the mother-country, and that the general defence of the province ought to devolve on the power whose policy had led to the war; whilst the inhabitants should be ready to give the imperial troops every assistance in the localities where they are actually resident.

CHAPTER V.

Arrive at Cornwall—The St. Lawrence—Gossip on India—Aspect of the country—Montreal—The St. Lawrence Hall Hotel—Story of a Guardsman—Burnside—Dinner—Refuse a banquet—Flags—Climate—*Salon-à-manger*—Contrast of Americans and English—Sleighs—The "Driving Club"—The Victoria Bridge—Uneasy feeling—Monument to Irish emigrants—Irish character—Montreal and New York—The Rink—Sir F. Williams—Influence of the Northerners.

IT was noon ere we reached Cornwall, a place some seventy miles from Montreal, where a rough *restaurant* at the station enabled us to make a supplement to the deficiencies of our simple repast. The people who poured in and out of the train here were fine rough-looking fellows, with big, broad, sallow faces and large beards, wrapped up in furs, wearing great long boots,—men of a new type. Several of them were speaking in French; but the literature which travelled along with us was American, mostly New York, in the matter of periodicals: it was of course English, and pirated, in the more substantial forms. The frost still clung to the outside of the windows; inside, the foliage and broad tracery of leaves, and cathedral aisles, and plumes of knight and lady, tumbled down in big drops, and by degrees the sun cleared away the crust on one side, so that we could look out on the flat expanse of snow-covered forest.

On our right, now and then glimpses could be caught of a pale blue riband-like streak across the dazzling white plain. "That's the St. Lawrence you see there. Pitty it's friz up so long. We wouldn't envy the Yankees anything they've got to show us if we had a port open all the year," quoth an honest Canadian beside me. For the first time I began to feel sympathy for a country that "can't get out" for five mortal months, and that breathes through another man's nostrils and mouth. A horrible semi-suffocated sort of existence. No wonder the Canadians look longingly over at that bit of land which Lord Ashburton yielded to the United States and the State of Maine.

A——n and I, by way of counteracting the influence of the atmosphere and external scenery, talked of India. Some poor creatures half the world's girth away, whom we were speaking of at that moment, would have given a good deal for some of the despised ice and snow around us, groaning no doubt under that sun which even in February knows no coolness in Central India in mid-day. How oddly things turn up! I had ever firmly believed that a young soldier friend of mine had slain many enemies in that great rebellion, and had, Achilles-like, sent many souls of sepoys to Hades, and so in that faith speaking, suddenly I was interrupted by A——n. "What are you talking of? *He* kill so *many* budmashes at Nulla-Nullah! Why, I don't believe he ever fired a shot or made a cut at a nigger in his life." *My* fierce little friend had done both, and many a time and oft. And so, as he knew, away went a reputation, within thirty miles of Montreal; thermometer 10°.

Hereabouts were seen many snug homesteads rising up through the snow, with farmhouses, and outhouses —all clad in the same livery. The country looked well cleared and settled; sleighs glided over the surface, and were drawn up at the stations to carry passengers and luggage. Anon we came upon a great frozen river, and crossed it by a series of arches too great for a bridge; but this was nevertheless the Ottawa itself rolling away under its ice coat, as the blood flows through an artery, to rush unseen into the cold embrace of the St. Lawrence. These two great bridges must be worth visiting when they can be seen in the full exercise of their functions. The river forms an island here which the ice now continentalises.

About four o'clock, very much as land looms up in the ocean, we saw the dark mass of Montreal rising up in contrast to the whitened mountain at the foot of which it lies; the masts of vessels frozen in, and funnels of steamers, mingled with steeples and domes; and as the sun struck the windows a thousand flashes of glowing red darted back upon us. Then the train ran past a "marine factory," whatever that may be, and a suburb of stone and wooden houses intermixed, and a population of children whose faces looked preternaturally pale, perhaps from the reflection of the snow, and of women in pork-pie hats with thick veils over their faces, and of men, mostly smoking, in great fur coats and boots; and at last the train reached the terminus, where a great concourse of sleigh-drivers, who spoke as though they had that moment left Kingstown jetty, Ireland, claimed our body and property. These were promptly routed by the staff of the St. Lawrence Hall, who carried off our party to an omnibus without wheels, which finally bore us off to the hotel so called.

The soldiers about the streets were all comfortably clad in dark overcoats, fur caps with flaps for the ears, and long boots; but the dress takes from their height, and does not conduce to a smart soldier-like appearance.

The streets through which we passed were lined with well-built lofty houses. It might scarce be fancy which made me think that Montreal was better built than American cities of the same size. In the great cold hall of the hotel there was excessive activity: befurred officers of the regiments sent to Canada during the Trent difficulty, before Mr. Seward had made up his mind and persuaded the President to give up the Southern envoys, were coming in, going out, or were congregated in the passage. Orderlies went to and fro with despatches and office papers. In fact the general-in-chief, Sir Fenwick Williams of Kars, and staff, the commanding officer of the Guards, Lord G. Paulet, and staff, were quartered here, and carried on their office business; and the Commissary-General, Power, and the Principal Medical Officer, Dr. Muir, were also lodging in the hotel, with a host of combatant officers of inferior grade.

There was no rush to the *table-d'hôte*, after the American fashion, but the dinner itself was very much in the American style. I was much amused at the distress of a Guardsman who made his appearance at the doorway during dinner, with a letter in his hand for one of the officers. He halted stiffly at the threshold, and stood staring at the brilliancy of the splendid ormolu ornaments, and the array of lacquered chandeliers and covers. In vain the waiters pointed out to him the officer he sought; he would not intrude on the gorgeous scene, nor would he trust his missive to another hand. At last, after gazing in a desperate manner on space, and balancing from one leg to another, he took a maddening resolve, put his hand to his cap, held the other out with the letter in it as his dumb apology and in mitigation of punishment, and marching straight to his mark, trampling crowds of waiters in his way, only halted when he came up to the table he sought, where, with eyeballs starting, he put the missive to the level of the captain's nose, saluted, and ejaculated, "By order of Colonel Jones, sir." "All right." With a wheel round and a salute, the perturbed warrior countermarched and escaped into the prosaic outward world. A Frenchman would have come in with the most perfect self-possession, and possibly with some little grace. An American would probably have turned his chew, have addressed some remarks to the waiters on his way, have given the captain a tap on the back or a nudge of the elbow, and would rather have expected a drink. And which of the three, after all, is to be preferred?

I met a whole regiment of men I knew, and after dinner adjourned with some of them to my rooms. They all growled of course, found fault with Canada and abused the Government, and seemed to think it ought not to snow in winter.

I received a most interesting letter from a friend of mine with the Burnside expedition, which revealed as large an amount of bad management as could well be conceived. Burnside, personally, has enough ingenuity, but is quite wanting in self-reliance, presence of mind, and vigour. The expedition from which so much was expected did more than might have been thought possible at one time under the circumstances.

A telegram from Toronto informed me that it was in contemplation to invite me to a public banquet, and desired me to state my wishes. Very much as I appreciated such an honour from my countrymen and fellow-subjects, it was inconsistent, as I conceived, with my position, as it certainly was with my sense of the merits attributed to me, to accept the very great compliment offered to me. It came all the more agreeably as it was in such contrast to the manner in which I had been received in the United States for the last few months; and it touched me very sensibly, more than my friends at Toronto could have imagined.

A——n came in rather wroth about a matter of flags. He had been to see some Frenchmen, whether real or true Zouaves of the Crimea I know not, who gave out on tremendous posters that they were the identical children of the Beni Zoug Zoug, who had acted before us all in that theatre on the Woronzow Road once so charming and well filled; and he had been seized with indignation because they, in that Canadian city, under the British flag, had dared to perform under the folds of the tricolor, and the stars and stripes of the United States. I explained that the British flag was metaphorically and properly supposed to float above both; all which much comforted him, and so to bed—cold enough, in despite of stoves and open fire. The servants here are Irish men and women, with a sprinkling of free negroes.

Next day the weather was not at all warmer. In winter time the cold is by no means unbearable in this

Canadian clime, when one is well furred and clad; to the poor it must be very trying, for furs and fuel are dear, and even clothing of an ordinary kind is not cheap. The emigrant, in his rude log hut open in many chinks, must shrink and shiver and suffer in the blast. What do they, who follow, not owe to the hardy explorer who has opened up wood and mountain, and laid down paths on the sea for them?

A thick haze had now settled down on all things, a cold freezing rime, which clung and crept to one, and almost sat down on the very hearth. Descending the stairs, which were in a transition state and in the hands of carpenters, to the long "salon-à-manger," I found the tables well filled by guardsmen, riflemen, and members of the staff, military and civil, who gave the place the air of a mess-room under disorderly circumstances.

I had before this seen many such rooms in American hotels in cities filled with soldiery, and I am bound to say the difference between the two sets of men was remarkable. The noise, gaiety, and life of these grave English were exuberant when compared to the silence of American gatherings of the same kind, which are, indeed, disturbed by the clatter of plates and dishes, and the horrible squeaking of chair legs over the polished floors, but otherwise are quiet enough. Here, men laughed out, talked loud, shouted to the waiters, aired their lungs in occasional scoldings and objurgations, having reference to chops and steaks and tardy-coming dishes; "old-fellowed" their friends; asked or told the news. I don't know that the Englishmen were better looking, taller, or in any physical way had the advantage of the men of the continent, except in ruddier cheeks perhaps, and in frames better provided with cellular tissue; but the distinction of style and manner was marked.

The Americans usually came into the salon singly; each man, with a bundle of newspapers under his arm, took a seat at a vacant table, ordered a prodigious repast, which he gobbled in haste, as though he was afraid of losing a train, and then rushed off to the bar or smoked in the passages, never sitting for a moment after his breakfast. The Englishmen came in little knots or groups, exhibited no great anxiety about newspapers, ordered simple and substantial feasts, enjoyed them at their ease, chattered much, and were in no particular hurry to leave the table. The taciturnity of the American was not well-bred, nor was the good humour of the Briton vulgar. It may be said the comparison is not just, because the Americans were engaged in a fearful war, which engrossed all their thoughts; whilst the English officer was merely sent out on a tour of duty. But in the bar-room, *restaurants*, or streets, the American did not maintain the same aspect: he put on what is called a swaggering air, and was not at all disposed to let his shoulder-straps or his sword escape notice.

The good people at home would have been greatly surprised to hear the way in which the officers spoke of their exile to the snows of Canada; but though they growled and grumbled when breakfast was over, probably till dinner time, they would have fought all the better for it. Indeed there was not much else to do.

The streets were piled with snow; and at the front of the hotel, sleighs, driven by Irishmen, such as are seen managing the Dublin hacks, wrapped up in fur and sheepskins, were drawn up waiting for fares, to the constant jingle of the bells, which enlivened the air. It was too early and too raw and cold for many of the ladies of Montreal to trust their complexions to the cruelties of the climate, thickly veiled though they might be; but now and then a sleigh slid by with a bright-eyed freight half-buried in *fourrures*, and some handsome private vehicles of this description reached in their way as high a point of richness and elegance as could well be conceived. The horses were rarely of corresponding quality. The guardsmen and other soldiers, "red" and "green," strode about in cold defiant boots, and seemed to like the town and climate better than their officers. Mr. Blackwell, the amiable and accomplished chief of the Grand Trunk Railway, called for me, and drove me out to an early dinner.

It was a matter of some ceremony to set forth: a fur cap with flaps secured over the ears and under the chin, a large fur cloak, and a pair of moccasins for the feet, had to be put on; and then we clomb the sides of the boat-like sleigh, and started off at a rapid pace, which produced a sea-sick sensation—at least what I am told is like it—in very rough places where the runners of the sleighs have cut into the snow. On our way we were rejoiced by the sight of the "Driving Club" going out for an excursion, Sir Fenwick Williams leading. All one could see, however, was a certain looming up of dark forms through the drift gliding along to the music of the bells, which followed one after the other, and were lost in the hazy yet glittering clouds tossed up by the horses' hoofs from the snow. In the afternoon the rime passed off, and the day became clearer, but no warmer.

At about three o'clock, we sleighed over by rough roads to the terminus of the railway, close to the Victoria Bridge, where a party of the directors and some officers — Colonel Mackensie, Colonel Wetherall, Colonels Ellison and Earle of the Guards, and others recently arrived—were assembled to view the great work which would stamp the impress of English greatness on Canada, if her power were to be rooted out to-morrow. The royal carriage—a prettily decorated long open waggon, with the Prince of Wales's coat of arms, plume, and initials still shining brightly— was in readiness; and as cold makes one active, or very lazy, as the case may be, we lost no time in starting to explore the bridge, which threw its massive weight in easy stretches across the vast frozen highway of the St. Lawrence—so light, so strong, so graceful, for all its rigid lines, that I can compare the impression of the thing to nothing so much as to that of the bounds of a tiger.

The entrance, in the limestone rock, is grandly simple; but ere we could well admire its proportions the car ran into the darkness of the great tube. The light admitted by the neatly designed windows in the iron sides of the aërial tunnel was not enough to enable us to pierce through the smoke and the fog which clung to the interior. The car proceeded to the end, the thermometer marking 6°. Statistics, though I have them all by me, I am not about to give, as the history of the bridge is well known; but Mr. Blackwell showed me a table which indicated that the monster suffers or rejoices like a living thing, and contracts and expands and swells out his lines wondrously, just in proportion as the temperature alters.

From this end of the magnificent bridge one could see, nearly a hundred feet below him, the rugged surface of the ice, beneath which was rolling the St. Lawrence. It was distinguished from the snowy expanse covering the land by the bluish glint of the ice, and by the torn glacier-like aspect of the course of the stream, where the frozen masses had been contending fiercely with the current and with each other till the frost-king had clutched them and bound them in the midst of the conflict. You could trace the likeness of spires, pinnacles, castles, battlements, and alpine peaks in the wild confusion of those serried heaps, which were tilted up and forced together; but the haze did not permit us to follow the course of the stream for any great distance. It was too cold for enthusiastic enjoyment, and we got into the car and backed into the darkness till we reached the centre of the bridge.

I confess, when it occurred to me that great cold makes iron brittle, the uneasy feeling I experienced of suspense, *malgré moi*, in passing over any of these great engineering triumphs, was aggravated so far that it required a good deal of faith in the charming diagram of the effects of temperature on the bridge, to make me quite at ease. I suppose it is only an engineer who can be quite above the thought, "Suppose, after all, the bridge does go at this particular moment." And then the iron did crackle and bang and shriek most unmistakeably and demonstratively.

At the centre of the bridge we got out, and had another look at the river, some sixty feet below. Remarked the *thinness* of the iron; was informed it was on purpose, every plate being made specially for its place. Examined carefully a bolt driven in by the

G

Prince of Wales; rather liked its appearance, as it was well hammered and seemed sound. Then the car received us, and we were drawn through this ghastly cold gallery once more, and were divulged at the railway station among a crowd of furred citizens.

Thence through the city over the rough road in our carrioles and sleighs. On our way I remarked a stone obelisk standing out of the snow close to the railway, in a low patch of ground near the river. "That," said my companion, "is a memorial to six thousand Irish emigrants who died here of ship fever." What a history in those few words—a tale of sorrow and woe unutterable—I hope, not of neglect and indifference too! The railway engineers have thoughtfully erected the monument of the nameless dead, and so far rescued their fate from oblivion.

I am not so philosophic as to witness the desolating emigrations which leave the homes of a country waste, and fill the lands of future kingdoms and possible rivals with an alienated population, without regret. Above all, I pity the fate of the poor pioneers whose hapless lot it is to labour unthanked and despised, to build up the stranger's cities, to clear his forests, and make his roads, to found his power and greatness, and then to sit at his gate waiting for alms when the hour cometh that no man can work.

It is most strange, indeed, and yet too true, that a race which, above all others, ought to seek the material advantages and the substantial results of hard work, should be the most readily led astray by windy agitators and by political disputes and passions. Here we are driving through the streets of Montreal, which owes much of its existence to Irish labour, and the labourer lives in filth and degradation, in the back slums of the city, intensely interested in elections and clerical discussions, little better cared for or regarded than the dogs thereof till his vote is required.

The city is now in its winter mantle, but it shows fair proportions. The Roman Catholic chapels are well placed and handsome, and excel in size and numbers the Protestant churches. The Quarter-master-General, who has had to hire one of the Catholic colleges to serve as barracks for the troops, says the priests are remarkably keen practitioners at a bargain: good Churchmen always were in old times. The metal-covered domes and spires, the roofs of houses sheeted with tin, now began to glisten in the sun, and gave a bright look to the place which did not make it all the warmer.

Montreal is a much finer-looking place than I had expected. The irregularity of the streets pleased the eye, wearied by straight lines and regular frontage. The houses of stone with double windows have plain bare fronts, and do not present so good an appearance as the best of New York; but the character of the residences as a whole is better, and the effect of the city, to compare small things with great, very much more interesting and picturesque.

Our destination in this drive was the Rink, or covered skating-ground, which is the fashionable sporting resort of Montrealese in the winter time. The crowd of sleighs and sleigh-drivers around the doors of a building which looked like a Methodist chapel, announced that the skaters were already assembled.

Anything but a Methodist-looking place inside. The room, which was like a large public bath-room, was crowded with women, young and old, skating or preparing to skate, for husbands, and spread in maiden rays over the glistening area of ice, gliding, swooping, revolving on legs of every description, which were generally revealed to mortal gaze in proportion to their goodness, and therefore were displayed on a principle so far unobjectionable. The room was lighted with gas, which, with the heat of the crowd, made the ice rather sloppy; but the skating of the natives was admirable, and some hardened campaigners of foreign origin had by long practice learned to emulate the graces and skill of the inhabitants.

It was a mighty pretty sight. The spectators sat or stood on the raised ledge round the ice parallelogram like swallows on a cliff, and now and then dashed off and swept away as if on the wing over the surface, in couples or alone, executing quadrilles, mazurkas, waltzes, and tours de force, that made one conceive the laws of gravitation must be suspended in the Rink, and that the outside edge is the most stable place for the human foot and figure. Mercy, what a crash! There is a fine stout young lady sprawling on the ice, tripped up by Dontstop of the Guards, who is making a first attempt, to the detriment of the lieges. How delighted the ladies are, and pretend not to be; for the fallen fair one is the best contortionist in the place! She is on her legs again—has shaken the powdered ice and splash off her dandy jacket and neat little breeches,—yes, they wear breeches, a good many of them,—and is zigzagging about once more like a pretty noiseless firework.

The little children skate, so do most portentous mammas. A line of recently arrived officers, in fur caps and coats, look on, all sucking their canes, and resolving to take private lessons early in the morning. Some, in the goose-step stage, perform awful first lines with their skates, and leave me in doubt as to whether they will split up or dash out their brains. The young ladies pretend to avoid them with unanimity, but sail round them still as seagulls sweep by a drowning man. And if a fellow should fall—and be saved by a lady? Well! It may end in an introduction, and a condition of "muffinage." And what that is we must tell you hereafter. I can't answer your question as to whether the women were pretty; eyes dark generally, and good complexions. The Rink is a bad place to judge of that point.

I paid my respects to Sir Fenwick Williams, who has his quarters in the hotel. The general has plenty of work to do at present, and did not seem quite so well as when I saw him after his return from Kars. There is a general impression that the Federals will keep their armies in good humour at the end of the war, by annexing Canada, if they can. No one asks what they will do with them when that work has been accomplished. Dined at the house of the Hon. John Rose, member for Montreal, and formerly a member of the Government. He had, after his hospitable wont, some young officers to dine also; and, after an agreeable evening, I slid home in a bitter snow drift to the hotel, and so to bed. Here is a page from my diary.

February 6.—The severe cold makes the head ache, and stupefies me *ultra modum*. I wrote to Mr. Hope, stating my reasons for declining the great compliment of a public dinner intended for me at Toronto. As I move about here, I feel that society is much under the influence of the unruly fellow, our next neighbour.

There is no great love for him; but his prodigious kicks and blows, his threats, his bad language, his size and insolence, frighten them up here. There is great anxiety for the American news; and I am bound to say, the Northern Americans must have done something to make the Canadians dislike them, as there is little love for them even where little is felt for England. I saw a great many of the principal personages *to-day*. Called on the Bishop, whose sweet, benevolent face is an index of his mind. He spoke in high terms of his Roman Catholic coadjutor; indeed, it would be difficult to quarrel with Dr. Mountain. In education, they work harmoniously together. Mr. D'Arcy M'Ghie called on me. He is now a member of the Canadian Parliament, and is giving his support to the authority of the British Crown. His loyalty is, of course, stigmatised by some as treason to what they call the cause of Ireland; but I believe the atmosphere of Canada is found to have a vapour-dispelling, febrifuge character about it which works well on the mind of the Irish immigrant. A most entertaining, witty, well-informed barrister, also an Irishman, paid me a visit, and gave some admirable sketches of Canadian society, of the bar, of the working of parties, as well as his own ideas on all points, in a peculiarly terse and pleasant way.

CHAPTER VI.

Visit the "lions" of Montreal—The 47th Regiment—The city open to attack—Quays, public buildings—French colonisation—Rise of Montreal—Stone—A French-Anglicised city—Loyalty of Canadians—Arrival of Troops—Facings—British and American Army compared—Experience needed by latter—Slavery.

I REMAINED several days at Montreal, examining the lions, and making the most of my brief stay. Here are living a knot of Southern families in a sort of American Siberia, at a very comfortable hotel, who nurse their wrath against the Yankee to keep it warm and sustain each other's spirits. They form a nucleus for sympathising society to cluster around, and so germinate into innocent little balls, sleigh-parties, and occasional matrimonial engagements.

"Waiting for his regiment," too, was old General Bell—the veteran who saw his first shot fired in the Peninsula, and his last, forty-four years afterwards, before Sebastopol. There were parades of the 47th Regiment and inspection-drills on the St. Lawrence in snow-shoes; and Penn marched out his Armstrongs in beautiful order, on their sleighs, for all to see.

The position of this fine city leaves it open to attack from the American frontier, which is so near that the blue tops of the mountain ridges of the bordering States can be seen on a clean day. The rail from the centre of New York runs direct to it, through the arsenal and fort of Rouse's Point on Lake Champlain; and there are two other lines converging on it, so that an enormous force could be swiftly sent against it. The frontier is here a mere line on the map, so drawn as to leave the head of Lake Champlain and Rouse's Point in the hands of the Americans. Its importance, its beauty, and the feeling of the inhabitants would render it tempting to the Northern armies; and the fierce, relentless, and destructive spirit which has been evoked in their civil war, might lead them to destroy all that is valuable and handsome in a city which stands in strong contrast to the hideousness of American towns, if they were, as of old, obliged to abandon the city.

The quays of Montreal are of imperial beauty, and would reflect credit on any city in Europe. They present a continuous line of cut-stone from the Lachine Canal along the river-front before the city, leaving a fine broad mall or esplanade between the water's edge and the houses. The public buildings, built of solid stone, in which a handsome limestone predominates, are of very great merit. Churches, courthouses, banks, markets, hospitals, colleges, all are worthy of a capital; and these would present a very different appearance to an invader from that which was offered by the poverty-stricken and insignificant Montreal of 1812.

There are a few guns mounted on a work on the left bank of the river above the city, but for military purposes the place may be considered perfectly open. There are more than 90,000 people in the city, but it is said not to be a fighting population; and there are many foreigners and emigrants of an inferior class, who taint the place

FOUNDATION OF MONTREAL.

with rowdyism. The British element was active in volunteering when I was there, and figures in uniform were frequently to be seen in the streets; but the time was unfavourable for any public displays, and I never saw any of the volunteers working *en masse*.

Here, as elsewhere, the jealousies of claimants for command, local and personal rivalry, have impeded the good work; but such obstacles would vanish in the presence of danger. National feeling has tended to make the organisation of corps too expensive, and the question of drafting for the militia has also interfered with the full development of the movement.

It would be unjustifiable to assert that the enterprise of the French people, and their capacity for colonisation, have been diminished by republican institutions; but, unquestionably, the great convulsions which have agitated society since the fall of the monarchy appear to have concentrated the energies of the race upon objects nearer home, even though they have annexed Algeria, established a protectorate over Tahiti, and are engaged in war with the Cambodians. Where is the enterprise which, more than 200 years ago, originated a company of merchant adventurers, who pushed out settlements into this wilderness, and founded factories among the Iroquois and the Mohawks? In those days, indeed, the zeal of Jesuits and other Roman Catholic missionaries preceded the march and directed the course of commerce.

Montreal owes its existence to a certain Monsieur Maisonneuve, the factor of the Commercial Association in 1642. More than 100 years afterwards it was nearly destroyed by fire; and ten years after the conflagration the troops of the insurgent colonies took possession of the town, which was a favourite object of attack in the two American wars.

In spite of many misfortunes—fire, hostile occupation, insurrection, riot—Montreal has flourished exceedingly, and the energy of its population has been displayed in securing for it a principal share of the trade between England and the Upper Provinces. Its railway communications have been pushed with great energy, and the canals and quays are in imperial grandeur; but still, in case of war with the States, the only outlet in winter (by rail to Portland) would be effectually blocked up.

The city contains nearly 100,000 inhabitants, of whom 60,000 are Roman Catholics—representing a great variety of nationalities, with a predominance, however, of French-Canadians and Irish. An abundance of fine stone, found near the town, has enabled the inhabitants to build substantial houses in lieu of the wooden edifices from which they were driven by two great conflagrations; but the material is of a dull cold grey colour, and the streets, seen in winter-time, have in consequence a gloomy and melancholy aspect. Many of the cupolas and spires and the roofs of many of the houses are covered with metal plates, which shine out in the sun, and give the city a bright appearance from a distance, which is not altogether maintained on a nearer approach.

The mental activity of the population, displayed in a large crop of newspapers, doubtless indicates a close intimacy with the United States; but Montreal is, after all, French Anglicised, and, notwithstanding the disaffection of which it gave symptoms in the rebellion, the sympathies of its people are very far removed from the bald republicanism of the New England States.

Nuns and priests seem, to a Protestant eye, to be rather too numerous for the good of the people; but having seen the schools of the Christian Brothers, and having heard the testimony of all classes to the services rendered to morals and religion, to charity and to Christianity, by the various religious orders, I am forced to believe that Montreal is much indebted to their labours.

The number of hospitals, schools, scientific institutions —the libraries, reading-rooms, universities, are remarkable. They are worthy of a highly-civilised, wealthy, and prosperous community; but, in fact, the economy with which they are managed is not one of the least remarkable features about the Montreal institutions. Party animosities have now been softened: but there is no doubt of the satisfaction with which the Liberal Canadian points to the fact that those who were imprisoned and persecuted by the Government, for rebellious acts or tendencies, have since been called to office, and have served the Crown in high official positions.

The people of Canada are learning a useful piece of knowledge or two from what is passing so close to them. The annexation party are heard no more: in their room stand the people of Canada, loyal to the Crown and to the connexion, prepared to defend their homes and altars against invasion. So far as I have gone, in no place in the Queen's dominions is there greater attachment to her person and authority.

The Canadians see with sorrow the ills which afflict their neighbours, in spite of all the ill-advised menaces of the Northern Press; but they felt naturally indignant at being spoken of as if they were a mere chattel, which could be taken away by the United States from Great Britain in order to spite her. With such turbulent and dangerous elements at work close to them, they will no doubt eagerly assist the authorities in their efforts to secure their borders and their country, by putting the militia on a proper footing. The patriotism of the Legislature can be relied on to do this. England will do the rest, and give her best blood, if need be, to aid this magnificent dependency of the same Crown as that to which she is herself subject, in maintaining the present situation.

It was most agreeable to hear praise instead of grumbling, and to know that amid no ordinary difficulties the troops were landed and conveyed across the snows of Nova Scotia and New Brunswick in the month of January without casualty or mishap worth mentioning, and that the arrangements were worthy of every commendation. It made us feel proud of our army when we saw the cheerfulness, soldierly look, cleanliness, and deportment of the men, and learnt that they had conducted themselves in the most exemplary manner, though exposed to great temptation by the hospitality of the New-Brunswickers and the cheapness of intoxicating liquors.

And what wonderful vicissitudes of service those officers and men have seen! Here is a face yet burned by the suns of India, encircled in fur-cap, and peering into the railway carriage to welcome some well-known friend from China or Aldershot. There marches a sturdy Guardsman, one of the few who remain of the men of Alma and Inkerman, with that small ladder of glory on his breast. Here is one of the old Riflemen

—alas, most gracious Queen! they feel proud in sadness of their name now—one of "the Prince Consort's Own Rifle Brigade," who heard, that bright evening when our good ship was gliding through the blue waters of the Dardanelles, the rich chorus of those manly voices, most of which are silenced for ever:—

"Soldiers, merrily march away!
Soldier's glory lives in story,
His laurels are green when his locks are grey,
Then hurrah for the life of a soldier!"

Firm and clean and straight as of yore, under all his load of greatcoat, furs, and boots, struts the soldier of the 47th, mindful of De Lacy Evans, "little Inkerman," and of the greater in which it was eclipsed. Will he be as trim and neat, I wonder, if they take away his white facings? Of the old "fours"—the second brigade of the division which with the light divided the "general" fighting—the 41st and 47th, though perhaps no better, always looked better than the 49th, because of their facings.

The influence of facings, indeed, goes much further than that in general society. The hotel in which I live (a very attentive host is doing his best to complete the resemblance by extensive dilapidations) is as like a barracks as can be. The "St. Lawrence Hall" is in a military occupation. The obstacles in way of "alterations" are bestridden by Guardsmen, Riflemen, and Engineers, on their way to breakfast and dinner, as if they were getting through breaches. In the hall abundance of soldiers, anxious orderlies with the quaint quartoes full of orders, and military idlers smoking as much as you like, but, I am glad to say, not chewing—nor, as a New York paper calls the

Republican Senators, " tobacco-expectorant." To appreciate this boon properly, pray be prepared to limit the suffrage immensely. In the passages more orderlies and soldier-servants, who now and then do a little of what is called flirting with the passing *demoiselles de service;* tubs outside in the passage; doors of rooms open *à la caserne;* military chests and charts on the table.

It would have given those who admit that war is necessary sometimes, as the sole means of redressing national grievances, considerable satisfaction to have seen the difference presented by the regular troops of Great Britain in Canada and the vast masses of volunteers assembled on the Potomac by the United States. It is not that the British are one whit finer men: taking even the Guards, there are some few regiments there which in height and every constituent of physique, except gross weight, cannot be excelled.

As a whole, perhaps, the average of intelligence, taken there to mean reading and writing, may be higher among the United States volunteers than among the British regulars;—not much, however. The Sanitary Commission of New York, a very patriotic and thoroughly American body, did not attempt to claim more than three-fifths of the United States armies as of American *birth*. The immediate descendants of Irish and German parents are thus included among native-born Americans, though they are in all respects except birth Irish and Germans still. Very probably they have not partaken to the full, or to any great extent, of the advantages of public education.

But, taking the statement of the Commissioners— which, by-the-bye, is a very serious reflection on the patriotism of the Northern populations—it may be doubted whether in reading, writing, and arithmetic there is any great superiority on the part of the United States troops over the British. I admit that in some regiments of the New England States there is a higher average of such knowledge as may enable a man to argue on the orders of his officers, and of such intelligence as may induce him to believe he is competent to criticise the conduct of a campaign.

There is an immense amount of newspaper reading and letter-writing, the former taste predominating; but our own mailbags are ample enough to satisfy any one that the same preponderance which is maintained by London over New York in correspondence is to be found in the English army over the American. Many Irish and Germans here have no inducements to write letters, but there are few who are unable to read their newspapers.

What is it, then, one may reasonably ask, which would satisfy the grumbler, who finds fault with the expenditure of standing armies, that he has got value for his money when he contrasts the British troops here with the battalions on the Potomac? It is the efficiency produced by obedience, which is the very life of discipline: the latter is obedience incorporated, and, in motion or at rest, acting by fixed rules, with something approaching to certainty in its results.

The small army in Canada could be massed together, with its artillery and transport, in a very short time, and directed with precision to any one point, though it is a series of detachments on garrison duty rather than a *corps d'armée*, and it has neither cavalry nor baggage animals. With all the liberal (if not occasionally extravagant) outlay, and the cost of transporting it, the force in a few weeks would be far less expensive than an American corps of the same strength; and it is no disparagement to the latter to say they would be less efficient than the British. I do not speak of actual fighting; for our battlefields in Canada tell how desperate may be the encounters between the armies. Our force would be under the orders of experienced officers. The staff would consist of men who have seen service in the Russian war, in Asia, in India, and in China, and who have witnessed the operations of great European armies. The United States is laboriously seeking to acquire experience, at a cost which may be ruinous to its national finances, and a delay which may be fatal to its cause; but it cannot galvanise the inert mass with the fire of military efficiency, though it burns, we are told, with hidden volcanic energies, and is pregnant with patriotic life. The use of an army in war is to fight, to be able to move to and after its enemy, to beat and to pursue him.

It is not greatly to be wondered at if the work, which Great Britain has only partially accomplished, notwithstanding the greatness of its progress, should be only begun in the United States. The aptitude of a large mass of the inhabitants for arms, whether they be foreign or native-born, is marred by many things. There is the principle of equality intruding itself in military duty, confounding civil rights with the relations between superior and inferior—between officer and rank-and-file. There is the difficulty of getting men to follow officers who have no special fitness for their post. A soldier may be made in a year; a company officer cannot be made in three years. There are many officers in the American army of great theoretical and some practical knowledge; there are many in the British army lazy and indifferent;—but no one would think for a moment of comparing the acquirements, in a military sense, of the officers of the two nations.

In the Crimean war, when our army was enlarged at a time that severe losses had much diminished the number of officers, we saw that our standard was considerably lowered by the precipitate infusion of new men. No wonder, then, that the United States had and has great difficulty in procuring officers of the least value for a levy of more than half-a-million of volunteers.

But the system itself is a most formidable barrier to success. Under no circumstances can it reach a moderate degree of efficiency, unless the test of subsequent examination be rigidly enforced. There is no superiority of rank, of military knowledge, of personal character, of social position, to create an emulation in the mind of the private to be the obedient but daring equal of the officer in the time of danger. To such general remarks there are many and brilliant exceptions.

In the course of time, the personal qualities and the reputation for bravery and skill of officers would stand in the Republican armies in lieu of those influences which move the British soldier. No one is foolish enough to think or say that the private follows his officer because the latter has paid so much money for his commission or has so much a year. The gradual rise from one rank to another is a guarantee of some military knowledge—at all events, of acquaintance with drill. Social position counts for much. Men who are equal before the law are very unequal in the drill-book.

It would be lamentable to see so much faith in a

cause, such devotion, zeal, boundless expenditure, and splendid material comparatively lost—to behold the petted Republic wasting away under this influence, and the *vis inertiæ* of the force it has called into being, were it not that the spectacle is a lesson for the nations. It has not yet come to its end.

If standing armies there must be, let them be as complete in organisation as possible. If an empire must rely on volunteers as its main defence, let care be taken that they are organised and officered so as to be effective, and regulated on such principles of economy that they may not overwhelm with debt the country they are engaged in protecting by their arms.

It is quite true that the Confederates suffer from the same disadvantages as those which affect the Federals, but in a far less degree. Mr. Davis, early in the war, got hold of the army and subjected it to discipline. It was not so difficult to do so in the South as in the North, owing to the difference in the people. The officers were appointed by him. The men were animated, as they are now, by an intense hatred of their enemy. Their armies were in a defensive attitude; a large number, comprising some of the best, of the United States officers sided with them. They are operating besides on the inner lines.

But, after all, if the possession of the seaboard, the use of navies, the vast preponderance of population, the ability to get artillery and arms, and the occupation of the heads of the great river communications be not utterly thrown away, the North must overrun the South, if only the Northerners can fight as well as the Southerners, and if the North can raise money to maintain the struggle.

Let us leave out of view the slave element for once. The Abolitionists assert that the most formidable weapon in the United States armoury is the use of the emancipated slave; but it is rather difficult to see how the slaves could assist the North as long as they remain obedient and quiet in the South, or how the North can get at them by a mere verbal declaration till it has conquered the Slave States. Above all, it is not clear that it would benefit the penniless exchequer of the North to have 4,000,000 black paupers suddenly thrown on it for support.

Slavery is to me truly detestable; the more I saw of it the less I liked it. It is painful, to one who has seen the system at work and its results, to read in English journals philosophical—pseudo-philosophical treatises on the subject, and dissertations on the "ethics and æsthetics" of the curse, from which we shook ourselves free years ago with the approbation of our own consciences and of the world.

Before I speak of the defence of Montreal in connection with the general military position of the Canadian frontier, I shall continue my brief narrative of my tour through Canada.

CHAPTER VII.

First view of Quebec—Passage of the St. Lawrence—Novel and rather alarming situation—Russell's Hotel—The Falls of Montmorenci, and the "Cone"—Aspect of the City—The Point—"Tarboggining"—Description of the "Cone"—Audacity of one of my companions—A Canadian dinner—Call on the Governor—Visit the Citadel—Its position—Capabilities for defence—View from parapet—The armoury—Old muskets—Red-tape thoughtfulness—French and English occupation of Quebec—Strength of Quebec.

It was early in the morning when the train from Montreal arrived at Point Levi on the right bank of the St. Lawrence, a little above Quebec. The impression produced on us by the heights of Abraham, by the frowning citadel, by the picturesque old city glistening in the sun's rays, and by the great river battling its way through the fields of ice and the countless miniature bergs, which it hustled upwards with full-tide power, can never be effaced.

It required some faith to enable one to believe the passage could be made by mortal boat of that vast flood from which the crash of ice sounded endlessly, as floes and bergs floating full speed were dashed against each other—flying fast as clouds in a wintry sky up the river, the banks of which resembled the sheen sides of an Alpine crevasse. The force of the stream is so great as to rend through and rupture the coat of ice which is thickened daily, and the masses thus broken, tossed into all sorts of singular shapes, jagged and quaint, are borne up and down by the flood till they are melted by the increasing warmth of spring. An ice bridge is occasionally formed by the concentration of the ice in such masses as to resist the action of the water, and then sleigh horses cross by a path which is marked out by poles or twigs stuck in the snow, but it more usually happens that the river opposite Quebec remains unfrozen, and offers the singular spectacle of the ice rushing up and down every day as the tide rises and falls, to the great interest and excitement of strangers who have to cross from one side to the other.

At first the attempt seems impracticable. The deep blue of the St. Lawrence can be only seen here and there through the bergs and floes, like the veins beneath a snowy skin, but those glints are for ever varying as the ice passes on. The clear spaces are no sooner caught by the eye than they are filled up again, and every instant there are fresh refts made in the shifting surface, which is at once as solid as a glacier and as yielding as water. In this race the bergs are carried with astonishing force and rapidity, and a grating noise; and a grinding, crashing sound continually rises from the water.

At the station there was a goodly crowd of men in ragged fur coats and caps, pea jackets, and long boots, of an amphibious sort, who did not quite look like sailors, and who yet were not landsmen. These were clamouring for passengers, and touting with energy in a mixture of French and English. "Prenez notr' bateau, M'sieu'—La Belle Alliance! Good boat, Sar! Jean Baptiste, M'sieu': I well known boatman, Sir." "The blue boat, Sir, gentleman's boat, Mon Espoir," "L'Hirondelle," and so on at the top of their voices. And sure enough there, drawn up on the snow near the station, was a range of stout whale boats, double planked on the sides, and provided with remarkably broad keels.

We selected, after a critical inspection, the captain of one of these—a merry-eyed, swarthy fellow, with a big beard and brawny shoulders—as our Charon, and following his directions we were stowed away in a sort of well between the steersman and the stroke oar, where we sat down with our legs stretched out very comfortably, and were then covered up to the chin with old skins, furs, and great coats. When all was ready, a horse was brought forward with a sling bar, to which a rope was attached from the bow, and we glided forward along the road towards the most favourable point for crossing at that stage of the tide. The boat was steadied and guided by the crew, who ran alongside with their hands on the gunwales. Houses by the road side snowed up—shop windows with French names—sallow-faced, lean people looking out of the grimy windows—some large ships on the stocks, roughly placed on the river bank—these met the eye as we passed over the snow road towards the point opposite the city now looming nearer. With cheap timber and labour it is not surprising that the ship-building trade of Quebec flourishes.

For more than a mile and a half the boat careered eastwards, in active emulation with several other boats which were in our track, and the citadel on the opposite shore already lay behind us, before the horse was detached at the side of a deep incline leading to the river, and in another moment the boat was gliding down the bank and rushing for a blue rent in the midst of the heavy surface, into which we splashed as unerringly as a wild duck drops into a moss hole. The moment the bow touched the water, all the crew, some seven or eight in number, leaped in and seized their oars, which they worked with a will, whilst the skipper, standing in the bow, directed the course of the steersman.

We were now in a basin of clear water surrounded quite by ice, which only left the tops of the small bergs and the high banks on each side visible to us seated low down in the boat; and as we looked the floes were rapidly closing in upon us; but the skipper saw where the frozen wall was about opening, and forced the boat to the point of the advancing and narrowing circle, in which suddenly a tiny canal was cleft by the parting of the bergs, and the opportunity was instantly seized by the boatmen.

The ice was already closing and gripping the timbers as soon as we had fairly entered, and in an instant out leaped the crew on the treacherous surface, which here and there sank till they were knee-deep, and by main force they slid the boat up on a floe, and rocking her from side to side as a kite flutters before it makes a swoop, they roused her along on the surface of the ice, which was floating up towards the city very rapidly. With loud cries to a sort of chorus, the crew forced the craft across the floe till they floundered in some half-frozen snow, through which the boat dropped into the water. Then in they leaped, like so many Newfoundland dogs coming to land, all wet and furry, took the oars again, and rowed across and against the tide-set as hard as they could. Now in the water, then hanging on by the gunwales, this moment rowing, in another tugging at the boat ropes, clambering over small ice rocks, running across floes, sinking suddenly to the waist in the cold torrent, the men battled with the current, and by degrees the shore grew nearer, and the picturesque outlines of the city became more distinct in the morning sun.

What with the extraordinary combinations and forms of the ice drifts, the inimitably fantastic outlines of the miniature ice architecture, and the novelty of the scene, one's attention was entirely fixed on what was passing around, and it was not till we had nearly touched land that we had time to admire the fine effect of the streets and citadel, which, rising from the icy wall of the river-bank, towered aloft over us like the old town of Edinburgh suddenly transplanted to the sea.

We found an opening in the blue cold water-rocks near the Custom-house landing-wharf, at which place there was a shelving bank; a stout horse was attached to the boat by a rope, on which the crew threw themselves with enthusiasm; and in a few seconds more we were on the quay, and thence proceeded to Russell's Hotel, which was recommended to us as the best in the place. One may find fault with American hostelries; but assuredly they are better than the imitations of them which one finds in Canada, combining all the bad qualities of hotels in the States and in Europe, and destitute of any of the good ones.

The master of the hotel was an American, and he had struggled hard "under the depressing influences of the British aristocracy" to establish an American hotel, and he only succeeded in introducing the least agreeable features of the institution; but the attendants were civil and obliging, and there was no extravagant pressure on the resources of the place, so that we fared better than if we had been down south of the frontier. Even the landlord, though not particularly well disposed towards one so unpopular among his countrymen as myself, yielded so far to the *genius loci* as to be civil. The rooms were small, and not particularly clean; but as painting and papering were going on, those who follow me may be better provided for.

A short rest was very welcome; but what fate is like that which drives the sightseer ever onwards, and forces him, with the rage of all the furies, from repose? " The Falls of Montmorenci were but a drive away, and the ' Cone ' was in great perfection."

" What is ' the Cone ?' " The effect of our ignorance on the waiter was so touching—he was so astonished by the profound barbarism of our condition—that we felt it necessary for our own character to proceed at once to a spot which forms the delight of Quebec in the winter season, and to which the *bourgeoisie* were repairing in hot haste for the afternoon's pleasure.

A sleigh was brought round, and in it, ensconced in furs, we started off for the Falls, which are about eight miles distant. It was delightful to see anything so old on this continent as the tortuous streets of the city, which bear marks of their French origin, after such a long contact as I had endured with the raw youth of American cities in general, but it was impossible to deny that the antiquity before us had a certain air of dreary staleness about it also. The double-windowed flat-faced houses had a lanky, compressed air, as if they had been starved in early life, and the citizens had the appearance of people who had no particular object in being there, and set no remarkable value on time. A considerable sprinkling of priests was perhaps the most remarkable feature in the scene, and occasionally knots of ruddy-faced riflemen, in all the glory of winter fur caps and great coats, disputed the narrow pavement, alternating with the "red" soldiers of the line.

The city is built on very irregular ground, and some of the streets are so steep that it is desirable for new comers to have steel spikes screwed into the foot-gear to combat the inclination to proneness on the part of the wearers. Emerging through a postern in the ancient battlemented wall we came out in an uninteresting suburb of small houses, from which a descent led to the margin of the water. Far as the eye could reach a vast snow plain extended, with surface broken into ridges, mounds, and long dark lines, and dotted with opaque blocks from which the church steeples sprung aloft, indicating the sites of villages. The ridges were the hills over the St. Lawrence, the mounds its islands, and the lines its banks, which expand widely on the left to embrace the sweep of the St. Charles Lake, on which stands the projecting ledge of the eastern part of the city.

As we approached the Lake, over which our route lay, black specks, which were resolved into sleighs, or men and women on foot, were visible making their way over the ice, which was marked by lines of bushes and branches of trees dressed up in the snow so as to indicate the route, and far away similar black specks could be made out crossing the St. Lawrence below, which has now become the great highway. But not a very smooth road. The surface is far from being level, and consists indeed of a succession of undulations in which the profound cavities sometimes give one a sense of insecure travelling.

On the whole, however, the expedition was much

to be enjoyed, the air was bracing, and the cold not intense, and the scene "slid into the soul" with all its deep tranquillity. Doubtless it produced a very different effect on the red-nosed Britons who were keeping watch and ward on the ramparts of the citadel, or on the poor "habitant" trudging patiently beside his sleigh-load of wood, and knowing that snow is his portion for the next five months.

On our right a continuous movement of white rugged masses, to all appearance like a stream of polar bears, betokened the course of the unfrozen St. Lawrence; on our left rose the high bank of the lake over which we were travelling, and cottages of the villagers; before us the sleighs were streaming towards a point which ran out into the river and beyond which there seemed to be a shallow bay. This was the point at which the Montmorenci river, recovering from its fall, expanded into a broad sheet at its junction with the greater river. Here we arrived in about an hour.

At the Point there were a few houses, some vessels imbedded in the snow, and piles of sawn timber and deal planks, and a great concourse of sleighs; and beyond it, looking up to the left, at the distance of some half-mile, we saw a glistening sugarloaf of snow, on the summit of which the creaming, yellow-tinged mass of the Falls apparently precipitated itself from the high precipice which bars the course of the stream. On the snow between us and the sugarloaf, and up the white sides of the latter, little black objects were toiling with small progress, but at intervals one of them, gliding from the top of the cone like a falling star in the Inferno, rushed prone to the base, and thence carried by the impetus of the descent skimmed over the ice towards us for hundreds of yards, like a round shot till its force was spent.

Of the crowd gathered at the Point nearly every one had the small hand-sleigh, something like a tiny truck with iron runners, under the arm, known in the vernacular as a "tarboggin," of the derivation of which it is better to confess ignorance. A few were provided with sleighs of ampler proportions, and all the visitors were bent on tarbogginiug it, either from a shoulder of the Cone or from the summit of the mass itself.

As we approached over the snow the natives, men and women, flew past us on their way after a rush down the Cone, shouting to the bystanders to take care. Sometimes two were together, the lady seated on the front part of the machine, the man behind lying on his face with his feet stretched out so as to guide the sleigh by the smallest touch against the ice. At a distance the pleasure-seekers looked like some hideous insects impelled towards us with incredible velocity. As they came near and flew past, the expression of their countenances by no means indicated serene enjoyment.

Near the Cone itself a crowd of "tarboggin" hirers and guides beset us and guaranteed a safe descent, but it seemed a doubtful pleasure at best, and there was some chance of breaking limb, as we were told happened frequently during the season. We ascended to the lower shoulder of the Cone by steps in the snow and gazed on the scene with some curiosity. Not only were the people launching themselves from the Cone, but more adventurous still there were who, climbing up the steep side of the precipice, tarboggin under arm, at last reached some vantage snow, by the side of the Fall, where they threw themselves flat on the sleigh, and then came rushing down with a force which carried them clear up the side of the lower ledge of the Cone and over it, so that they were once more plunged downwards and were borne off towards the St. Lawrence.

It could now be very plainly seen that the Falls fell behind the Cone into a boiling turbulent basin, which fretted the edge of the ice and repelled its advances. Although much diminished in volume the body of water, which makes a leap of 250 feet down a sheer rock face into the caldron, was sufficiently large to present all the finest characteristics of a waterfall, but it was at times enveloped in a mist of snow, or rather of frozen spray, which blew into eyes, mouth, ears, and clothes, and penetrated to the very marrow of one's bones. And it is of this ever-falling frozen rain the Cone is built, and as the winter lengthens on the Cone grows higher and higher, till in favourable seasons it reaches an altitude of 120 feet. It is as regular as the work of an architect, and, I need not say, much more beautiful. At present it had not attained its full growth, and was only 80 feet in height—but its symmetry was of Nature's own handiwork. The Falls are in a narrow concave cup of rock crested with pine forests, and its sides now forbid the ascent, which is practicable in summer time by a series of natural steps in the strata. The waters cover this young cone with wings of spray and foam, and flittering, tremulous, and unsubstantial as they are, it is nevertheless from their aerial vapours that the solid and sturdy ice mountain grows up.

Of its substantial nature we had an excellent proof—of a human, practical kind: for, obeying many invitations, we walked along a snow path which led to a portal cut in the solid oxide of hydrogen, and entering found ourselves in a hot and stuffy apartment excavated from the body of the Cone, in which there was an Americanised bar, with drinks suited to the locality, and as much want of air as one would find in a house in the Fifth Avenue of New York. It was full of people, who drank whiskey and other strong waters.

I know not by what seduction overcome, but, somehow, so it happened, that one of my companions, on our return to the outer air and light, was led to sacrifice himself on a tarboggin, and yielded to a demon guide. I watched him toiling on, with painful steps and slow, doggedly up the path towards the slippery summit, and, when he had gained it, I slid down below to observe the result of the experiment, and judge whether it looked pleasant or not. He was but an item among many, but I knew he was among the *braves des braves*, and had received a baptism of fire in the trenches of Sebastopol, which had rained a very font of glory in India, and scarcely paled in China. I watched him assuming the penal attitude to which the young tarbogginer is condemned, and after a balance for a moment on the giddy height, his guide gave a kick to the snow, and down like a plunging bomb flew the ice-winged Icarus. He passed me close; I could see and mark him well. Never, to judge from facial expression, could man have been in deadlier fear. With hard set mouth, staring and rigid eyes, and aspect quite antipathetic to pleasure, he careered like one who is falling from a house top, and his countenance had scarce assumed its wonted placid look when I met him gasping and half faint. And yet he had the astounding audacity to say, " It was delicious. Never had a more delightful moment," when he came back pale and panting from his flight.

We returned from the Falls by a hilly, rough road over the bank of the Lake, and arrived at our hotel in time to dress for dinner, to which I was invited at the house of a Canadian gentleman, I think an Englishman by birth, who entertained us right hospitably.

There is a wonderful calm in the conversation of the Canadians, perhaps a little too much so, but it is a relief from the ambitious restlessness of the common American. The Canadian mind suffers as the mind of every country which is not a nationality must suffer, and caution assumes the place of enterprise. If the Americans knew the business of diplomacy a little better, and could but restrain the democratic vice of boastful threatening and arrogant menace, they could have alienated Canada from our cold rule long ago, even though Canada would have lost by the change many privileges and a cheap protection to her industry, commerce, and social expansion.

February 10*th*.—To-day I paid my respects to His Excellency the Governor, Viscount Monck, and proceeded to visit the citadel, which is now occupied by a battalion of the 60th Rifles under Colonel Hawley. Independently of the historical associations which attach to this commanding-looking work, I was attracted to it by the consideration that it has twice saved Canada to Great Britain. I am bound to say that, in my poor opinion, it will never do so again, if left in its present condition. The works, once strong, have lost much of their importance since the introduction of long-range artillery, and the armament is in a very imperfect condition, consisting of old-fashioned pieces of small calibre, which could furnish no reply to a battery established on the heights across the St. Lawrence.

The citadel itself has in its construction some of the points of a regular fortress after Vauban, and on the river side the parapets tower aloft from a steep rock, which puts one in mind of the site of the platform at Berne; but on the east side it is hampered by houses and by the suburbs of the city; and it could be approached without much difficulty from the other side, as soon as a lodgment could be effected on the heights of Abraham. The fosses and ditches were partially filled with snow, which obscured the ground and the adjacent country, if such whiteness can obscure anything. Colonel Hawley was good enough to show us over the works and point out the objects of interest as far as they could be discerned. Among them were some ancient iron guns on which Great Britain ought not to rely for very effective service in the defence of the place.

But some new heavy guns have recently been mounted, others are to follow, and as the ordnance stores in Canada will soon be replenished with the best description of pieces, there then need be no apprehension for Quebec on the score of weak artillery: or for a position that is the key of Quebec, which is most emphatically the master-key of Canada.

The outworks of the citadel itself, however, are not by any means in a satisfactory condition; even the high parapet overlooking the lower town might be crumbled away and expose the interior of the place; in one particular part of this work the guns are masked by blocks of houses, the windows of which actually look into the interior of the citadel, and the fire of the place could be so impeded, and the defence so cramped by the existing enceinte, that I very much doubt whether it would not be better to remove the latter altogether.

We trudged patiently around the long lines of parapet in the snow, now looking down upon the river clamorous with its burden of ice, and on the tortuous streets of the old-fashioned town. In summer and in the open months the St. Lawrence is thickly studded with ships; and dense forests of masts line the course of its banks; but now the only specimen of commercial enterprise on its bosom consisted of a few canoes struggling backwards and forwards through ice and water with their scanty freights.

Inside the citadel, cherry-cheeked riflemen were playing like schoolboys in the snow. In spite of temptation the regiment was in good condition; and although in modern days some objection might be taken to the closeness of their quarters in summer, the British soldiers who served under Wolfe would have been greatly astonished if they could have seen the comforts enjoyed by, and the cares bestowed on, their descendants. Even those much-neglected, injured Penelopes, the soldiers' wives, are tolerably well off in their quarters, somewhat too crowded, it is true, but still more comfortable than at Aldershot or the Tower.

After a long march along the parapet, in which I stumbled across more rotting gun-carriages, useless mortars, and bad platforms than I care to mention, we visited the Armoury, which is near the parade-ground of the citadel. The stock of firearms is arranged with great taste, and the cleanliness and effectiveness of all the material reflected credit on the storekeeper.

Some of the contents consisted of very interesting rifles of renowned makers in former days, with carved stocks, flint locks, and barrels encrusted with gold, intended as presents to Indian chiefs and warriors of tribes sufficiently strong to cause us injury by their hostility or render us service by their alliance. Old flint-lock muskets of inferior quality, with barrels like so many feet of cast-iron piping, intended for the indiscriminate destruction of friend or foe; horse-pistols of the fashion in vogue one hundred years ago, and the like, were to be found in the same spacious apartment, which contained specimens of the most recent improvements in firearms. Formerly flint pistols were served out to the frontier patrols, but of course percussion locks have, for many years, been given to all those employed in the service of the Crown in a military capacity. Some worthy official at home, however, still continues to send out barrels of flints with laudable punctuality, as he has not been relieved by superior order from the necessity of keeping up the supply of these articles. We have all heard of the forethought evinced by the home authorities, when they sent out water-tanks for our lake flotilla, forgetting that they were borne on an element quite fit for drinking. But I heard in the citadel of a still more remarkable instance of thoughtfulness.

A ship arrived at Quebec some time ago with an enormous spar reaching from her bowsprit to her taffrail consigned to the storekeeper. It had been the plague of the ship's company, it had been in everybody's way, and had nearly caused the loss of the vessel in some gales of wind. The whole resources of the quarter-master-general's department were taxed to get it safely on shore, and transport it to the heights. And what was it? A flag-staff for the citadel. And what was it made of? A stout Canadian pine, which had probably been sent from the St. Lawrence in a timber ship to the government officials at home; who, having duly shaped and pruned it into a flag-staff, returned it to the land of its birth at some considerable expense to John Bull.

The citadel is of no mean extent, but covers about forty acres of ground, and necessarily requires a very strong garrison; if they were exposed to shell or vertical fire from the opposite side of the river, or from the western side of the place, as there is no defence provided, they would certainly suffer great loss. It is obvious that a permanent work must be built at Point Levi, to sweep the approaches and prevent the establishment of hostile batteries on the river. A regular bastion with outworks should be constructed on the heights above the point, in order to make Quebec safe.

There are also dangers to be apprehended from the occupation of the railway terminus at Rivière du Loup which do not affect Quebec immediately, but are, nevertheless, to be carefully guarded against. In the event of war appearing imminent, a temporary work to cover the terminus on the land side, and sweep the river, would be necessary.

There exist the remains of some outworks in advance of the citadel, which are so well placed that it would be very desirable to reconstruct defences on their sites.

They are called the French works, and their position does credit to the skill of the engineer who chose it.

The British flag has waved for just 102 years from Cape Diamond, but the Fleur-de-lys had fluttered on the same point for 220 years, with the exception of the three years from 1629 to 1632, when Sir David Kirke placed Quebec in our hands.

Nothing proves the inaccuracy of artillery in those days more strikingly than the inability of the French, on Cape Diamond, to prevent the British transports landing their men at Point Levi, although the St. Lawrence is little more than 1000 yards broad opposite the citadel. By our bombardment, however, we nearly laid Quebec in the dust before the action.

On account of the very natural remembrance of the glory of Wolfe's attack, his death and victory, it has almost been forgotten that our first attempt to land at Montmorenci was repulsed by Montcalm with the loss of 500 men; and it was only when the original scheme failed, that Wolfe conceived the plan of re-embarking his troops, and landing above the town. He had 8000 regular troops; the French had 10,000 men, but of these only five battalions were regular French soldiers. Montcalm believed no doubt that he could drive the British into the river, or force them to surrender, and he threw the force of his attack on the British right, which rested on the river. The French right, consisting of Indians and Canadians, was easily routed; the French left, deprived of the services of its general and of his second in command, was ultimately broken, and fled towards the town, covered in some degree by the centre battalions, which fell back steadily; nor was it till five days after the battle that Quebec fell into our hands. The fire must have been exceedingly close and desperate; and its effects speak well for the efficiency of old Brown Bess at close quarters, for out of the force engaged, the British lost over 630, and the French 1500, of whom 1000 were wounded or taken prisoners. There was little artillery engaged; for we had but one, and the French but two or three pieces on the heights. A very few months afterwards we had nigh lost that which we had so gallantly and fortunately gained.

On the 28th April next year, General Murray, following the example of Montcalm, and depriving himself of the advantages which a position inside the walls of Quebec would have given him, moved out on the heights of Abraham, with 3000 men and twenty guns, to oppose the French under the Chevalier de Levi, who were moving down upon the city. In an ill-conceived attack on the enemy, Murray lost no less than 1000 men and all his guns, and had to retreat to the city. He was only relieved by the arrival of a British squadron in the river, which compelled the French to retire with the loss of all their artillery.

Looking down upon the narrow path below the parapet, one must do credit to the daring of Arnold, Montgomery, and the Americans in their disastrous attempt to carry the citadel by an escalade. Arnold, after his astonishing march and desperate perils by the Kennebeck and Chaudière—which has been well styled by General Carmichael Smyth one of the most wonderful instances of perseverance and spirit of enterprise upon record—followed the course pursued by Wolfe; and embarking at Point Levi, occupied the heights of Abraham, but when Montgomery joined him from

Montreal, it was found they had no heavy artillery. Thus they were forced either to march back again, or to try to carry the place by storm. Two columns, led by Arnold and Montgomery, endeavoured to push through the street at the foot of the citadel, one from the east and another from the west.

The Canadians say, that after Montgomery carried the entrenchment, which extended from the foot of the cliff to the river, he rushed at the head of his column, followed by a group of officers, towards a second work, on which was mounted a small field-piece. The Americans were just within twenty yards when a Canadian fired the gun, which was loaded with grape. Montgomery and the officers who followed him were swept down in a heap of killed and wounded, and the column at once fled in confusion. Arnold, who had forced his way into the houses under the citadel, was carried back wounded soon after his gallant advance: and the Canadians again claim for one of their own countrymen, named Dambourges, the honour of having led the sortie from the citadel which charged the Americans, and forced those who were not slain to surrender.

Certainly the Canadians showed upon that occasion, as no doubt they would again, a strong indisposition to fraternise with the American apostles of liberty, equality, and fraternity; they harassed their communications, and, under their seigneurs, cut off several detachments. The attempt on Quebec was never repeated; and the Americans fared but ill in both their Canadian campaigns.

A well-organised expedition made in winter-time would now be attended with far greater danger than it was in former days, and if the snow remained in good condition, artillery, provisions, and munitions of war could be transported with greater facility than on the ordinary country roads. Quebec would, under these circumstances, be deprived of the co-operation of the fleet; but with the improvement in the defence which would be effected by the erection of a regular work at Point Levi, and by the alterations indicated in the citadel itself, Quebec would be in a position to resist any force the Americans might direct against it, and would have nothing to fear except from regular siege operations, which there was no chance of interrupting or raising. It would be most important to have the feelings of the inhabitants enlisted on our side. I fear there is reason to believe that they are antagonistic to the Americans, rather than violently enamoured of ourselves.

Having enjoyed a view from the Flag-staff Tower, 350 feet above the river, which in summer must be one of the grandest in the world, and which even now was full of interest, my visit to the Citadel was terminated by lunch in the mess-room, and I returned homewards through the city. I was encircled with people enjoying the keen bright air, though the thermometer was twenty degrees below freezing point.

Not the least interesting to me of the people were the habitans in their long robes gathered in round the waist by scarlet or bright-coloured sashes, with long boots, and fur caps, and French faces, chatting in their Old-World French; and the monks, or regular clergy, who moved as beings of another age and world through the more modern types of civilisation—such as fast officers in fast sleighs, and the Anglicised families in their wheelless calèches. I had the honour of an invitation to dine at the club called Stadacona, which is a corruption or modification of Indian words signifying "the site of a strait," where I met a number of the citizens of Quebec at an excellent substantial dinner, which had far more of English tastes than of French cookery about it. The conversation did not disclose any symptoms of the tendency towards Americanisation which the Northern journals are so fond of attributing to the people of Canada; but it was perceptible that a war with America was regarded as an evil which could only fall on Canada because of her connection with Great Britain, and that Great Britain ought therefore to take a main part in it. The Canadians are proud of the part borne by De Salaberry and others in the former war; but, greatly as the country has advanced, I doubt if there is now such a population of ready, hardy fighting men as then existed: for most of the hunters, lumberers, and nomad half-castes, who cannot be called settlers, have been absorbed in cultivated lands and settled habits. The appointment of British officers to organise and command the volunteers has given offence; and I think it would be advisable, if not necessary, in case of actual war, to let the volunteers choose their officers within certain limits, and to give the authorities corresponding to our lords-lieutenant of counties power to name the commanding officers of corps, under the sanction of the Governor-General.

CHAPTER VIII.

Lower Canada and Ancient France—Soldiers in Garrison at Quebec—Canadian Volunteers—The Governor-General Viscount Monck—Uniform in the United States—A Sleighing Party—Dinner and Calico Ball.

I AM afraid that in this Lower Canada just now we do but occupy the position of a garrison. The aspect and the habit of the popular mind are foreign, but they are not French any more—at least modern French; rather are they of an Old-World France—of a France when there was an ancient faith and a son of St. Louis; when there was a white flag blazoned with fleur-de-lys, and a priesthood dominant—a France loyal, chivalrous, and bigoted, without knowledge and without railways, content to stand on ancient paths, and hating reform and active mutation. What a change has occurred since the old Bourbon struck the medal with its inscription, "Francia in Novo Orbe Victrix, Kebeca Liberata. 1690." There may be many in Canada who cannot forget their origin and their race, kept alive in their memories by a common tongue, ancient traditions, and antipathy to a foreign rule exercised from a far-off land, and sometimes manifested by rude, rough instruments, and by a mechanism of force; but it would be well for them to remember that, whilst France has passed through many convulsions, Canada has been saved from external and internal foes, with the exception of the American invasion in 1812, and the troubles caused by her own disaffected people at a later period, whilst as an appanage of France she must have undergone incessant anxieties and assaults. She has been spared the agonies of the Revolution, the exhaustive glories and collapse of the Empire, the reaction of the "Desired one"—the consequences of the convulsions of 1830, of 1848, of 1852. Great Britain, too, is bound to remember that she is dealing with a brave and ancient race, delivered to her rule under treaty, who have, on the whole, resisted many temptations, and preserved a firm attachment to her government in the face of an aggressive and prosperous Republic. Our soldiers must be taught to respect the people of Canada as their equals and fellow-subjects—a hard lesson perhaps for imperious islanders, but not the less necessary to learn, if we would preserve their attachment and our territories.

In justice to them I must say that the 60th Rifles gave no occasion to the people to complain, though Quebec is not destitute of its "rough" fellows, and of provocations; and that during my stay in Canada I only heard of one instance in which officers or men could be accused of indiscretion or want of respect for the people. Whiskey is shockingly cheap and atrociously bad, and public-houses are only too numerous, so that the base upon which the evils which afflict the soldier rest is not wanting here any more than at home.

A garrison rule must be very galling unless the officers and men are minded to behave themselves, and it would cause me regret if my observations of some regrettable circumstances in that relation were confirmed by larger experience. Of course the peasants are provoking; they are heavy and coarse, relying on their *vis inertiæ*, and aggressively passive. The other day, for instance, when Lord Monck was leading his sleigh party, several country carts came down from the opposite direction in the deep track, and it was with the utmost difficulty the driver of our party avoided collision with them, as the habitans would not get out of the way. Still one does not like to see young Greenhorn of the Invincibles flicking up the bourgeoisie with his whip as he whisks round a corner, for not getting out of the way. A gallant captain of volunteer artillery complained greatly of matters of this kind, but he also expressed very unreasonable jealousy respecting the appointment of English officers to superintend, and organise, and command the force.

February 11*th.*—Still more snow falling, and the cold sharper than ever. Visited the Parliament Houses and Library, of which more hereafter; saw the Ursuline Chapel; called on Mr. Cartier, Mr. Macdonald, Mr. Cauchon, and Mr. Galt, members of the Ministry, to whom I had introductions. In the evening dined with the Governor-General and Lady Monck at Government House. Although His Excellency has been but a short time in the country, and succeeded an able, energetic man, he has already gained the confidence of men difficult to win, and gives fair promise of administering the affairs of the provinces with sagacity and vigour. It occurred to me, considering the position of Canada, that, to escape from the consequences of divided views and command, it would be desirable to have the military and civil administration in one hand at critical junctures, or to send out a soldier as Governor-General. To be a good soldier one must be gifted with the faculties which constitute a good ruler, and the civilian can only possess those same qualities minus the special knowledge of the professional military man. Lord Monck, however, has applied himself with ability and zeal to the consideration of the provincial defences.

The table of the Canadian Viceroy was elegant and hospitable; and it was a relief to the eye to catch such semblance of state as was afforded by the scarlet uniforms and gold lace of the aides-de-camp, military secretary, and others of His Excellency's household, who were at dinner, after the long monotony of American black. Not but that now and then uniform was creeping in at private dinner-tables in the States also, principally on the persons of foreign-born officers. But it is, or rather it was, opposed to the custom of the country.

I remember Mr. Seward telling me one day, when we met in Washington, that it was contrary to etiquette for a foreigner to wear the livery of his royal master or mistress in the United States. Soon afterwards I saw at table a colonel in full uniform of the French infantry; but, on inquiry, I learned he was in command of a New York regiment composed of his exiled compatriots; and a very gallant regiment—in spite of its Anglophobia, loudly expressed during the Trent affair—it proved itself. Even here let me tell a story. When the colonel in question, who had been for many years a journalist in New York, appeared in Washington, after getting his commission, he repaired to the house of an astute and witty diplomatist, with whom he had an ancient intimacy. "Ah! my dear colonel," exclaimed the Minister, "by accepting the command of your regiment, you have cut short the friendship of ten years." "How is that, Excellence?" "Why, how can we ever meet again as of yore? I cannot dine with you; for how dare I present myself in your camp?" "Why not, Excellence?" "Why, my dear friend, do you think I could ever get my hair dressed well enough to please the five hundred French coiffeurs in your regiment?" "But, at all events, my dear Minister, I can come and dine with you!" "Impossible, my friend! How could I venture to ask a man to dinner who has under his orders five hundred French cooks!"

More snow. The landlord is rather impressed with the news that the Union army is positively about to march on Richmond at once; and, indeed, it is only the sceptical mind, with some knowledge of facts, that can resist the effect of the constant iteration of falsehoods in the American papers, which never loses its influence on the American mind.

February 12*th*.—Notwithstanding a slight fall of white rain, Lord Monck had a sleighing party to Lorette, an Indian village, where we repaired in great force, ladies and gentlemen, furred and muffed, and enjoyed ourselves greatly, lunching in a very pleasant rustic sort of auberge, half-buried in the snow. These sleighing parties render a Canadian winter tolerable, and there is a certain degree of " chance of being lost " which commends them to the adventurous and forms a theme for many small stories. On our coming home, we had nigh experienced one of these mild adventures, for the snow fell again and obscured the face of the country—a very white and well-washed face indeed, with no remarkable features in it,—and it was by chance we got on the track at a certain turn in the road, which was only marked out by the summits of the submerged fences and hedges peering over the drift, and looking uncommonly like each other all over the country. This little experience of travel rather dispelled notions I had of the great practicability of a winter campaign, for it would be quite impossible to move guns and troops with *certainty* in a country where all movements depended on the snow not falling, in opposition to the probability that it would do so.

The officers of the 60th Rifles entertained His Excellency at dinner in the evening, and I had the honour of being invited to meet him. The entertainment took place in the mess-room of the citadel. Little more than a century ago, M. de Montcalm may have been dining on the same spot with the regiment of Musketeers of Guienne. Who may dine there in 1962? The evening was ended at a " calico " ball for the benefit of the poor of the city, which was attended by the townspeople only, the ladies being dressed in calico, which was afterwards, I believe, with the receipts, distributed to the indigent.

February 13*th*.—Accompanied Mr. Bernard, who kindly placed his knowledge and good offices at my disposal, to see some of the lions of the city; and, thus ably conducted, I visited the Parliament Houses, the Library, the Ursuline Convent, the Rink, and many other places; I dined in the evening with Mr. Galt, the Finance Minister, whom I had the pleasure of meeting at Washington some time before. Mr. Cartier, the head of the Administration, and nearly all the Ministers, were present. Afterwards attended a ball at Mr. Cauchon's, one of Mr. Galt's colleagues, which was an assemblage of the *élite* of the old French society of the place. My companions left me to-day for England, where one was anxious to take his seat on the opening of Parliament, and the other went with him, I suppose, for companionship's sake.

CHAPTER IX.

Canadian view of the American Struggle — English Officers in the States—My own position in the States and in Canada—The Ursulines in Quebec—General Montcalm—French Canadians— Imperial Honours—Celts and Saxons—Salmon Fishing—Early Government of Canada—Past and Future.

WHILST I was in Quebec the American papers ceased not to record great Union successes, impending expeditions, and, as is their wont, to throw out hints of some inscrutable woe conceived by the head of Stanton, and to be wrought by the arm of McClellan on the South. " Jeff. Davis going to Texas or Mexico— The neck of the rebellion broken—Our young Napoleon preparing for the last grand campaign." Many of our officers were very anxious to visit the Federal armies, but the tone of the Northern press was so exceedingly virulent and insulting toward Englishmen, that the authorities, mistaking their license for the real opinion of Americans, discouraged applications for leave as much as possible. This was to be regretted; the more so that those officers who went from Canada to the States were not provided with any official letters, and were, indeed, in some instances, misguided so far as to conceal their military character. It could not but have been most useful to our officers to have been enabled to take fair measure of the system and capability of an American army, North or South; to have formed an estimate of their generals and of the value of their several arms—cavalry, artillery, and infantry, each of which presented conspicuous examples of what to avoid, more especially the first, whilst the second had peculiar features worthy of study, and the third was a very wonderful illustration of the volunteer principle.

When I represented the importance of sending officers to the armies for the special purpose of examining and reporting on their condition, I was met by the reply that it would be a violation of neutrality to dispatch commissioners to the Federal army, unless similar officers were sent to the Confederate headquarters; and that it would not be possible to adopt the latter step, as the Washington Government would not grant them leave to go through the lines, and would resent the proposal. When some officers were at last dispatched with an official sanction to the army at Yorktown, they made their appearance in a forlorn, destitute, and helpless condition, which made their companions in arms blush for them.

For myself, I had every reason to believe that no objection would be made to my accompanying the army under General McClellan. Several senators who had given me their good wishes, were most desirous that I should be able to set off an account of a victory against the narrative of the retreat from Bull Run. Although I had been recovering a little from the effects of the ludicrous and malignant falsehoods circulated against me up to the Trent affair, I was *très mal vu* in some quarters in Washington, and of course I was included in the general outburst against all British subjects with which the surrender of Mason and Slidell was accompanied.

In Canada I had recovered health and spirits; nay, more—some small shreds of popularity in the States. The secretaries of literary institutions renewed their requests for lectures, the autograph hunters sought the post-office once more with their flattering though ill-spelt missives; but there was no inducement to return to the States till the army of McClellan was actually about to take the field. The exploits of the army of the West had, indeed, attracted my eyes in that direction. The capture of Fort Henry and Fort Donelson promised well for its future career, but if I travelled so far out of my way I should have lost my chance of seeing the most brilliant and important campaign. The chief interest was certainly concentrated on the Potomac, and in the operations against Richmond. The West was far away, and it would have been a chance against my letters reaching home so as to anticipate the exaggerated illusions of the New York journals. And so I quietly waited and watched till the news from the States became so triumphant and decided that it behoved me to return, lest some important movement should take place on the Potomac. As I could not be with more than one army, I then resolved to follow the fortunes of McClellan's great host, which indeed was regarded by Americans themselves with the greatest anxiety. And so, after a few days, I set about leaving cards and paying farewell visits to those who had so kindly entreated me in the City of the Strait.

The learned institutions, the libraries, the machinery of education, the various literary and scientific associations, and the admirable seminaries of Quebec, are most creditable to the community; they would place that city on a level with some of the most learned of European cities of far greater antiquity; and the public spirit and intelligence of its citizens have been fully evinced in the aid and support they have rendered to institutions designed for the spread of knowledge.

The public buildings have also the stamp of respectable antiquity upon them; none of them possess any considerable architectural merits, but several are exceedingly interesting. Constant fires have proved nearly ruinous to the buildings erected by the original settlers; and those which have been subsequently built are not remarkable for beauty—indeed, I may say that the Laval University is one of the plainest buildings it has ever been my lot to behold.

On all sides it is admitted that the nuns of the Ursuline Convent have conferred the greatest benefit upon the city by their unceasing devotion to the task of education. Many people of respectability— Protestants as well as Catholics—send their children to be educated by these excellent women, representing the system inaugurated more than 200 years ago by Madeleine de Chauvigny, who, moved by grief for the loss of her husband to devote herself to Heaven, and to the spread of the Christian faith, sailed forth from France, and, landing at Quebec, established schools for the Indian girls to learn the faith of the white race, which was destined to destroy their own.

The Ursuline Convent is a massive building, ugly as most convents of modern date are, standing amidst the houses of the city. The day I visited it there were no means of seeing the schools, and I was obliged to be content with a sight of the chapel instead. On ringing the bell by the side of a massive iron-bound door, I was admitted to the front of a *grille*, through which I conveyed my wishes to the unseen lady who demanded the purport of my visit; and, after a short delay, the clergyman attached to the service of the church was ready, and an old Swiss or porteress conducted me to the entrance of the chapel, which is of large size, of no pretensions to architectural beauty, and of little interest to me for anything but the fact that within its walls lie the bones of Montcalm.

The Ursulines, however, are of opinion that they have got a collection of paintings of merit, and I was called upon to admire some extraordinary specimens of art very nearly approaching the class denominated daubs, which were not recommended even by antiquity. Although the priest bore a pure Irish patronymic, he had never been in the British isles, having been educated in France, where he was born, whence he came out to Canada in the course of his ministry. He was an agreeable, intelligent, gentlemanly man, but he had evidently no faith in the pictures, and probably not much greater in some other remarkable decorations exhibited within the holy walls. The altar-piece and two or three subjects belonging probably to the old convent, rescued the collection from entire condemnation.

On the wall of the chapel, on the left-hand side from the entrance, there is a marble slab, on which are engraved the following words: "Honneur à Montcalm! Le destin en lui dérobant la victoire l'a récompensé par une mort glorieuse!" The graceful words are due to Lord Aylmer. Montcalm received his death-wound from a ball fired by the only piece of artillery which we could get up the heights; but like his great rival and conqueror he was wounded in the fight by a musket-shot at a comparatively early stage of the battle. Like Wolfe, too, Montcalm loved literature: "également propre aux batailles et aux académies, son désir était d'unir aux lauriers de Mars les palmes de Minerve."

The following is a translation of the inscription and epitaph written by the Academy of Inscriptions and Belles Lettres of Paris in 1761, and inscribed on a monument which that body had designed to erect in Quebec, but which never reached that city, the vessel on which it had been embarked having been lost at sea:

"HERE LIETH
In either hemisphere to live for ever,
LEWIS JOSEPH DE MONTCALM GOZON,!
Marquis of St. Véran, Baron of Gabriac,
Commander of the Order of St. Lewis,
Lieutenant-General of the French army;
not less an excellent citizen than soldier,
who knew no desire but that of
TRUE GLORY;
Happy in a natural genius, improved by literature;
Having gone through the several steps of military honours
with an uninterrupted lustre;
skilled in all the arts of war,
the juncture of the times and the crisis of danger;
In Italy, in Bohemia, in Germany,
an indefatigable general:
He so discharged his important trusts,
that he seemed always equal to still greater.
At length, grown bright with perils,
sent to secure the province of Canada,
with a handful of men,
he more than once repulsed the enemy's forces,
and made himself master of their forts,
replete with troops and ammunition.
Inured to cold, hunger, watching and labours,
unmindful of himself,

> he had no sensation but for his soldiers:
> An enemy with the fiercest impetuosity;
> a victor with the tenderest humanity;
> adverse fortune he compensated with valour;
> the want of strength with skill and activity;
> and, with his counsel and support,
> for four years protracted the impending
> fate of the colony.
> Having, with various artifices,
> long baffled a great army,
> headed by an expert and intrepid commander,
> and a fleet furnished with all warlike stores,
> compelled at length to an engagement,
> he fell—in the first rank—in the first onset,
> warm with those hopes of religion
> which he had always cherished;
> to the inexpressible loss of his own army,
> and not without the regret of the enemy's,
> XIV September, A.D. MDCCLIX.
> Of his age, XLVIII.
> His weeping countrymen
> deposited the remains of their excellent General in a grave
> which a fallen bomb in bursting had excavated for him,
> recommending them to the generous faith of their enemies."

Had his counsel been taken by de Vaudreuil, we never could have occupied Point Levi, and in all probability the expedition to Quebec would have failed.

There is something exceedingly touching in the death of the two generals in the same battle. My guide, however, was more interested in calling my attention to the ornaments of the altar, and to a skull, which he assured me was that of Montcalm.

> " Through each lack-lustre eyeless hole,
> The gay recess of wisdom and of wit,
> And passion's host that never brook'd control,"

was seen filled with dust, and the priest held in his hand, like a cricket-ball, the home of the subtle intellect of the man who raised to such a height the power of France in the western world. When the old Indian chief told Montcalm—"Tu es petit! mais je vois dans tes yeux la hauteur du chêne et la vivacité des yeux des aigles," how little the politic, gallant Frenchman ever thought his skull would be kept in a box in a priest's cupboard, and shown as a curiosity to strangers from that barbarous Britain.

I cannot say that the priest succeeded in pointing out anything as interesting among the pictures as even the skull of the Marquis de Montcalm.

So far as I can ascertain, no Canadian painter has yet been inspired by the faith and devotion which wrought such miracles and wonders in mediæval Europe, to concentrate his talents on church pictures.

There is not much good fellowship between the French Roman Catholics and their Irish co-religionists; and I was told that few of the latter ever entered the chapel of the Ursulines, though they constitute an appreciable proportion of the population. The Canadians, indeed, retain a good deal of the old French sentiment, and regard the Irish very much as their ancestors, under St. Ruth, looked on the poor vassals of the Irish Jacobins. The Irish are, however, more energetic and restless, and do not lose by comparison with the unenterprising inhabitants.

The feelings and faith of the French Canadian tend to keep up all that is French in his nature. Small wonder that it should be so. But it may be doubted whether he has much sympathy with the Empire, though he is proud of the glory and renown attained by the parent stock under the "Great Gaul" who founded it.

In visiting the beautiful and well-ordered Library of the Houses of Parliament, the state of which does honour to the excellent curator, I observed several very handsome volumes of the most costly works marked with the French imperial cipher. They had, it appeared, been presented to the Canadian Parliament by the Emperor Louis Napoleon, and they were pointed out to me with much pride and pleasure; but I looked in vain for any such outward and visible sign of favour and policy on the part of the reigning House in England. The conduct of France towards Canada in former times, if not always just to the settlers, was indeed exceedingly liberal to the landed interest; on one occasion some sixteen country gentlemen were raised to the French peerage. The most a Canadian can hope for now is a barren baronetcy or the honours of the Bath. By conferring on our colonies, dependencies, and provinces very liberal democratic forms of government institutions, and at the same time refusing to give the counterpoise which an extension of the aristocratic system to them would bestow, we hasten the coming of the day when separation becomes inevitable. When separation takes place, the difference of institutions begets opposition of views and of policy, distrust, and, finally, collision.

One of my New York acquaintances, who professed to be somewhat of a philosopher, said, one day, he was quite sure the colonies never would have revolted, no matter how high tea was taxed, if the king had made a few of the leading Americans peers of the realm. The dream of an Imperial Senate with representatives from all the portions of the wide-spread territories of Great Britain may excite the imagination, but it is not likely to be ever realised. The honours which have been conferred on such men as Sir Etienne Taché and Sir Narcisse Belleau, are highly prized, and a more liberal bestowal of the cheap defence of nations would do much to gratify the reasonable ambition of the Canadians.

That there should be some—and not a little—jealousy of foreign interference and usurpation of places, profits, and honours, by the English families, is not unnatural. I am not persuaded that it was right to hand over the whole direction of the volunteer and militia organisation to British officers, who are by the many often identified with the last noisy ensign who has been playing pranks in the Rue de Montagne. The remembrances of the old rebellion have not altogether died out, but it appeared to me that the Canadians are a mild, tractable race, fond of justice, a little too fond of law, and quite content to live under any rule which secured them equal rights, and gave them facility for moderate litigation and religious exercises.

While I was in Quebec some foolish young men stormed a house under a misapprehension as to its character. The same thing might have happened in Great Britain; it would have excited no feeling—the perpetrators might have compounded for their folly, or have suffered the penalty. Here the matter was hushed up, and some of the Canadians were vexed and angry. Provincials must necessarily be jealous of the smallest appearance of disrespect or show of distinctive justice between the two races.

There are very few persons in England acquainted with the many ancient and glorious memories which endear Quebec to the French Canadians. Jacques

Cartier is to them a greater discoverer and navigator than Captain Cook is to us, and a long list of names thoroughly French illustrate the early history of the city. De Frontenac, Le Chevalier de Levi, Dambourges and others are not known to those who are well acquainted with Wolfe and Montcalm.

Quebec, though doubtless the oldest city existing on the continent, is in a very different condition from that in which it was for many a year after it was founded by Champlain, more than two centuries and a half ago. It is quite delightful, after a sojourn in the United States, to ramble through the tortuous streets, lined by tall narrow-windowed houses with irregular gables, even though an air of something like decay has settled upon the place. There is no trace in Quebec of the feverish activity of American cities—no great hotels nor eager multitudes thronging the pavements; but in summer the quays present a most animated appearance, for the noble waters of the St. Lawrence are then laden with stately ships, and traffic is carried on extensively in the exchange of the exhaustless forest-produce of the back country for the manufactures of Europe.

The Indian squaws and their people have well-nigh vanished from the scene, and it would almost seem as though they were unfit to learn the doctrines of Christianity—it is certain they had not qualities to permit of their flourishing in the midst of Christians. Other coloured races brought in contact with the white man have saved themselves from extermination by service; but the individual Indian is feudatory to no man—he says "Ich Dien" to no created being. The result is, that, slowly and surely, he is driven further and further out into the waste, or is caught up in the waters of civilisation, and held, like the fly in amber, as a curious instance of the incompatibility of one substance with the surrounding particles of another. He will never again play a part in any contest which may take place between the British and Americans; notwithstanding the efforts made by the Confederates to use the Southern Indians in the present war, no adequate results have been obtained for the trouble.

In the War of Independence the Indians served on both sides, but the odium of employing them in the first instance against the colonists must undoubtedly rest on the British ministry of the day.

Although the distance from Montreal to Quebec, taking the course of the river, is but 180 miles, there is considerable difference in climate. The scenery around the capital of the Lower Province, and the present seat of Government, is more elevated and picturesque; but the quality of the soil is not so favourable to agriculture. The habitant is a very different being from the Scotch or English farmer; he regards with aversion agricultural implements of the new school, and woos the earth to yield its fruits with the most simple appliances; he is stubborn in his attachment to antique customs, and if he has most of the virtues, he assuredly has some of the faults of a purely rural agricultural population.

The events of the rebellion induced us, perhaps, to underrate the military capacity of the French Canadians, but they may point with pride to the deeds of their ancestors in defence of their soil against American invasion, and they would, no doubt, maintain in the field the reputation of the race from which they spring. The great defect of the native is, perhaps, his want of enterprise. He rarely emigrates to new scenes of labour, and even the inhabitant of the town shrinks from an encounter with the active American or Anglo-Saxon. Thus it is, at the present moment, that nearly all the agricultural and industrial enterprises of Lower Canada have originated with or been developed by persons of a different stock. Want of capital is the great evil which afflicts the inhabitants of both Canadas, and even the oil-wells and gold mines have, to a large extent, fallen into the hands of the solid men of Boston, and of the hard men of New England; but the Canadians would behave in the face of an enemy with the spirit, courage, and conduct which they have exhibited on their own limited battle-fields.

It would be of little value, within the limits of this volume, to attempt a recapitulation of the principal events of Canadian history, either in connection with its early founders or with the English government; but surely the materials are not wanting for an interesting record of the struggles of the enterprising Europeans who contended so fiercely with barbarous races and an inclement clime to found what already promises to be a great nation. The savage has died out, or he has been civilised into a degraded creature for whom no place seems left at the great table of nature, and the civilised man his successor has learned to control and mollify the influences of climate, and to extort from the soil fruits in abundance. But Canada is by no means as cold as it has been painted, or rather, it would be more proper to say, the cold there is not so intolerable as we think. It would astonish many people in this country to learn that the Northern States of America suffer more from cold than does the vast frontier region of Canada which borders on the Lakes. In Iowa, for instance, the cold is more intense than at Montreal. Grapes and peaches ripen on the Canadian shores of the great lakes; plums, melons, tomatos, and apples thrive and grow to perfection in the provinces. As cultivation advances the rigour of winter is appreciably diminished, although the farmers, with that customary want of submission to the will of Providence which characterises all people who live in dependence on the seasons, complain that the frost is not as severe as it was in the good old times, and that they are deprived of the advantages of long-enduring snow and rigid winters.

What glorious visions of shooting now and of fishing in spring had opened before me, if the Federal army would only stay quiet! Not, indeed, that there is much sport for the rifle or fowling-piece now left in this part of Canada in winter, except moose, for which I did not care much, but that such strange scenes could be visited and described. In open weather there is a little shooting of quails, partridges, and ground game; before winter sets in there is plenty of wild ducks, but it is in fishing that the province is most tempting. The Godbout, uncertain as it is, would tempt any fisherman to a pilgrimage—a river in which one man, Captain Strachan, played and landed forty-two salmon and grilse in two half-days. But then the black-flies and musquitoes! Well, of this more hereafter. Though little that more must be, as long as there is such a guide-book as that of Dr. Adamson—the charming, amiable, and accomplished gentleman, in whom I was rejoiced to recognise the type of *le vrai gentilhomme irlandais;* who knows every thing that ever was done or thought by Canadian salmon, and is ever willing to impart his knowledge.

To a young officer fresh from a Mediterranean or home station—unless he were at Aldershot or the Curragh, perhaps—Quebec must appear rather dull. He has none of the excellent sporting for great and small game which India affords. Society presents itself under a new aspect. A people speaking a different language are not his servants, nor his kith and kin, and yet he must protect and fight for them. He has no sympathy with a nationality which is prouder of Montcalm than of Wolfe, and which claims, nevertheless, the lions and the harp as "*notre drapeau.*" So if he be unwise and unreasonable, he takes dislikes and ascribes every inconvenience he endures, not to the policy of the mother-country he serves, but to the people of the province.

I was present one evening at a ball given by one of the ministers, a French Canadian, at which there was a large assemblage of all the best people in the city, and I was struck by the absence of young officers, although many of higher rank were present. A lady, to whom I mentioned the circumstance, said, "Oh! they rarely come among us, so we have left off asking them. If they do come, they stand with their backs against the wall criticising our style and our dresses, and never offer to dance till supper is over, when they vanish." This is by no means universally applicable to all societies or regiments, but it is no doubt the truth in some instances.

One must regret that the English language was not introduced into the law courts and legislature. Experience proves that there are no instruments so powerful in sustaining the existence of a nationality, as the tongue and pen. The Canadians of to-day affect to be French, more because they speak a French at which Paris laughs, than from any real sympathy founded on mutual interests or present history between France and Canada. I was assured by one earnest Canadian, that France had never forgiven the Bourbons for the fault of Louis XV., in ceding Canada to Great Britain. He had more reason probably for asserting that, but for the establishment of our supremacy in 1765, the rebellion of the thirteen colonies of North America would not have occurred when it did. But the conquest by Wolfe, confirmed by treaty, put an end to most cruel and barbarous massacres, outrages, and petty border wars, between the French and English settlers and their auxiliary tribes of Indians, and if it had been attended or followed by any wise and liberal acts of government, must have produced very great results on the tone and temper of the Canadian mind.

It would have been wonderful indeed, if, a century ago, when our statute book was written in blood, when our fellow-subjects at home were under the ban of religious disability, and beaten to the earth beneath the weight of penal enactments, any traces of wisdom had been exhibited in the management of a distant dependency. Keeping alive the feelings of a distinct nationality by the powerful machinery of different national laws and customs, the conquerors ruled the province by military law for more than ten long years; but the tempest which agitated the American colonies was already felt in the air. The ministry, anxious only to drain money from their distant dependencies, were engaged in devising taxes, whilst the colonists prepared to vindicate, by force of arms, their great principle, that representation was the basis of taxation. The two Acts of 1774 were passed to enable the government to raise revenues for the maintenance of the local government, and for the appointment of a council of government, nominated by the Crown. By the capitulation of Quebec, the free exercise of their religion was accorded to the Canadians. By the Act of 1774, the Roman Catholic Church was recognised as established, and the "Coutume de Paris" accepted as the foundation of civil and equity administration.

Is it not strange that Great Britain should have accorded such concessions to Roman Catholics and colonists, when the penal system was most rigorously enforced in Ireland? But is it not stranger still, that the people of the American colonies, who were about to set themselves up as the children and the champions of freedom of faith and conscience, should have taken bitter umbrage at those very concessions! The Americans of the North bore an exceeding animosity to the French Canadians. They remonstrated in fierce, intolerant, and injurious language with the people of Great Britain, for the cession of these privileges to the Canadians, and the Continental Congress did not hesitate to say that they thought "Parliament was not authorised by the constitution to establish a religion fraught with sanguinary and impious tenets."

In a strain of sublime impudence, considering the work they were ready for, the same Congress also expressed their astonishment that Parliament should have consented to permit in Canada, "a religion that has deluged your island with blood, and dispersed impiety, *bigotry*, persecution, murder, and *rebellion* through the world."

It may be worth while to notice the fact that the first notion of united action on the part of the British North American colonies may have been developed by the British government, and that the idea of independence was suggested by the very recommendations to self-defence which came from the mother country. The Convention of Delegates at Albany in 1754, which met in consequence of the advice tendered by the Home Government, adopted a federal system, which contained, in effect, the germ of the United States. Though this and similar propositions were not entertained, the growth of such an idea must have been rapid indeed. In the British Colonial system there was the breath of life—a little fanning, and the whole body was alive and active. In the Canadian system there was only the animating spirit of dependency on France, and on a system in France, which was perishing before the sneers of the new philosophy.

The French Canadians of the present day, in accusing the British government of a hundred years ago of want of liberality and foresight in the administration of their newly acquired territory, are wilfully blind to the sort of government which they received from the Bourbons. The dominion of a foreign race, however, is always galling, be it covered ever so thickly with velvet, and all its acts are regarded with suspicion and dislike. The concessions and liberality of the British government which drew forth such indignant protests from the bigoted New Englanders, was ascribed to fears of Canadian revolt, or to a selfish desire to conciliate the good-will of subjects who might become formidable enemies. If England lost the American colonies because she refused to accept a principle which, however sound and just, was certainly new and not accepted as of universal application, she needed not to apprehend the recurrence of a separation, forcible or peaceable, of Canada on any such grounds. It is impossible for a country to be held by a more slender cord; and in all but the actual exercise of the sovereign style, title, and attributes, Canada is free and independent. If the sentiment or the nationality of the Lower Canadians ever induces them to seek the protection or rule of any European State, they will no doubt at once come into collision with Upper Canada and the United States, and we can but pity their infatuation. If Upper Canada thinks to better herself by separation, and union with the Western States, Great Britain assuredly will never hold her by force. It would be useless to discuss the rights and obligations of a sovereignty and its nominal dependency in relation to mutual succour in time of war; but it seems only fair that the great permanent works necessary for strategical purposes, and as *points d'appui* for the forces of the protecting military power, should be made and repaired and garrisoned at the imperial expense, whilst on the mass of the population must be placed the task of rising to defend their country from invasion, assisted by such imperial troops as can be spared from the occupation of the fixed points of defence. The Canadians must not content themselves with the empty assertion that if their country should be invaded Great Britain alone is attacked. Let them emulate the Old England colonies, and the conduct of their ancestors in 1812. The United States bear them no good will; and as the only power from which Canada has anything to fear, the Americans would be just as likely to make war against the Province as against the Empire, and trust to their own impregnability, except at sea, as a guarantee against any dangerous consequences.

The future is beyond our ken. There are prophets who long ago predicted the amalgamation of the Upper Province with the West, and who now find greater hope for the realisation of their soothsayings in the approaching dissolution of the Federal States. Others there are who see at no distant time the re-establishment of a French dependency on the northern portion of the Anglo-Saxon States, already hemmed in on the slave border by the shadowy outlines of an empire under French protection. When we see what has taken place on that continent within the last hundred years, it is not to be said that combinations and occurrences much more wonderful will not come to pass before the present century closes. The policy of a State, as the duty of an individual, is to do what is right and leave the future to work out its destiny.

CHAPTER X.

Canadian Hospitality—Muffins—Departure for the States—Desertions—Montreal again—Southerners in Montreal—Drill and Snow Shoes—Winter Campaigning—Snow Drifts—Military Discontent.

ALTHOUGH my residence in Quebec was very short, I left the city with regret. Compared with the cities of the States, its antiquity is venerable and its ways are peace; but from what I heard of public amusement in summer time I should say that life here would be found dull, as compared with existence in a European capital, or in a city so vainly gay and profitably festive as New York. There is no great wealth among the people, but a moderate competency is largely enjoyed, and neither wealth nor poverty attains undue dimensions.

I found at Quebec a very agreeable society, the tone of feeling which prevails in a capital, the utmost hospitality. Had I had a hundred mouths they would here all have been kept busy. Invitations came in scores, and were to be resisted with difficulty. Knowing all this I am the more astonished at the recent statements which I have heard, that the Canadians have not extended any civilities to our officers. If so, a great change must have taken place. I am not now talking of sleighing parties, but of the hospitality of the inner house. The fair Canadians may have been too kind in accepting the name and position of "muffins" from the young Britishry; but the latter cannot say they have suffered much in consequence. A muffin is simply a lady who sits beside the male occupant of the sleigh—*Sola cum solo,* " and all the rest is leather and prunella."

The social system is intended rather for the comfort of the inner life, and for the development of domestic happiness, than for such external glare and glitter as Broadway delights in, or for such unsound social relations as mark the America of hotels. The great artists who adorn the drama or the lyric stage can rarely be bribed sufficiently high to visit these northern regions; but I doubt whether there is not a better taste in art among the people of Quebec than there is to be found in most cities of the same size in the United States.

On a gloomy winter evening I was once more battling with the ice on the St. Lawrence; and, after a long passage, left Point Levi for Montreal.

A weary life-long night it seemed, and a still wearier day in the train. It was close upon twenty-one hours of stuffy, foodless travel, ere we arrived at Montreal. Nor can I remember anything worth recording of all that linked weariness, long drawn out, except that, halting at a roadside station in the night, I came on a detachment of the Scots Fusilier Guards, who had come up from Rivière du Loup, after their passage in sleighs over the snows of New Brunswick, and were in high spirits, looking very red in the face, and bulky in comparison with the lean habitans. "Misthress," quoth one of them to the woman at the bar, "wad ye gi'e me a dhrap av whuskie?" The Hebe complied with this request, and for some very small pecuniary consideration filled him out nearly a tumblerful of the dreadful preparation known in the States as "Fortyrod." The soldier tasted it, blinked his eyes, squeezed them close, pursed up his lips, smacked them, gave a short watery cough, smelt the mixture, and, looking at his comrades, exclaimed, "My Gude! Hech! I'd jist as soon face a charge of baynets." After that proem I was prepared to see the hardy warrior eject the fluid, but he proceeded to a most inconsequent act: for, nodding his head, he said, "Sae, here's t'ye, my lads," and tossed down the fire-water incontinent.

There were several companies of H.M.'s 63rd Regiment in the train, also going up to Montreal. It did not escape me that at the station pickets were looking sharply out for intending deserters, who might have cut away in the darkness; and I was told, and felt inclined to believe it might be worth their while, that there were Yankee crimps lying in wait at all the stations to help the deserters across the frontier, if they could induce them to leave their colours. The anxiety and annoyance caused by desertion, and by the chance of it, add to the dissatisfaction which is now expressed in our army in Canada; but I must say I cannot quite sympathise with the violence and exaggeration in which that dislike finds vent.

Captains of companies suffer losses, but in many instances they have only themselves to blame. The men, seduced by high pay, either in the States or as farm-labourers in Canada, are seized with an irresistible desire to quit the service abruptly, "without leave," and resort to ingenious artifices to escape.

Sometimes a whole guard will march off bodily, non-commissioned officers and all; occasionally one of the number will submit to be handcuffed, and will be marched by his comrades through the post as a deserter, or a man will put on a sergeant's jacket or sew chevrons on his coat sleeve, and march off his party as if they were going out on picket or patrol duty. Such artifices cannot always be successfully encountered, but they are to be met to some extent by increased vigilance.

I need not say that it was with satisfaction I exchanged my railway van for a comfortable room in the house of Mr. Rose at Montreal. The news of an immediate advance of the army of the Potomac which had been received from New York turned out to be untrue; no immediate hurry was there need for to go down to the seat of war. I dined at the club, where we had a very agreeable party, enlivened by the fervent conversation of some Southern gentlemen of the little colony of refugees which finds shelter in Montreal under the British flag. There is some work of Nemesis in the condition of these gentlemen. Here are Charleston people, who claimed the right to imprison British subjects because they had dark skins, now taking refuge under the British flag, from the exercise of the very power which enabled them to maintain their claim, and apologising to Englishmen for the peculiar institution on the ground that they treated their niggers better than the Yankees do.

The snow again falling, and the day cold. On the Sunday after my arrival, I walked into town in moccasins, and attended service in Christchurch, where the ritual was in close imitation of the cathedral formula at home. I saw a party of the Guards marched to church, who had an air of profound discontent on their manly features. Some Canadians near me evidently regarded them as hardened heretics going to a place of punishment, and at the same time deserving it as foreign mercenaries; but the Guards certainly did not seem to care one farthing for their opinion, if they understood the expression of it. The building is very handsome; but, in spite of the cold outside, I found the atmosphere unbearable, owing to the stoves, iron pipes, or some other undesirable calorific apparatus. The sermon was respectable and frigid.

I spent the next day visiting the remarkable places and persons passed over in Montreal on my last brief visit. In the evening I dined with Colonel Kelly and H.M.'s 47th Regiment, who entertained Sir Fenwick Williams and the officers of the Guards then in garrison, and on the following morning at 9 o'clock I drove over to the Barracks to see a drill of the regiment on the St. Lawrence in snow shoes. Sir Fenwick Williams and some staff officers were on the ground. The regiment was admirably handled by Colonel Kelly, and the scene was very novel and amusing. The regiment was in excellent condition: the men seemed rather to like the fun with the snow shoes, and when skirmishers were thrown out or called in at the double, there was certainty of a fall or two from unlucky privates tripping up in their shoes and tumbling in the snow, which flew like puffs of musketry. Fresh from parades of volunteers I felt the force of Lord Clyde's maxim—" The first duty of a soldier is to obey"—as I looked at the measured tread even at the quickest, and the alert, agile formations of the men to whom discipline was the whole scope of military intellect. There was, I thought, in that complex machine of many parts, but of only one animating, moving power, what would be cheaply bought by the United States by many hundreds of thousands of dollars for the purposes of war, though man to man one of their regiments might be more intelligent, and quite as capable of deeds of valour as the old 47th, of whom indeed not many had the Crimean medal, though the campaign is now but a few years old.

In the evening I dined with the Commander-in-Chief, Sir Fenwick Williams, and met Mr. Cartier, Mr. Galt, and Mr. Rose.

The letters from England which came by every mail showed that the position was not much understood, as it was believed there would be a speedy movement of the army of the Potomac, which I knew to be buried in mud. The American papers of course deluded their readers by constant assurances that McClellan was about to move next week. It would seem, after all, that in new countries the practice of going into winter quarters, which prevailed among sixteenth and seventeenth century generals, was founded on good reason; but that as the land became better drained, and the roads were improved by civilisation and populations, the necessity for inaction was diminished. Napoleon astonished Europe by some wonderful escapades in the field; but even in the Peninsula the British suffered greatly in winter movements. In the old French war, operations in Canada were usually over in August or early in September; but the Americans, in their bold and skilful campaign of 1775, commenced their invasion or dash late in the year—managed so well that they broke in almost simultaneously at Montreal and Quebec, on the British, who had only one regular regiment in the Provinces, in November—and it was on the last day of the year that Montgomery and Arnold made their brilliant and unsuccessful attempt to carry the citadel by escalade.

Again, in 1812, it was as late as October before the Americans opened their campaign on the Niagara frontier; and it was about the middle of November when they directed their ill-managed and abortive demonstration against Montreal. They again moved in January, 1813, and several actions took place in the early months of the year, nor did the approach of winter drive the contending parties from the field; and a good deal of sharp fighting took place in December. In the following year the Americans began the offensive at a later period, though the corps intended to operate against the Montreal district was in motion in the first week of March. Our defeat at Plattsburg occurred on September 11th. The Americans make much of it—with great justice. They defeated the best regiments of an army which had proved itself, in face of the picked troops of Napoleon, the first in Europe. When winter is well established in these high latitudes, perhaps it is, under ordinary circumstances, more favourable to military operations than it is in lower latitudes, where tremendous rains alternate with heavy snow storms, which do not form permanent deposits over which to move men or guns.

On the following day I dined with Mr. Chamberlain, of the "Montreal Gazette," Mr. Rose, Mr. Ryland, Major Penn, and a number of gentlemen connected with the Canadian press, at a famous old-fashioned English tavern, kept by an old-fashioned John Bull cook, who would have fainted outright at the sight of a *vol-au-vent* and died of an *omelette glacée*, where we had much old-fashioned English talk. On our issuing into the outer world there was a snow-fall going on, the like of which I, unaccustomed, had never seen before; and my voyage out to Mr. Rose's was diversified by attempts of the sleigh-driver to get over boundary-walls and into gardens, till we came to a dead stop just as the fall cleared off a little, and permitted us to get a glimpse of the moon. But the moon gave no assistance, for its rays only lighted up great snow mounds and a universal whiteness, and the road seemed as doubtful as ever. As I was deliberating what was best to be done, a sleigh-bell was heard jingling in the distance, and the vehicle gradually approached us. We hailed the occupant, and I heard a well-known voice in answer: it was that of Colonel Lysons, an inmate of the same hospitable abode as that I occupied. Our united efforts at last discovered the mansion.

The snow-storm continued next day: the fall was so great that Lysons, who was bound to Quebec on duty connected with the Militia Bill, and started early, was compelled to return *re infecta* in the morning. Towards the afternoon the storm ceased, and left a thick outer garment over the body of the country. The younger people of the house considered the occasion favourable for snow-balling, and I was included in some diffusive arrangements, very unfavourable to literary composition, for the spread of the white artillery, directed by willing hands and unrelenting aim at short range. I dined with the artillery mess—went afterwards to a ball given by H.M.'s 16th Regiment at the Donegana, which is the head-quarters of Secessiondom—and finished the evening by a visit to the house of Mr. Judah, who gave a dance which was attended by Lord F. Paulet and a number of soldiers, and, above all, by a lovely American, who created a strong current in favour of the Union, of which she was a staunch advocate.

As already hinted, I have heard of complaints from officers of the Guards and other regiments that the Canadians during the period in question did not treat them with the hospitality for which they were once celebrated. Of that point I am not well able to judge; but I must say, that during the whole period of my stay in Canada, I never was in any society in which I did not see British officers, and never knew of their having had reason to complain of neglect till lately. If there was any want of hospitable civility, I must think the officers were in some measure to blame for it: for among those stationed any length of time in Canada, or who knew the country in former years, I always heard unreserved praise of those Canadians who had the means of entertaining visitors. It must be remembered that there are few Canadians who are wealthy enough to give set dinners, and that the reserve which guards the family of the Frenchman existed in the times from which his descendants in Canada take their traditions and manners. Many people in Montreal, well inclined to show every attention in their power to the officers quartered among them, were deterred by the very prestige of the Guards' social position from offering them ordinary civility; and by degrees in many cases an estrangement grew up.

I saw nothing to account for the discontent of officers who were quartered at Montreal, save and except the fact that they were on foreign service, that they were not in England or London among their friends, and that they did not like the people,—all grounds which they might unfortunately allege against any other part of the world in which the British army is forced to serve. The subject is only important, in so far as it exercises an influence over the relations of the two countries; a common expression of dislike on the part of men who exercise a great influence among the most powerful classes in this country must increase any tendency to regard with indifference the possession of the great territory which it is my belief we should seek to attach to the Crown by every possible legitimate means, Professor Goldwin Smith and the political economists of his school notwithstanding.

After a stay of some days in Montreal, I received intelligence which rendered it necessary for me to depart at once for the United States, and I returned to New York by Rouse's Point, travelling night and day. I had seen enough of Canada to inspire me with a real regard for the people, and a sincere interest in the fortunes of such a magnificent dependency of the Crown, and I resolved, as far as in me lay, to attract the attention of the home country to a region which offers so many advantages to her children, and promises one day to be the seat of flourishing communities, if not of a vast and independent empire.

CHAPTER XI.

Extent of Canada—The Lakes—Canadian Wealth—Early History—
Jacques Cartier—English and French Colonists—Colonial and
Acadian Troubles—La Salle—Border Conflicts—Early Expeditions
—Invasions from New England—Louisburgh and Ticonderoga—
The Colonial Insurrection—Partition of Canada—Progress of
Upper Canada—France and Canada—The American Invasion—
Winter Campaign — New Orleans and Plattsburg — Peace of
Ghent—Political Controversies—Winter Communication—Sentiments of Hon. Joseph Howe—General View of Imperial and
Colonial relations.

A VICTORY won not a century ago gratified the animosities of the American colonies, and added to the countries ruled by the Sovereign of Great Britain a tract of territory thrice the size of his kingdom. From Labrador to the western limit of Lake Superior, a line drawn east and west within the boundaries of Canada, is 1600 miles long; but the breadth of the country from its Southern frontiers to the ill-defined boundary on the North, is but 225 miles. This vast region is divided into Upper and Lower Canada. The former lies between long. 40° and 49° N., and lat. 74° and 117° W. The latter lies between 45° and 50° North and 57° and 80° W. The three hundred and forty thousand square miles thus bounded present every variety of scenery and of soil. The climate is mainly influenced by the relations of the land to the enormous inland seas and great rivers which occupy such a space in the map of British North America. From Lake Superior, which is larger than all Ireland, flows the mighty stream which feeds Lake Huron by the River St. Mary. Huron

is nearly 250 miles long and 221 miles broad. From
Lake Huron the river and lake of St. Clair lead
the flood into Lake Erie, which is 280 miles long and
63 miles broad. From Lake Erie the current runs
with quickening pace, till it rushes in ceaseless flight
into the fathomless depths of Niagara, and whirls on-
ward to melt into the waters of Lake Ontario. The
last and smallest of these seas, Ontario, is 180 miles
long and 50 miles broad. The St. Lawrence, winding
through many islands, emerges from its eastern
extremity and commences its uninterrupted career of
700 miles to the Atlantic. The land of this northern
continent in fact reverses the part of Ocean, and
enfolds sea after sea within its arms. The water blesses
the land for its protection; it yields an easy way to the
progress of civilisation; transports the produce of the
settler's labour to distant markets, and lays open to his
enterprise the wide-spreading forests and plains which,
but for them, would still be the heritage of the Indian
and of his prey. Among the greatest proofs of enterprise in the world are the canals by which the people
living on the shores of the lakes have rendered navigation practicable from the sea to Lake Superior. The
display of the natural and artificial products of the far-
reaching lands watered by the giant St. Lawrence at
the Great Exhibition of 1862, came to the eyes of most
of us with a sort of shock. It was surprising indeed to
behold such evidences of wealth given by a dependency
which was associated in the popular mind with frost
and snow, with Niagara, Labrador, and French insurrection—Moose, moccasins, and Indians. There we saw
an exuberance and excellence of growth in timber and
in cereals—in all kinds of agricultural produce, com-

bined with prodigious mineral riches. Sir William Logan, assisted by the zealous, skilful, and indefatigable staff of Canadian geologists, showed what a future Canada may expect when capital and population combine to disinter the treasures which now lie hid within its rocky ribs.

According to Jesuit Hennepin, the name of Canada furnishes a proof of an ignorance and deficient appreciation of the true value of the country that still mark the workings of the European mind in reference to the resources of Canada. According to him, the word Canada was derived from a corruption of the Spanish words Capo da Nada, or Cape of Nothing, which they gave to the scene of their early discoveries when, under a conviction of its utter barrenness and inutility, they were about abandoning it in disgust. The derivation may be well doubted, but the implication may be true enough. The mainspring of Spanish, and indeed of all European enterprise in those days, was the hope of gold, and although there is reason to know that the precious metal is associated with others scarcely less valuable in Canada, of course it was not found lying in heaps and blocks on the sea-shore, and therefore the Spaniards concluded that it did not exist. It has been conjectured, with greater appearance of probability, that Canada is a modification of the Spanish word signifying "a passage;" because the Spaniards thought they could find a passage to India through Canada; as others, with greater reason, believe there may yet be found a permanent practicable way to the shores of the Pacific through its wide expanse of lake and mountain.

The accounts of the first discovery of Canada, meagre

as they are, possess a romantic interest which is never likely to assume any very precise or substantial form. Although Cabot, who discovered Labrador and Hudson's Bay, was the first person who suggested or projected the establishment of colonies or settlements in these newly-found regions, and English merchants actually established some small colonies there, it is to Jacques Cartier, of St. Malo, that the credit of the first real establishment of Europeans in Canada must be assigned. Cabot discovered the Gulf of St. Lawrence: it was Cartier who found that the Gulf was but the mouth of a vast river; and who urged his little craft among its unknown dangers till he came to the site of Quebec. It was no ordinary man who, having accomplished thus much, pressed onwards till he reached Hochelaga, the site of Montreal. He was impelled by the love of gold and precious stones, and believed that here he had found them, but they were indeed only Lagenian mines. Cartier, and many another gallant sailor, found glittering mica and crystals on the shores of their new found lands, which in their innocent faith they believed to be gold and diamonds, and so filled ship and were off to sea again. The failure of these early adventures cast Canada into disfavour with those who led the enterprise of the East. Whilst the English merchants and navigators were, with uncertain steps, seeking some solid resting-place on the eastern shores of America below the St. Lawrence, Canada was left in the possession of the Indians—not a peaceable possession, because the great Tribes were as irreclaimably belligerent as the Highland Clans or the Irish Septs. It is curious to reflect on the fact, indeed, that little more than two hundred years ago the whole of the vast region between Massachusetts and Hudson's Bay was in the hands of the Red Man. But he was then yielding ground rapidly before the imperious strangers who had seized his shore farther south. The merchants of Bristol and of London turned their attention to Virginia before the French of St. Malo had well established themselves on the shores of the St. Lawrence. Both English and French alike were encouraged and stimulated in these early efforts by the Crown. About the time that James the First was granting charters and framing corporations for colonies in Virginia, Champlain was establishing French settlements at Tadousac and Quebec, in Nouvelle France. The early dealings of English and French with the natives are discreditable to both nations; both fomented or availed themselves of dissensions among the Tribes, and when hostilities broke out, threw their weight on one side or the other. Whilst the New England Puritans were encouraging themselves in the work of destroying the Red Man by quoting passages from the Old Testament, which clearly showed how they the chosen people of God were called upon to slay the Canaanite, Champlain, with his Roman Catholic priests, was quite as busy in rooting out Iroquois in the name of Heaven and of the Church. Of the two invading races, indeed, the French were the least exclusive, for they neither burned nor banished Dissenters. So great was the liberality of France in those days, that Protestant and Roman Catholic emigrants shared in the same enterprise, and abode in the same settlements. But the Brethren of New Plymouth took a very limited view of Christian fraternisation, and at the very outset the colonists of the Northern and of the Southern

States were animated by principles so opposed that even in the grub state they bit and stung each other.

English and French colonists were alike undergoing the spasmodic influences of the jealousy and intrigue which usually preside over the birthplace of colonies, when the operations of the war which broke out between France and England in 1628, were extended to those distant regions. The growing power of England at sea enabled her to strike a tremendous blow at New France. Champlain, with all his garrison, was starved into capitulation by Sir David Kirke; but on the restoration of peace and of the colony to France, in 1633, he returned to Canada, where he died two years afterwards. Champlain, with all his faults, was undoubtedly a man noteworthy, politic, and valuable in his time and generation, and his name will ever be associated with the early history of the continent. Priests and nuns and missionaries after his death swooped down on the Indians, who began to hate each other worse than ever they had done before, whilst at the same time they learned to entertain a savage dislike for the race which they had welcomed to their shores so courteously and gently. Thousands of Indians were indeed converted, as it was called, to Christianity; but it was only that they might rage with greater cruelty and fierceness against their brethren. Massacres of Christians and of converts by furious savages fanned these unholy flames. Little is left of either the Indians or of their Christianity now. A common animosity to the aborigines brought about the first "rapprochement" between the French and British colonists. The New English and the New French first met in America to consider the propriety of an alliance against their Indian enemies, which should not be broken by war between the parent countries, but the status of the two offshoots of the great European rivals was very different. The French in Canada at one time displayed a wonderful amount of enterprise, energy, and perseverance in their dealings with the savages, which can only be appreciated by those who have studied their early records, but it contrasts strongly with the quiescence and political folly of their descendants. Their early explorations were characterised by a spirit worthy of the countrymen of Cartier. Among these, the voyage of La Salle from Niagara deserves to be mentioned, as indicative of the highest qualities of a traveller. In a little craft of some sixty tons, he ascended the rapid river above the Falls of Niagara, amidst difficulties which we can but little understand, and gained the broad expanse of Lake Erie; thence boldly steering westward, he came upon the narrow river or strait of Detroit, crossed the lucid waters of Lake St. Clair, and was at last rewarded by the grand discovery of Lake Huron. Still boldly pursuing his course westward, La Salle at last came to Lake Michigan, whence in company with Father Hennepin, his jesuit historian, he undertook the feat of penetrating to the head waters of the Mississippi. Nor did he stop when he reached the mystic stream; he trusted himself to the mighty flood, and never turned round or bated breath till he floated out, 2000 miles below, on the turbid waters of the Gulf of Mexico. Whilst the hierarchy of France were busy founding bishoprics, building churches, and establishing seminaries, the English, distracted by internal convulsions, left their American colonies pretty much to themselves. France sent out governors, councillors, and bishops to New France; England dispatched her Puritans, adventurers, younger sons, Catholic cavaliers, and Nonconformists; but the natives were sure to suffer, no matter in what form the colony was ruled, or of what Europeans it was composed. Terrible diseases, although known in Europe for two hundred years previously, according to contemporary writers, appeared suddenly, and without European communication, among the indigenes, and ravaged the miserable tribes, already decimated by intestine war and ruin. Christians were naturally held accountable for all the evil; and for a large part indeed they were.

Whilst James the Second was making a last stand for his Crown against the victorious Dutchman, La Salle, with a patent of Governor, was sailing from La Rochelle, for the dependency of Louisiana, which now completed the vast semicircle over which the King of France claimed authority, and which enclosing the British settlements in a belt from Newfoundland through the lakes, swept thence by the Ohio down to the Gulf of Mexico, far away to the *terra incognita* under the setting sun. The superior trading resources of the Indians of the South, the favourable conditions for the expansion of trade possessed by the British on the Hudson over the French, who had to struggle with longer frost, and the wintry storms of the St. Lawrence, and the greater commercial enterprise of the English colonists, nullified that vast territorial superiority. The French governors thought, by displays of vigour and violence towards the natives, to alter the course of trade; but they could not compete with their neighbours, and quarrels and petty wars vexed the life of both colonial systems. In 1690,

M. de Frontenac launched three little corps of invading savages, aided and led by French troops, against the British settlements in the New England Colonies. Schenectady in New York, Salmon Falls in New Hampshire, Casco in Maine, were surprised and burned, and the colonists were given to the sword and the scalping-knife. For a time the survivors of the massacre had something else to do besides persecuting each other to death for witchcraft or torturing their heretics. They set to work to avenge their slaughtered saints. Sir William Phipps, a native of Massachusetts, led his Puritan hosts to Port Royal in Nova Scotia, but was obliged to retreat ingloriously from an attempt against Montreal. His rival, De Frontenac, had no better fortune in a projected attack by land and sea against New York. The war which raged between the colonists was terminated by the Peace of Ryswick; but peace did not last long, and the declaration of war by Great Britain against France and Spain revived the bloody contests between the borderers. The British Government sent out Marlborough's veterans, and those sailors who had swept the seas of every enemy, to aid the colonists. An immense expedition, which seemed capable of destroying any trace of French rule in Canada, sailed from Boston in 1710, against Quebec, but failed miserably at sea and in the St. Lawrence ere it reached the city. The Peace of Utrecht, in 1713, brought about a cessation of hostilities, but not of jealousies, or of Indian wars and massacres. By that time the predominance of the white man was well established, and the faces of the Indians were turned steadily towards the setting sun, and their footsteps followed his course towards the forests of the west. Fort after fort encroached on their decreasing domain, and Englishman and Frenchman, each after his kind, sought to reproduce in the New World those features of the mother country which he loved or admired or respected most.

In the period which elapsed between the Treaty of Utrecht and the declaration of war in 1745, both the Colonies and Canada prospered, but the increase of the former was to that of the latter as the increase of grain compared with that of moss. The people of Massachusetts, led by their colonial chief, Pepperell, with contingents from Rhode Island, Vermont, and Connecticut, were joined by the British fleet under Warren, and set out on their darling project of reducing Louisburg, the great French arsenal and station at Cape Breton. On the 17th of August, 1746, after a siege of two months, the place surrendered with all its stores to the victorious Colonists. It was with difficulty that France could communicate with her menaced dependency, for the sea was nearly controlled by the British fleets, but her pride was aroused, and great armaments were prepared and dispatched to Canada. *Afflavit Deus et hostes dissipantur.* Two expeditions were nigh lost altogether on the waves. A third was destroyed by the fleet under Warren and Anson. The Peace of Rochelle put an end to the passionate efforts of France to retrieve her disasters, but the rivalries and excesses of the British and French fur-traders continued the strife between the Colonies and New France. The latter claiming the whole course of the Ohio, as it appears with some reason, forbade our traders to resort there. Forts were built to enable the French to exercise their jurisdiction and authority on ground which was regarded by the British Colonists as their own, and it is a remarkable fact, that George

Washington's first military service was in command of an expedition of Virginians to capture the works erected by the French, and that he was compelled to lay down his arms by De Villiers, after a brief and inglorious—not to say very badly-managed campaign. Although Great Britain made considerable efforts to aid the colonists in their wars, she could not very well continue to do so when she was at peace with France, if her distant subjects chose to carry on hostilities on their own account. The King's Government gave advice to the Colonies to unite for self-defence, which led in 1754 to the assemblage of a convention at Albany, at which Massachusetts, Rhode Island, New Hampshire, Connecticut, Pennsylvania, Maryland, and New York were represented. The delegates drew up a plan for what was in effect a Federal Union, but the plan fell to the ground. The Home Government refused to adopt it, because of certain encroachments which it contained on the prerogatives of the Crown; and the colonial assemblies, which had already exhibited a sturdy self-reliance and independence worthy of attention at home, were equally dissatisfied with the proposal. But the seed had been sown—the idea of Federal Union, of self-taxation, of levying troops and regulating trade, was busy in men's minds. In the same year the Colonists were preparing for their great attack on Canada—an attack which was made, not because France was the enemy of England, but because Frenchmen in Canada were rivals of the American colonists.

The lines of invasion of French Canada marked out by the American subjects of the British Crown, were very much the same as those of the American rebels against the Crown, when some twenty odd years afterwards they prepared to invade British Canada. It is singular that the men who, under the authority of the Crown of England, or using at least the pretext of a state of war between the home countries, waged war against the subjects of France in Canada, should have been foremost in the rebellion against England, and that, in the invasion of Canada, which was one of their first undertakings in pursuance of their rebellion, they should have found neither sympathy nor aid amongst the French Canadians, whose allegiance had been so recently transferred to the King of England. More singular still is it that France, which had received so many tremendous blows from these very colonists, and which suffered so much in her efforts to defend her Canadian dependencies from these inveterate assailants, should have been mainly instrumental in establishing their independence, and in leading their great revolution to a successful issue. The condition of the Scottish borders in the fourteenth and fifteenth centuries furnishes but a very poor parallel to the state of the debateable land which spread from the banks of the Ohio, by the great lakes, down to the Atlantic. Constant aggressions took place from one side or the other by trading parties, bands of Indians, or by armed parties with larger purposes of occupation or vengeance. Whilst the English colonies were enjoying the full fruit of the principles on which they had been founded, Canada, regarded as a mere dependency of the French Crown, vexed with the complicated and inconsistent form of government, was daily losing ground. The ill-paid governors were corrupt, or at all events exacting: the Intendants ground the province to powder to make the most of their office, and beneath each of these officers was an army of ecclesiastics, bent on appropriating, for that incarnation of the Church which appeared in their proper persons, the best of the land and the great tithes of all trade and commerce. Of the many encounters which took place on the borders, there are few authentic records: it is sufficient to know that neither the French nor the English succeeded at the period in effecting a permanent lodgment within the frontiers of the enemy. The Governors of Canada commemorated their victory, "*Rebellibus Novæ Angliæ Incolis,*" on medals and brasses, and Great Britain rewarded by various honours the colonial generals and governors who were supposed to have attained advantages over their Canadian neighbours. In 1756 war was again declared by Great Britain against France. Montcalm, availing himself of the utter imbecility of Lord Loudon, who commanded the British troops, speedily fell upon the important post of Oswego, on Lake Ontario, and captured it with its garrison, guns, flotilla, and stores. He followed up that great success in the following year, by the capture of Fort Edward, which surrendered, with its garrison of 8000 men under Monroe, who were massacred by the Indian auxiliaries. The officers who were sent from England to command the troops, and their continental allies at this period, must have inspired the American continentals with a feeling of profound contempt: but Lord Chatham, perceiving that the Colonists must be the mainstay of military operations, aroused the various New England settlements, by spirited despatches and promises of help, to make strenuous efforts against the enemy. Once more a British fleet under Admiral

Boscawen appeared upon the scene, and a force of 14,000 men, under Lord Amherst, was covered by its guns in the operations which led to the surrender of Louisburgh on the 26th of July, 1756. This success was tarnished by the defeat of a powerful army under Abercrombie, in an ill-judged assault against Ticonderoga, where 16,000 men were beaten back by the French garrison, which numbered only 3000; but Kingston, on Lake Ontario, surrendered to the British-American troops, and Fort du Quesne—in the advance against which Braddock lost his life in the former war—was abandoned without a blow by its French garrison, who would be somewhat astounded, if, revisiting the glimpses of the moon, they could gaze upon the Pittsburgh of the present day on the site of their ancient post. In July, 1759, three great expeditions were directed against Canada. The Ministry resolved at any cost to trample under foot every trace of French dominion on the American continent, and in that resolution they were mainly sustained by the passion and animosity of the New England colonists. A powerful corps under Lord Amherst was directed against Ticonderoga. Another corps, under Sir William Johnson, mainly composed of continentals and Indians, advanced against Fort Niagara, whilst an army commanded by General Wolfe, covered by the fleet, made an attack from the St. Lawrence against Quebec. Ticonderoga and Crown Point were abandoned by the French, and Fort Niagara was taken after an engagement with the enemy. How Wolfe fared all the world knows: an elaborate account of the great victory which gave Canada to the Crown would be out of place in this volume, but elsewhere I have made a few remarks concerning the events of that memorable battle. On the 18th of September the British standard floated from the citadel of Quebec. Ever since that time the country, handed over four years afterwards by the Treaty of Paris to the British, has remained under the protection of England, acquiring year by year a greater measure of freedom and self-government, till, at this moment, it may be considered as attached to the Empire solely by what Mr. O'Connell called "the golden link of the Crown." The whole population of the country then ceded was under 70,000. The population of the British colonies in America was at least twenty times as numerous. The American Colonists were at last gratified by a conquest which relieved them from a dangerous neighbour, who was backed by the power of France, and which opened to their enterprise not only the lakes and rivers of Canada, but Nova Scotia, Cape Breton, the St. Lawrence, and all the valuable fisheries of the sea-board. It was unfortunate that no attempt was made to define the exact boundary line between the Colonies and the new territory, although the Proclamation of 1763 no doubt was supposed at the time to be sufficiently accurate; but we shall see hereafter that the neglect proved very damaging to the interests of Canada. The Americans, perhaps, would have resented any attempt to define very nicely the frontier between the new conquest of England and the territories of the colonists who had contributed to some extent in effecting it; and there were not many who foresaw the rupture which divided the mother-country and her dependencies for ever.

For fifteen years Canada, content with the preservation of her ecclesiastical establishments, of freedom of religion, and of the "Custom of Paris," seemed perfectly indifferent to the transfer of her allegiance from one king to another, the change, perhaps, being more in the language of her rulers, and the blazon of her standard, than in the mode of government. In fact the British military governors were singularly like the French military governors; but it was felt at home, as soon as the difficulties with the colonies began, that Canada could not continue to be like a mere military division of a conquered country. In 1774, the Quebec Act was passed, which created a council to aid in the administration of the province, guaranteed the freedom of the Roman Catholic Church, and abrogated the Royal Proclamation of 1763. In lieu of the administration of a military pro-consulate, there was established a settled government, with some show of a representative basis. The American colonists were then upon the verge of the great rebellion, and as a proof of the spirit in which they acted, it may be remarked that the Continental Congress made a most violent remonstrance against the toleration of Roman Catholicism in Canada, guaranteed by the Quebec Act. The very next year the rebellious colonists captured Ticonderoga and Crown Point, and Montreal; and had their enterprise against Quebec succeeded, Canada might have become included in the territory which eventually became portion of the United States. So bent were the colonists on including Canada in the scope of their great design, that in 1776, immediately after their unsuccessful invasion, Franklin, who was one of the main movers of Wolfe's expedition, and two gentlemen, were sent by Congress to offer the Canadians a free press and State rights, and the free exercise of the faith which but two years before they had so bitterly denounced the British Government for guaranteeing, if they would but join in the revolt against Great Britain. In the war which followed between the British and the American colonists, Canada was made the base of operations against the colonies, which generally terminated in disasters, such as that of Burgoyne, though, in pitched battles, the British were almost invariably victorious. The habitans took little or no part in the contest, but on the Declaration of Independence, a number of Royalists emigrated from the States and settled in the country, in very much the same way as the Southern Americans are now taking refuge in Canada from the persecution of their Northern neighbours. The wish to give, in their new country, these devoted men some equivalent for that which they had lost, suggested a course which has been condemned by subsequent events. The Home Government resolved upon the unfortunate step of dividing the province into Upper and Lower Canada, with a governor-in-chief in Lower, and a lieutenant-governor in Upper Canada, so that the Royalists might not be quite swamped by the French element. The governors selected were often men without particular aptitude for administration, certainly destitute of the ability needed in dealing with the very peculiar state of society, trade, and interests prevailing in the provinces.

Although the legislative council and assembly of Upper Canada had equal privileges with that of Lower Canada, the condition of the people was very different, principally owing to the paucity of population. Governor Simcoe, to whom the care of Upper Canada was first confided, ruled over a wilderness, in which a few clearings around the trading stations on the lakes and rivers, and some huts gathered about the military posts, were the sole vestiges of the white man and civilisation. As the English colonists gained the upper hand in the constant strife which raged during the latter period of the French occupation, the habitans of the remoter settlements had gradually withdrawn towards Lower Canada, and had concentrated in the neighbourhood of the towns on the St. Lawrence, where they could find safety in case of danger, and transport should their friends be unable to protect them. It was not surprising that the whole French population flocked into the lower province; for under a foreign rule they gained confidence and ease by the contemplation of their numbers and the concentration of their masses. Although many American Royalists came into the lake country so abandoned, they were not equal in number to the population that fled. It required no small amount of courage and perseverance in Governor Simcoe to conduct the affairs of his little government, from the site which his sagacity pointed out to him as the most favourable for the development of his province. The Red Man's wigwam still clung to the border of the British posts, and the few intrepid men who ventured to fix their homes along the shore of the Upper St. Lawrence, found themselves amidst an uncongenial population of half-breeds and Indians, accustomed indeed to the chase, and to the rude barter which represented the only trade of those vast regions, but utterly averse to settled life and agricultural labour; obnoxious also to handicraft-men, mechanics, and the followers of the peaceful, regular pursuits which are the handmaidens of civilisation. Under these circumstances the advance of Upper Canada, slow as it was for some years, is surprising, and the rapidity of her subsequent progress is certainly worthy of admiration. In 1793 the revenue of Upper Canada was less than 1000*l.* a-year; and although the machinery of carrying on government and law existed, it was but imperfectly, if at all, worked. In theory the English law prevailed, and one cannot but admit, if we are to judge by its fruits, that it was far better calculated to promote the security and prosperity of the country; than the Custom of Paris, to which the French Canadians clung in virtue of the capitulation of Quebec. Even thus early the militia occupied the attention of the legislature, although they were obliged to do battle against the denizens of the forest, and to encourage the hunter by rewards for the destruction of bears and wolves. The regulation of trade between the provinces and the United States—the establishment of ports of entry—the adjustment of land titles, and other useful matters of the kind, were not neglected by the earliest Parliaments. Unhappily religious questions arose soon after the close of the last century in Lower Canada. The national feeling became associated with the ancient religion in opposition to the aims of the British Government and of the Protestant clergy. Whilst Dissenters and Presbyterians and other schismatics from the Church of England were allowed free scope in Upper Canada, the Government set itself to work to give to the Protestant Church in Lower Canada the prestige which belonged to the Catholic Church. The Canadians raised the cry—*Nos institutions! notre langue! et nos lois!*

When hostilities with America seemed imminent in

1807, the militia nevertheless responded to the call with enthusiasm in Lower Canada, and Acts were passed in Upper Canada for raising, training and billeting the force in case of need. Although the language for which the Lower Canadians cried out was that of France Acadianised, the institutions and the laws in which they took pride belonged only to a France of the past. The Republic had placed between Canada and France a barrier which the priesthood declared to be impassable. What had they to do with the Goddess of Reason and a calendar without a saint? What had a people steeped in feudalism, or the Custom of Paris, to do with the Code Napoleon? Nevertheless the rulers of Canada suspected the habitans of treason, whilst the habitans suspected the rulers of designs upon their faith; and so it was that want of confidence, one of the most formidable impediments to the good understanding between governor and governed which can exist, took root and grew apace. The second war with the United States was at hand. The animosity of the Americans of the Southern and Middle States against England was much augmented by the discovery of a project of the Canadian Secretary, Ryland, to detach the New England States from the Union, and to annex them to Canada. The bitter feelings which the old New England Colonists had entertained towards their French neighbours had been mitigated by the influence of a common language and the congenial religion and laws of the English rulers of Canada. Certain it is that the New England delegates opposed the war which was declared against Great Britain by the Government of Washington by every means in their power, though they were by no means complimentary to Canada, which they supposed it to be one of the objects of the war party in America to annex. On the declaration of war in 1812, the Canadians, with the exception of the inhabitants of one parish, turned out with the greatest alacrity, and in considerable force, to defend their country. General Hall, the American Governor of Michigan, seized upon Sandwich in July in the same year; but he was soon very glad to cross over to Detroit again, where he very ingloriously capitulated soon afterwards to General Brock, with 2500 men and 33 pieces of cannon, thus surrendering the whole State of Michigan to Great Britain.

The Americans, elated by their naval successes however, resolved to conquer Canada, although Massachusetts, Connecticut, and New York opposed the war with so much determination, that it seemed very probable the Union would be broken up by the persistence of the Southern statesmen in their policy. A corps under Colonel Van Rensellaer attacked the British and the Colonists under Brock at Queenstown, near Niagara, and although that gallant, intrepid, and able officer fell at the head of the 49th regiment, the British, aided by Canadians and Indians, captured or slew nearly the whole of the American invading force, under the eyes of a large number of American militia, at the other side of the river, who refused to cross to the aid of their countrymen. The Americans demanded an armistice, which was most injudiciously granted by General Sheaffe. The American General Dearborn, meantime, with a force varying, it is said, from 8000 to 10,000 men, invaded Lower Canada, but after some unsuccessful skirmishes retreated to Plattsburg. A few days afterwards the American General Smith made an attack on Fort Erie, which was characterised by pusillanimity, and ended in disgraceful failure. When the campaign opened in January, 1813, it was not auspicious for the invading Americans. General Winchester's force was defeated by Colonel Proctor, near Frenchtown; Ogdensburg was taken; but the Americans, nevertheless, continued the war with characteristic perseverance and foresight, and set to work to use the water communications which we had neglected, and thus gained an assured advantage. General Sheaffe was driven out of Toronto by an expedition which landed under the guns of a newly-created American lake fleet, commanded by an experienced and brave sailor, Commodore Chancey. The capture of Fort George followed; but an attempt to overrun Lower Canada ended in utter defeat, Prevost, however, being beaten back in an attack upon Sackett's Harbour, and Proctor being repulsed in an assault on Sanduskey, so as to moderate any undue exultation on the side of the British on account of their success.

This war excited little attention in England, where men thought only of their great naval victories, in which their ships captured, sunk, or dispersed whole fleets of the enemy, or of the grand operations in Spain, where Wellington was worsting in succession the best generals of the Empire. All the strength of the United States was put forth in their war against Canada, and it is only astonishing that the Americans did so little with the means at their disposal. In July a British expedition, covered by two sloops of war, destroyed stores, barracks, and property at Plattsburg, Burlington, and Swanton, whilst the Americans burned the British stores at York. It must be remembered that the Americans had every facility in the command of the lakes, and in the command of the waters. The connection between Lower and Upper Canada was carried on by rapid and dangerous rivers, and by lakes which were constantly patrolled by the Americans, the roads being simply tracks through a forest, or causeways of a most rudimentary character. For some time both sides contended for the supremacy of the Lakes. On the 31st of July the British, under Sir J. Yeo, captured two of Commodore Chancey's squadron, which was further reduced by the loss of two gun-boats, which capsized in trying to escape from the victorious English. But Chancey repaired damages in Sackett's Harbour, and on the 28th of September attacked the British flotilla, which eventually retreated under the guns of Burlington Heights. For the time, therefore, the Americans were masters of Lake Ontario, and they used their advantages in capturing British stores and reinforcements. On the 10th of September the British lost the command of Lake Erie also. An American squadron of nine vessels under Perry, far superior in size, number of men, and in calibre of guns, defeated a British squadron of six vessels under Barclay. The result of this defeat was that the British under Proctor had to evacuate Detroit and Amherstburg, and fall back to open communication with their base of supplies. On the river Thames the pursuit became so severe, that Proctor turned to bay, but he was overwhelmed by the Americans under Harrison, who numbered 3500, whilst the British did not exceed a third of that strength. Michigan was lost to us, and the only port retained by the British west of Burlington was Michilimacinac, which they had taken early in the war.

Nothing less than the conquest of Lower Canada would now satisfy the Americans. A force of 12,000 men was assembled to operate against Montreal. On the 20th of September, Colonel de Salaberry, a Canadian in command of a post of militia, and a few Indians, checked the advance of the enemy, and fell back to Chateaugay, where in a most creditable and gallant action he defeated an American column under Hampton, which was intended to co-operate with an expedition down the St. Lawrence, against Montreal. Another portion of the force was defeated at Chrystler's Farm, with some loss, by a body of British regulars, Canadian militia, and Indians. The attack on Montreal was precipitately abandoned, and the Canadians, who had done so well, were sent back to their homes. But winter did not put an end to the war. The British determined to drive the enemy out of Canada, and the Americans retired before them. On the 10th of December the enemy abandoned and burned the town of Newark. On the 18th of December the British surprised Fort Niagara with all its garrison, and gave Lewiston and Manchester to the flames. Buffalo and Black Rock were captured and destroyed by the British under Riall, and the whole country-side was laid waste in retaliation for the burning of Newark. Sir George Prevost was able to meet the Canadian Parliament with pride, and to congratulate it on the conduct of the provincial militia in the field, and the loyalty of the people. Before the coming of spring had loosed the lakes and rivers, the Americans returned to the attack on Canada, and in March, 1814, Macomb crossed Lake Champlain; but a part of his force was repulsed in an attack on Lacolle, and he retired to Plattsburg. In May, Sir J. Yeo fitted out an expedition from Kingston, which sailed on the 4th of May, captured Oswego, and destroyed some military stores, but did not succeed in a similar attempt against Sackett's Harbour. On the 3rd of July a strong force of Americans landed near Chippewa, and defeated a body of British, Canadians, and Indians, of inferior numbers, under Riall. A very bloody and determined contest ensued on the 25th, near the same place, in which the Americans made repeated efforts to break the British, but were repulsed, and finally retired to their camp, whence they retreated towards Fort Erie, destroying their baggage and stores. The British followed, and were beaten in a desperate attack to storm the fort. Whilst these small yet sanguinary actions were breaking out sporadically along the Canadian frontier, the Government at home made use of a part of the forces liberated by the peace with France, and resolved on giving the Americans a little diversion from their pursuit of glory and conquest in Canada. A British force under Ross defeated the American army at the Races of Bladensburg, captured Washington, and destroyed public buildings and property of all kinds. A demonstration against Baltimore did not succeed because the fleet could not co-operate, although the British troops routed the American covering army with the utmost ease, and at New Orleans our troops endured a humiliating repulse. The war did not languish in Canada. The British took Prairie du Chien in the west, and seized on all the country between the river Penobscot and New Brunswick. The most important part of the State of Maine thus fell into British possession, and a provisional government was established over it till the end of the war, when Maine was restored to the United States. To compensate for these successes, the British flotilla was beaten by the Americans under McDonough, and Sir George Prevost sustained a discreditable defeat at the hands of a very inferior force under General Macomb, on the 8th of September, at Plattsburgh. The Americans, however, abandoned Fort Erie on the 5th of November, which was the last vestige of their great plans for the conquest of Canada. The Peace of Ghent put an end to a contest in which the United States would have soon found itself opposed to the whole power of Great Britain. The conditions of that Treaty were disastrous for Canada, as they shut her out from any seaport for several months of the year. In fact, Admiral Gambier, Mr. Goulburn, and Mr. Adams, knew nothing at all about their business, and exercised neither diligence, research, nor caution, in examining the stipulations of the treaty. They accepted all the American conditions and statements without inquiry or hesitation. They never bestowed a thought on the effect of such observations as "the high lands lying due north from the source of the river St. Croix, and the head of the Connecticut river not having been ascertained;" " part of the boundary between the two powers not having been surveyed," and the like, which many years after became essential and powerful arguments in the discussion. In the war the Canadians had displayed courage and spirit, and the best American generals and statesmen were very speedily satisfied that they could effect very little in the way of conquest. They were but too glad to make peace. The war had not only damaged their resources, but threatened the very existence of the

Union. The northern delegates at the Hartford Convention had not merely objected to the proceedings of the Federal Government, but had entered upon the discussion of fundamental changes in the constitution. In the Treaty of Ghent no concession was made on any of the points on which the declaration of war was made. In some respects the contest with the United States proved of decided benefit to Canada; the money spent by the army enriched the country, and the incidents of the campaign tended to raise the reputation of the Canadians in England, and elevated the sentiment of self-respect among the people. Roads were made or projected for military purposes. Canals were discussed and planned, and steam began to contend with currents and rapids. The revenue exceeded the expenditure, although nearly 27,000*l*. figured as an item for militia services the first year after the war.

Had it not been for political and civil complications, the progress of Canada would have been still more rapid; but truth to say, progress encountered a considerable obstacle in the character of the people of Lower Canada. Probably not less than 35,000 of the whole population were of French descent, strongly attached to their institutions, and therefore indisposed to change—influenced by traditions of a most conservative character, and by territorial arrangements which perpetuated the very essence of feudalism. Nevertheless, emigration was encouraged, free passages were given to some immigrants, food to others, one hundred acres of land to all. Banks were established; but through all the extent of the upper province in 1817, there were not quite seven persons to the square mile. In some instances injudicious governors exercised their power to counteract the good disposition of the House of Parliament, and occasionally Parliament marred the excellent intentions of the representatives of the Crown. Impeachment of judges, imprisonment of journalists, questions of privilege and the like arose, which interrupted the good feeling so necessary to the progress of colonial life. Constant fears of sedition, privy conspiracy, and rebellion, haunted the minds of governors, whilst the colonists and the habitans struggled for greater freedom of action. Although the Canadians had resisted the Americans with the greatest energy, they were suspected of a desire to coalesce with, or to imitate the institutions of, the enemy. England at this time was agitated by aspirations for reform, and those who led the masses certainly justified the suspicion with which their designs were regarded, by intemperance of language. Among the emigrants who flocked to Canada were men who were tinged deeply with the dye of dangerous democratic doctrine, and notwithstanding the great gulf fixed between the new comers and the French habitans, it was feared that the two parties would unite in founding a government which could not be congenial to one or the other. When Lord Dalhousie came out in 1820, he found however a tolerably prosperous community. The dissensions respecting the civil list which had occurred for several years previously, inaugurated Lord Dalhousie's administration. The Assembly would not grant a permanent civil list, and took the extraordinary step of appointing an agent, who was a member of the British Parliament, to represent them in England. The impolicy of dividing the country into two provinces became more apparent as questions connected with revenue arose, and the discussion of these questions was embittered by deficient harvests and commercial distress. Now it was seen how injuriously the want of a port open all the year affected the interests of Canada, which for five or six months was denied all access to the sea, unless through the United States. The union of the two provinces was agitated, but the French population did not support the project. They believed they would lose by amalgamation; that they would forfeit their privileges, and be deprived of the advantages they enjoyed in the free import of American produce. When it became known that the Government really had a project for the union of the provinces, Mr. Papineau, the Speaker of the Assembly, was dispatched to England with a petition against the proposed amalgamation, and it was deferred for a time. Financial difficulties increased the ill-temper of the governed, and the harshness and resolution of the Government widened the breach between them. Squabbles and ill-blood sprang up with greater vehemence and animosity every day, and the seeds of the evil which came to maturity in 1837, if not then first planted, were certainly invigorated. The energies of the English, Scotch, and Irish emigrants who flocked into the north were not to be repressed by these malign influences. The citizens of the old world pushed their way into Upper Canada, and finding lakes and rivers unfit for navigation, projected and carried out canals, and already grasped the probability of landing cargoes of Canadian wheat in Liverpool, from vessels loaded at Kingston and Montreal.

The Imperial negotiators who renounced all the

claims which they might have preferred in behalf of
Canada on the peace of 1815, would probably have
failed to secure for the province a port on the sea,
although the British, who held so large a portion of the
State of Maine, might have fairly sought some equivalent for it. At all events no strenuous effort was
made to obtain such an advantage—nor was there any
attempt on our part to ascertain what the precise
boundaries were which the Americans claimed. We
will just see how a British negotiator many years
later consented to draw a line which placed the land
communications of the mother country with the provinces in war time at the mercy of an enemy for many
miles of its course—Canadian interests and Imperial
considerations being alike neglected—peace and war
alike hampered, by want of foresight, prudence, or
statesmanlike consideration. The increasing prosperity
of Canada forced her to enter into closer relations
with the United States, and to accede to arrangements
with the Federal Government, which were of course
regulated by Imperial agency, and which were not
always characterised by wisdom. But there was no
alternative—at least not one which could then be
adopted. The idea of a great confederation of the
British Provinces, which would enable Canada to avail
herself of the ports of New Brunswick and Nova
Scotia, if it presented itself at all, was seen to be surrounded by embarrassing obstacles and conflicting
sentiments. The skill in the conception, and the
energy displayed in the execution, of the canal system,
which is the grandest and most extensive in the world,
have made a practicable passage of more than 2000
miles from Anticosti up to Superior City; and works

proposed or in progress by land and water attest the enterprise and resolution with which the Canadians contended against the only impediments in the way of their prosperity and greatness. The claims of Canada to Imperial aid against invasion are strengthened by concessions made by the Imperial agents, which clear away the path of the invaders. Although all the border States had their representatives and champions, the voice of Canada was not heard in the deliberations of the Commission. It was British territory which was in debate—there are some who hold that Canada is alone called upon to defend it. Although the land may be invaded because it belongs to Great Britain, so far that Great Britain is actually attacked by aggression upon it, Canada, involved in war because of its dependency on the British Crown, must bear the brunt of defending that which British diplomacy has rendered peculiarly liable to invasion. It is plain that those who insist on leaving Canada to defend herself, are advocating a policy which tends to separate Canada from the British Crown. The provinces are ruled by a British viceroy, and are under the British flag, which would be the cause of an American attack. Canada can do nothing to provoke hostility, but the English may be struck with effect as long as the provinces are ruled by the Crown, and contain a company of British soldiers.

It would be interesting to inquire whether the Canadians would be better off by themselves than they are at present, supposing always that the new theories are likely to prevail, in case of war. Notwithstanding the violence and exaggerated language of the American press, it is only right to conclude that Canada is far less liable to insult and aggression under British protection than she would be without it. But that remark can only hold good in cases where the Americans do not feel more than usual irritation against Great Britain. The Canadians must feel that if they stood alone, pretexts would not long be wanting to treat the provinces as Texas was served. Canada has at present the power of England at her back, and the threat to deprive her of it by no means implies that she will be left to fight single-handed in the day of need. On the whole, balancing the chances of aggression on account of England against the chances of aggression if she stood alone, it is certain that Canada gains more than she loses by her present connection. The growth of great states along her frontier, and the excessive weakness of a water boundary in face of a maritime power, have caused us at home to insist on the engineering impossibility of defending the whole of the land and lake boundaries, but it by no means follows that the conquest of the country would be equally easy. With the full command of the sea and all its advantages—with commerce free—with a wonderful unanimity in the object of the war—with immense exaltation of spirit, and unparalleled expenditure of money, the Northern Americans have not yet subdued the Southern States, though they have more than tested the quality of their inner armour. Canada, with its narrow belt of inhabited territory, flanked by inland seas and vast rivers, offers no resemblance, it is true, to the South, but aided by Great Britain and her army, her fleet, and her purse, she might defy subjugation if she could not escape invasion. It must be noted that the Americans frequently dwell on ideas for a long time ere they attempt to carry them out, but that generally they do make an effort to give practical effect to those theories which have taken hold of the popular mind. For many years before the annexation of Texas and the war with Mexico took place, the people were prepared for both by the constant inculcation of their necessity. It is only justice to the Government of the United States to declare that their action has been generally restrictive, and that it has acted as a drag on the wheels of the popular chariot. There is in fact a great people standing between the fringe of the noisy democracy and the highlands of Federal authority, which breaks the force of the popular wave, and hears unmovedly the beatings of the turbulent press, and raging voices of the Cleons of the hour. Shame it is indeed to them that they so often permit the worth, and sense, and honour of the nation to be represented by the worthless, foolish, degraded scum that simmers in its noisy ebullitions on the surface of the social system. We cannot be sure how far the Americans are actuated by the feelings which find expression in the most scandalous public paper of New York, but we do know that the paper in question is largely read, and that its favourite topic, when there is a lack of subjects for abuse or menace, is the forthcoming doom of Canada, "when this weary war is over."

In case of an invasion caused by any quarrel with Great Britain, or by any policy for which the Canadians are not responsible, what ought they to expect from us? Everything but impossibilities. Among the greatest of impossibilities would be protection of the whole of the frontier, with all the aid they could give us. The greatest would be the defence of their territories without all the aid they could afford. The Canadians tell us that in the hour of danger they will be ready, but as yet they have fallen short of that degree of preparation which we have a right to expect. If the blow falls at all it will come swift and strong, but if they do their duty to us there can be no fear of our failing them in the time of peril.

The Honourable Joseph Howe has vindicated the claims of the colonies to the care, protection, and assistance of the mother country. He has pointed out the defects in our system, from which the inevitable necessity arises, that the colony shall become detached from the mother country, to become its rival, or probably its enemy at some future stage of its existence. Though California—3000 miles away—is represented at Washington; "though Algeria is represented at Paris;" the provinces of North America have no representation in London.

" Our columns of gold," he exclaims, " and our pyramids of timber, may rise in your Crystal Palaces, but our statesmen in the great council of the empire never. Saxony or Wirtemberg are treated with a deference never accorded to Canada, though they are peopled by foreigners. The war of 1812-15 was neither sought nor provoked by the British Americans. It grew out of the continental wars, with which we certainly had as little to do. Whether a Bourbon or a Bonaparte sat upon the throne of France, was a matter of perfect indifference to us. We were pursuing our lawful avocations —clearing up our country, opening roads into the wilderness, bridging the streams, and organising society as we best could, trading with our neighbours, and wishing them no harm. In the meantime British cruisers were visiting and searching American vessels on the sea. Then shots were fired, and, before we had time to recall our vessels engaged in foreign commerce, or to make the slightest preparation for defence, our coasts were infested by American cruisers and privateers, and our whole frontier was in a blaze.

"You count the cost of war by the army and navy estimates, but who can ever count the cost of that war to us? A war, let it be borne in mind, into which we were precipitated without our knowledge or consent. Let the coasts of England be invaded by powerful armies for three summers in succession; let the whole Channel from Falmouth to the Nore be menaced, let Southampton be taken and burnt, let the Southdowns be swept from the Hampshire hills, and the rich pastures of Devonshire supply fat beeves to the enemy encamped in the western counties, or marching on Manchester and London; let the youth of England be drawn from profitable labour to defend these great centres of industry, the extremities of the island being given up to rapine and to plunder; fancy the women of England living for three years with the sound of artillery occasionally in their ears, and the thoughts of something worse than death ever present to their imaginations; fancy the children of England, with wonder and alarm on their pretty faces, asking for three years when their fathers would come home; fancy, in fact, the wars of the Roses or the civil wars back again, and then you can understand what we suffered from 1812 to 1815. Talk of the cost of war at a distance; let your country be made its theatre, and then you will understand how unfair is your mode of calculation when you charge us with the army estimates, and give us no credit for what we have done and suffered in your wars.

"Though involved in the war of 1812 by no interest or fault of our own; though our population was scattered, and our coasts and frontiers almost defenceless; the moment it came, we prepared for combat without a murmur. I am just old enough to remember that war. The commerce of the Maritime Provinces was not a twentieth part of what it is now, but what we had was almost annihilated. Our mariners, debarred from lawful trade, took to privateering, and made reprisals on the enemy. Our Liverpool 'clippers' fought some gallant actions, and did some service in those days. The war expenditure gave to Halifax an unhealthy excitement, but improvement was stopped in all other parts of the province; and, when peace came, the collapse was fearful even in that city. Ten years elapsed before it recovered from the derangement of industry, and the extravagant habits fostered by the war.

"A few regiments were raised in the Maritime Provinces, their militia was organised, and some drafts from the interior were brought in to defend Halifax, whence the expeditions against the French Islands and the State of Maine were fitted out. Canada alone was invaded in force.

"General Smith describes the conduct of the Canadian militia in the few but weighty words that become a sagacious military chieftain pronouncing a judgment on the facts of history.

"In 1812 the Republicans attacked Canada with two corps, amounting in the whole to 13,300 men. The British troops in the Province were but 4500, of which

3000 were in garrison at Quebec and Montreal. But 1500 could be spared for the defence of Upper Canada. From the capture of Michilimacinac, the first blow of the campaign, down to its close, the Canadian Militia took their share in every military operation. French and English vied with each other in loyalty, steadiness, and discipline.

"Of the force that captured Detroit, defended by 2500 men, but a few hundreds were regular troops. Brock had but 1200 men to oppose 6300 on the Niagara frontier. Half his force were Canadian Militia, yet he confronted the enemy, and, in the gallant action in which he lost his life, left an imperishable record of the steady discipline with which Canadians can defend their country.

"The invading army of yeomen sent to attack Montreal were as stoutly opposed by a single brigade of British troops, aided by the militia. In the only action which took place the Canadians alone were engaged. The enemy was beaten back, and went into winter quarters.

"In 1813, Canada was menaced by three separate corps. The Niagara district was for a time overrun, and York, the capital of the Upper Province, was taken and burnt. The handful of British troops that could be spared from England's European wars, were inadequate to its defence; but in every struggle of the campaign, disastrous or triumphant, the Canadian Militia had their share. The French fought with equal gallantry in the Lower Province. At Chateaugay, Colonel de Salaberry showed what could be done with those poor, undisciplined colonists, who, it is now the fashion to tell us, can only be made good for anything by

withdrawing them from their farms and turning
them into regular soldiers. The American general
had a force of 7000 infantry, 10 field pieces, and 250
cavalry. De Salaberry disputed their passage into the
country he loved, with 1000 bayonets, beat them back,
and has left behind a record of more value in this
argument than a dozen pamphlets or ill-natured
speeches in parliament."

"When the independence of the United States was
established in 1783, they were left with one half of the
continent, and you with the other. You had much
accumulated wealth and an overflowing population.
They were three millions of people, poor, in debt, with
their country ravaged and their commerce disorganised.
By the slightest effort of statesmanship you could have
planted your surplus population in your own provinces,
and, in five years, the stream of emigration would have
been flowing the right way. In twenty years the
British and Republican forces would have been
equalised. But you did nothing, or often worse than
nothing. From 1784 to 1841, we were ruled by little
paternal despotisms established in this country. We
could not change an officer, reduce a salary, or impose
a duty, without the permission of Downing Street.
For all that dreary period of sixty years, the Republicans governed themselves, and you governed us.
They had uniform duties and free trade with each
other. We always had separate tariffs, and have them
to this day. They controlled their foreign relations—
you controlled ours. They had their ministers and
consuls all over the world, to open new markets, and
secure commercial advantages. Your ministers and
consuls knew little of British America, and rarely con-

sulted its interests. Till the advent of Huskisson, our commerce was cramped by all the vices of the old colonial system. The Republicans could open mines in any part of their country. Our mines were locked up, until seven years ago, by a close monopoly held in this country by the creditors of the Duke of York. How few of the hundreds of thousands of Englishmen, who gazed at Nova Scotia's marvellous column of coal in the Exhibition, this summer, but would have blushed had they known that for half a century the Nova Scotians could not dig a ton of their own coal without asking permission of half a dozen English capitalists in the city of London. How few Englishmen now reflect, when riding over the rich and populous states of Illinois, Michigan, Missouri, and Arkansas, that had they not locked up their great west, and turned it into a hunting ground, which it is now, we might have had behind Canada, three or four magnificent provinces, enlivened by the industry of millions of British subjects, toasting the Queen's health on their holidays, and making the vexed question of the defence of our frontiers one of very easy solution.

" When the Trent affair aroused the indignant feeling of the empire last autumn, we were—as we were in 1812—utterly unprepared. The war again was none of our seeking.

" Nova Scotia and New Brunswick had thousands of vessels upon the sea, scattered all over the world. Canada had her thousand miles of frontier unprotected. Had war come, we knew that our money losses would have been fearful, and the scenes upon our sea-coasts and our frontiers, sternly painted as they must occur, without any stretch of the imagination, might well bid the 'boldest hold his breath for a time.' But, did a single man in all those noble provinces falter? No! Every man, ay, every woman accepted the necessity, and prepared for war.

"Again it was a question of honour, and not of interest. In a week we could have arranged, by negociation, for peace with the United States, and have kept out of the quarrel. But who thought of such a thing? Your homesteads were safe; ours in peril. A British—not a colonial ship—had been boarded: but what then? The old flag that had floated over our fathers' heads, and droops over their graves, had been insulted; and our British blood was stirred—without our ever thinking of our pockets. The spirit and unanimity of the provinces, no less than the fine troops and war material shipped from this country, worked like a charm at Washington. President Lincoln, like Governor Fairfield, saw clearly that he was to be confronted not only by the finest soldiers in the world, but by a united and high-spirited population. The effect was sedative; the captives were given up. And the provincials—as is their habit, when there is no danger to confront—returned to their peaceful avocations."

It may be necessary to make some allowance for the tinge of colonial patriotism in this passage, but after all the Hon. J. Howe is a transplanted Englishman. He speaks with the voice of some millions of people, and we must listen to it, or be prepared for a good deal of lukewarmness or "disloyalty." I have avoided any reference to the disputes which broke out into rebellion in 1837, because no useful end would be gained by an account of an unfortunate schism which was produced by want of judgment on the part of the Government at home, and by the extreme fanaticism of a party in the province. But the fanaticism has in no small degree been justified by what has since taken place. When "rebels" are pardoned, it may be a proof that the government which pardons is strong and generous. When "rebels" are not only restored to civic rights, but are invested with office, it is almost a demonstration that the government which permits them to exercise important functions under it, was in error in the contest which drove these men to resistance. The rebellion in Canada had, however, nothing to do with the great question we are now discussing. We are approaching the larger subject, which is opened by the consideration of the arguments which are used by Imperialists and Colonists in their controversy respecting the magnitude and relation of the empire and the colony in war.

It becomes of high practical value to consider what Canada can do, and what Canada has done in the direction of self-defence, should she be threatened with war, either from imperial or colonial causes. It can be no satisfaction to Canada to become a fief of the new Federal *quasi*-republic because Great Britain failed in her duty; and all the references to the patriotism and exertions of valour of Canadians in past times, would reflect all the greater discredit on them now, when they enjoy rights and privileges unknown to their hardy ancestors. Let us first see what her resources and defensive powers are, and then cast a glance at what Canada and the British Provinces in North America have got to defend. The only military force Canada can employ is the militia. Her present proud position should induce the people of Canada to make every effort to preserve the conditions under which they enjoy so much liberty, happiness, and prosperity; but she has in the future a heritage of priceless value, which she holds in trust for the great nation that must yet sit enthroned on the Lakes and the St. Lawrence, and rule from Labrador to Columbia.

CHAPTER XII.

The Militia—American Intentions—Instability of the Volunteer Principle—The Drilling of Militia—The Commission of 1862—The Duke of Newcastle's Views—Militia Schemes—Volunteer Force—Apathy of the French Canadians—The First Summons.

IN a country situated as Canada is, without well-defined obligations as regards the sovereign power, there can be but two kinds of military force available for defence—a militia and an organisation of volunteers. The first is essentially the proper constitutional force on which Canada must mainly rely in case of invasion. The second, notwithstanding its enormous importance and value, is but accidental. Unless Canada assumed towards us the relations of a protected state, like India, and raised an army officered by the British such as was that of Oude, or as that, to a certain extent, of some states at the present day, her volunteers could have no fixed and adequate value in a general scheme of defence. The Canadian militia must constitute the chief strength of Canada in operations on her territory. It would be impossible for Great Britain to do more than provide officers, money, arms, artillery, and ammunition—perhaps the head and backbone of the force which would be needed for a large system of campaigns. The only enemy Canada has to fear is the Northern Republic. I am quite willing to do every justice to the moderation of Mr. Seward, and to the pacific policy of Mr. Lincoln, but it cannot be disputed that the strength of the central Government will be much diminished on the cessation of the present conflict, and that whatever way it ends the Cabinet of Washington will be little able to oppose the passions of the people in the crisis which peace, whether it be one of humiliation or of triumph, will bring with it. Passion, the passion wrought of pride, love of dominion, national feeling, and the like, is far stronger than the silken bond of commerce. There is danger of war with Great Britain as soon as this war in America is over; and the question is, how far Canada will be able to aid herself? Because if she does not contribute largely to her own defence, it seems certain that British statesmen will not strive very strenuously to avert her doom. At the moment I write there is not, in a state of organised efficiency, one regiment of militia in the length, which is great, and the breadth, which is small, of Canada. Party violence has set at nought all warnings and all solicitations. The Canadians appear to rely on the traditions of the past, and on the result of the small campaigns in the war with America, without any appreciation of the vast changes which have taken place since. Northern Americans, reaching their boundaries with pain and many a toilsome march, filtered small corps upon their soil—far inferior in numbers and equipment to those which now represent the quota of the smallest state in the Union. In my letters from America I called attention to the significant fact that the northernmost point of the territory claimed by the Southern Confederacy was within 120 miles of the lake which forms the southern boundary of Canada. It may not be likely that the Confederacy will ever make good its claim to Western Virginia, and fix its standard in undisturbed supremacy at Wheeling, but it is nevertheless true that a strong passionate instinct urges the people of the North to consolidate the states of the West and those of the East by the absorption of Canada, which, with its lakes and its St. Lawrence, would be ample recompense for the loss of the South; and, with the South in the Union, would be the consummation of the dream of empire in which Americans wide-awake pass their busy restless lives. The Americans are well aware of the vast advantage of striking a sudden blow. The whole subject of Canadian invasion lies developed in well-considered papers in the bureau drawers of Washington. At the time of the Trent affair I was assured by an officer high in rank in the government that General Winfield Scott had come back from France solely to give the State the benefit of his counsels and experience in conducting an invasion of Canada; and (I cannot think it doubtful that the Federal Government would, in four or five weeks after a declaration of war with England, be prepared to pour 120,000 or 150,000 men across the British frontier. What has Canada done to meet the danger? In May, 1862, the Honourable John Macdonald proposed that a minimum of 30,000 men or a maximum of 50,000 men should be enrolled and drilled for one month every year for three or for five years, but it was considered that Canada could not spare so large a number of men from the pursuits of trade, and above all of agriculture, during the open season when drill would be practicable. The measure was rejected. Mr. Sandfield Macdonald, after the failure of this proposal, introduced and carried a measure which gave the Government a permissive power to call out the unmarried militiamen for six days' drill in every year, and which provided that militia officers might be attached to the regular regiments serving in Canada for two months every year in order to learn their duties. By the fundamental law of Canada the Government has the power of calling out in time of war, first, all eligible unmarried men between 18 and 45 years of age; secondly, married men between 18 and 45; and finally, those males fit to carry arms between 45 and 60 years of age. Under these laws Canada should have a force of 470,000 men available for service, and of these there are actually on the muster rolls of the militia 197,000 unmarried men between 18 and 31 years of age, whose service would be compulsory in case of need. The Canadian Parliament voted half a million of dollars in each of the years 1863 and 1864 for military purposes, but the greater proportion of these sums was expended on the volunteers and on the staff of the militia. There has been no adequate return for the heavy drain such a sum causes on the Provincial exchequer. The best commentary on the voluntary system in militia drills is to be found in the fact that less than 10,000 men have been in attendance on them.

With the experience we have had of the unstable character of volunteer forces in the field, it is not prudent for Canada to rely on her volunteers so much as she does. They have within their very body the seeds of dissolution. Some corps can decree their disbandment at two months', others at six months' notice —in other words, they may melt away at the very crisis of the war. Does American volunteering teach us nothing? In all human probability the South would have been struck to the earth at the first Battle of Bull Run, if the Pennsylvania volunteers had not presented to the world the extraordinary and disgraceful spectacle of whole battalions under arms marching off from the field, as their unfortunate General McDowell expressed it, "to the sound of the enemy's guns." That was no isolated case. The desertion, at the same time, of other volunteer battalions under the equally unfortunate General Patterson in the Shenandoah Valley, left him unable to prevent the Confederate General Johnston marching with all his men to the aid of Beauregard. Over and over again the Federal leaders have been paralysed by similar defections, and it was not till they became strong enough to hold the volunteers by force, as Meade did before he made his attempt against Richmond, that the evil was cured. Had the Federals gained Bull Run, they were ready to have marched on Richmond at once—they would have found the city defenceless, and the South disorganised. Such a proof of Federal power as a decisive victory would, I believe, from what I saw in the South, have crushed the Secession party, and have strengthened the adherents of the Union, who were then numerous in many of the States. It might not have stopped the civil war, but it would have certainly given the most enormous preponderance to the North. The defeat mainly caused by McDowell's weakness in men, and the reinforcements received by the enemy in consequence of Patterson's inability to hinder their arrival, which was caused by the wholesale disbandment of volunteers, gave such an impetus to the Confederates, that their principle was carried triumphantly over the States, and crushed all opposition. We have seen what that defeat has cost the Federals since. In Canada the volunteers belong almost exclusively to the urban population—only a fifth come from rural districts; and as the towns in Canada are very small, it is plain that the volunteer system would operate very injuriously on the trade of the cities, and would in all likelihood break down, without any imputation on the courage and patriotism of the townsmen. It is, of course, beyond the power of Canada to cope with the people of the United States single-handed, but the agencies which England could bring to bear against the enemy on the American seaboard, and on all the seas furrowed by her ships, would damp the ardour which the Northerners would exhibit at the first onslaught. It would be, no doubt, a very deplorable and a very disgraceful contest, but Great Britain would not be responsible for the beginning of hostilities.

Just in proportion to the celerity and magnitude of their first successes would be the efforts of the Americans to secure their conquest. It is far easier to repel than to expel. A handful of militia, ill-drilled, supported by a similar force of volunteers of similar inefficiency, could offer no resistance to the swarms of invaders, and would but increase the stress to which the little army of Queen's troops in garrison here and there would be subjected at the outbreak of war. To all argument and entreaty, to insinuations and menace, Canada opposes the grand simplicity of her *non possumus*. She is burthened with debt, and even without any expenditure for the militia her outlay is considerably more than her income. A party in Canada called for a regular agreement with the Government at home to regulate the amount to be paid by Canada, and the troops to be furnished by her, as a part of the British Empire. These troops were to consist of militia of the first class, to be drilled by detachments in each succeeding year, till the whole number, whether it were 50,000 or 100,000, should be properly disciplined. It was proposed by some advocates of this scheme that each body of militia should be called out for six months; and that when that period expired the men should be entitled to immunity from further drills till war broke out, when they would become liable for ten years' service, after which they would go into a reserve only to be used in great emergencies.

Many modes of raising, maintaining, and drilling this force have been suggested; but as the principle was not adopted they are scarcely worth discussing. Drills for short periods are certainly of little or no avail; and if money cannot be borrowed to put 100,000 men in a state of readiness, the organisation of 50,000 men to be drilled for three months in each year in bodies of 12,000 or 15,000 does not seem at all unreasonable. The rate of wages in Canada is very high, and the lowest estimate for the support, pay, and clothing of a militiaman for six months comes to about £20 per man. It is, therefore, a simple sum in multiplication to arrive at the ultimate figure of Canadian *possumus* in regard to the paying power of the Provinces. It is not true that if one man can be kept for £20 for six months two men can be kept for the same sum for three months. The levy of 50,000 militiamen for six months would cost Canada, if she were alone, one million sterling. Mr. Cartwright has pointed out that Canada could discipline 100,000 militia, with half a year's instruction each, for as much as would support a standing army of 2,000 men for the same period. We may be very angry with the Canadians for their happy security. It is not so very long ago since the Duke's letters to Sir John Burgoyne startled us out of a similar *insouciance*. We may feel that the sudden development of the United States has placed us in a very doubtful military position. It is not so easy to shake off the obligations incurred by conquest and by emigration under the flag of Great Britain. In the face of very frigid warnings from the press, and very lukewarm enunciations of policy from her best friends, Canada had some reason to fear that there is a secret desire "to let her slide," and that nothing would please England so much as a happy chance which placed the Provinces beyond our care without humiliation or war.

The duty of Canadians to their own country is very plain indeed if the people of England refuse to give them distinct guarantees that under certain conditions they will give them the whole aid of money, men, and ships that is required; but these guarantees are implied in the very fact of suzerainty of the Crown. It must, however, be made known—if it be not plain to every Englishman—that the abandonment of Canada implies a surrender of British Columbia, of New Brunswick, Nova Scotia, Prince Edward's, Newfoundland, if not also the West India Islands. Many bitter words written and spoken here rankle in the breasts of the Canadians, and I have quoted the words in which a Canadian statesman has placed before Englishmen the terrible consequences which Canada may suffer from war, because she is a part of the British empire, engaged in a quarrel on imperial grounds with the Government of the United States. We do undoubtedly owe something to Canada, from the bare fact that for many years she resisted temptation, and remained under our flag unmoved by the blandishments and threats of the United States. In my poor judgment the abandonment of Canada would be the most signal triumph of the principle of democracy, and the most pregnant sign of the decadence of the British empire which could be desired by our enemies. No matter by what sophistry or by what expediency justified, the truth would crop out through the fact itself that we were retiring as the Romans did from Britain, Gaul, and Dacia, but that the retreat would be made in the face of united and civilised enemies, and that the sound of our recall would animate every nation in the world to come forth and despoil us.

As yet there is no reason for such a pusillanimous policy.

The Commission of 1862 laid it down as their opinion that an active force of 50,000, with a reserve of the same number, would be required for Canada; but as the bill founded on their report did not become law, the Canadian Government had no power to borrow arms from the home Government for the whole number, as would have been the case had they passed the bill. Lord Monck, however, procured from the home Government a considerable augmentation of the supplies in store of artillery, small arms, ammunition and accoutrements. But the rejection of the Militia Bill of 1862 filled the home Government with apprehension. The Duke of Newcastle, on the 20th of August of that year, wrote as follows:—

"If I urge upon you the importance of speedily resuming measures for some better military organisation of the inhabitants of Canada than that which now exists, it must not be supposed that Her Majesty's Government is influenced by any particular apprehension of an attack on the Colony at the present moment, but undoubtedly the necessity for preparation which has from time to time been urged by successive Secretaries of State is greatly increased by the presence, for the first time on the American Continent, of a large standing army, and the unsettled condition of the neighbouring States. Moreover, the growing importance of the Colony, and its attachment to free institutions, make it every day more essential that it should possess in itself that without which no free institutions can be secure—adequate means of self-defence. The adequacy of those means is materially influenced by the peculiar position of the country. Its extent of frontier is such that it can be safe only when its population capable of bearing arms is ready and competent to fight. That the population is ready, no one will venture to doubt; that it cannot be competent, is no less certain, until it has received that organisation, and acquired that habit of discipline which constitute the difference between a trained force and an armed mob. The drill required in the regular army, or even in the best volunteer battalion, is not necessary, nor would it be possible, in a country like Canada, for so large a body of men as ought to be prepared for any emergency; but the Government should be able to avail itself of the services of the strong and healthy portion of the male adult population at short notice, if the dangers of invasion by an already organised army are to be provided against.

"We have the opinions of the best military authorities, that no body of troops which England could send would be able to make Canada safe without the efficient aid of the Canadian people. Not only is it impossible to send sufficient troops, but if there were four times the numbers which we are now maintaining in British North America, they could not secure the whole of the frontier. The main dependence of such a country must be upon its own people. The irregular forces which can be formed from the population, know the passes of the woods, are well acquainted with the country, its roads, its rivers, its defiles: and for defensive warfare (for aggression they will never be wanted), would be far more available than regular soldiers.

"It is not therefore the unwillingness, or the inability of Her Majesty's Government to furnish sufficient troops, but the uselessness of such troops without an adequate militia force, that I wish to impress upon you.

"In your despatch of the 17th May last, you informed me that there were then 14,760 volunteers enrolled, besides others who had been more or less drilled. It is far, indeed, from my intention to discredit either the zeal or the efficiency of these volunteers, who have, I hope, greatly increased in number since the date of your despatch; but they constitute a force which cannot suffice for Canada in the event of war. They might form an admirable small contingent; but what would be required, would be a large army.

They might form a force stronger than is necessary in time of peace to secure internal tranquillity, but would be inadequate to repel external attack in time of war. Past experience shows that no reasonable amount of encouragement can raise the number of volunteers to the required extent.

"It appears to me that the smallest number of men partially drilled which it would be essential to provide within a given time, is 50,000. The remainder of the militia would of course be liable to be called upon in an emergency. Perhaps the best course would be, to drill every year one or more companies of each battalion of the sedentary militia. In this manner the training of a large number of men might be effected, and all companies so drilled should, once at least in two years, if not in each year, be exercised in battalion drill, so as to keep up their training.

"I put forward these suggestions for the consideration of the Canadian Government and Parliament, but Her Majesty's Government have no desire to dictate as to details, or to interfere with the internal government of the Colony. Their only object is so to assist and guide its action in the matter of the militia as to make that force efficient at the least possible cost to the Province and to the mother country.

"The Canadian Government will doubtless be fully alive to the important fact that a well organised system of militia will contribute much towards sustaining the high position with reference to pecuniary credit, which, in spite of its large debt, and its deficient revenue for the past few years, the Colony has hitherto held in the money markets of Europe. A country which, however unjustly, is suspected of inability or indisposition to provide for its own defence, does not, in the present circumstances of America, offer a tempting field for investment in public funds or the outlay of private capital. Men question the stable condition of affairs in a land which is not competent to protect itself.

"It may, no doubt, be argued on the other hand, that the increased charge of a militia would diminish rather than enlarge the credit of the Colony. I am convinced that such would not be the case, if steps were taken for securing a basis of taxation sounder in itself than the almost exclusive reliance on Customs duties. It is my belief that a step in this direction would not only supply funds for the militia, but would remove all apprehension which exists as to the resources of the Colony.

"Whatever other steps may be taken for the improved organisation of the militia, it appears to Her Majesty's Government to be of essential importance that its administration, and the supply of funds for its support, should be exempt from the disturbing action of ordinary politics. Unless this be done there can be no confidence that, in the appointment of officers, and in other matters of a purely military character, no other object than the efficiency of the force is kept in view. Were it not that it might fairly be considered too great an interference with the privileges of the representatives of the people, I should be inclined to suggest that the charge for the militia, or a certain fixed portion of it, should be defrayed from the consolidated fund of Canada, or voted for a period of three or five years.

"It has further occurred to me, that the whole of the British Provinces on the continent of North America have, in this matter of defence, common interests and common duties. Is it impossible that, with the free consent of each of these Colonies, one uniform system of militia training and organisation should be introduced into all of them? The numbers of men to be raised and trained in each would have to be fixed, and the expenses of the whole would be defrayed from a common fund, contributed in fair proportion by each of the Colonies. If the Governor-General of Canada were Commander-in-Chief of the whole, the Lieutenant-Governors of the other Colonies would act as Generals of Division under him; but it would be essential that an Adjutant-General of the whole force, approved by Her Majesty's Government, should move to and fro, as occasion might require, so as to give uniformity to the training of the whole, and cohesion to the force itself.

"As such a scheme would affect more than one Colony, it must, of course, emanate from the Secretary of State, but Her Majesty's Government would not entertain it unless they were convinced that it would be acceptable both to the people of Canada and to the other Colonies; and they desire to know, in the first instance, in what light any such plan would be viewed by the members of your Executive Council. I understand that the Lieutenant-Governors of Nova Scotia and New Brunswick, availing themselves of the leave of absence lately accorded to them, intend to meet you in Quebec in the course of the ensuing month. This visit will afford you a good opportunity for consulting them upon this important question.

"The political union of the North American Colonies has often been discussed. The merits of that measure, and the difficulties in the way of its accomplishment, have been well considered; but none of the objections which oppose it seem to impede a union for defence. This matter is one in which all the Colonies have interests common with each other, and identical with the policy of England."

The Government of the day presented a scheme which was rightly characterised by Lord Monck as containing no principle calculated to produce effective results, and to be entirely illusory and nugatory as far as the enrolment of the militia was concerned. Lord Monck enclosed the heads of a plan for the reorganisation and increase of the active militia, based mainly on the voluntary principle, with rules for the erection of armouries, drill-sheds and rifle-ranges, and the appointment of brigade-majors and sergeants, &c., and other means of a perfect organisation. The scheme was to raise an active battalion for each territorial division of the country corresponding with the regimental district of the sedentary militia, to be increased in number as needed, each active battalion to be taken from the subdivision of the district. Mr. Macdonald thought no Government could exist which would venture to recommend the raising of 50,000 partially trained militia, although the cost, spread over five years, would scarcely exceed the annual appropriations. In fact, at the root of all these various schemes and plans lay the evil of uncertainty. Canada did not know how far England would go in her defence, and seemed fearful of granting anything, lest it might be an obligation which the mother country would have otherwise incurred, whilst England, by withholding any definite promise, or indulging only in vague remonstrances, sought to make the Canadians show their hands. Each was anxious for an answer to the question, " How much will you give us?" The Military Commissioners reported that Canada ought to provide 150,000 men, including the reserves, which force, large as it is, would be less than that furnished by states of smaller population in the Northern Union; but Canada is very poor, and not unnaturally makes the most of the argument that she can have no war of her own, and that her defence should be our affair. No one, I apprehend, will allow himself to be beaten to death because there is no policeman by.

In February, 1863, a report of the state of the militia of the Province was prepared by Lieutenant-Colonel de Salaberry and Lieutenant-Colonel Powell, of the Adjutant-General's of Militia Department in Lower and Upper Canada, respectively, from which it appears that there were then 25,000 volunteers organised, of whom 10,230 belonged to Lower, and 14,780 belonged to Upper Canada. Of these there were proportionately 33 for every 1000 in the cities, and $7\frac{1}{3}$ for every 1000 in the counties; those in the upper section contributing less than those in the lower section, and Upper Canada contributing a larger number on the 1000 than Lower Canada. In the enumeration of the various companies—field batteries, troops of horse, companies of artillery, engineers, rifles, infantry, naval and marine companies—it is to be observed that only one naval company appears as having performed twelve days' drill. Some steps should be taken to develop naval and marine companies in the passes along the shores of the lakes. The importance of having trained sailors and gunners stationed just where they are wanted cannot be exaggerated, but it is not very likely that Brigade-Majors will look after such a force. It must be remembered that the national force of Canada consists of two different organisations—the volunteer militia and the regular militia. Canada is divided into twenty-one military districts, eleven in Lower and ten in Upper Canada. In each district there is a Brigade-Major to superintend the drill and instruction of all volunteer companies, furnish monthly reports thereon, and by inspections and active organisation to promote the efficiency of the volunteer service as far as possible. The appointment of these officers has been attended with very good results in this branch of the Militia Staff. In August, 1862, forty-six non-commissioned officers were sent out by Government, and paid by the Canadian Parliament, to drill volunteers; and sixty-eight sergeants were subsequently applied for to meet the increasing demand for instruction. The report of the Deputy Adjutant-Generals of Militia, presented to Lord Monck in 1863, stated—

"Taking population as a basis, these Volunteer Corps are distributed as follows:—

" Population all Canada (census 1861), 2,506,752,—present Volunteer force, 25,010, or say 10 Volunteers for each 1,000 inhabitants.

" Population—Lower Canada.
1,110,664 Volunteers, 10,230,—or say $9\frac{1}{4}$ for each 1,000.

Upper Canada.
1,396,088 Volunteers, 14,780,—or say $10\frac{2}{3}$ for each 1,000.

2,506,752 25,010

" Population all Canada, showing proportion of Volunteers in cities and counties.

Cities,   257,273   Volunteers 8,525,—or say 33 for each 1,000.
Rural, 2,249,479   „   16,485,—or say 7½ for each 1,000.

       2,506,752   25,010

"Population of Cities.
Lower Canada, 153,389   Volunteers, 5,500, or say 36 for each 1,000.
Upper Canada, 103,884   „   3,025, or say 29 for each 1,000.

       257,273   8,525

"Population of Rural Parts.
Lower Canada,   957,275   Volunteers, 4,730, or say 5 for each 1,000.
Upper Canada, 1,292,204   „   11,755, or say 9 for each 1,000.

       2,249,479   16,485

"It will thus be seen that in the cities of Canada, those in the Upper Section of the Province contribute less, in proportion to their population, than do those in the Lower Section; while in the rural parts, Upper Canada contributes a larger number for each 1,000 inhabitants than does Lower Canada.

"The volunteering, thus far, has been the free-will offering of the people, and it is gratifying to observe that in the counties of Upper Canada, with the exception of three, nearly every one has furnished its quota of the 25,000 now organised, while in many instances they are considerably beyond the proportionate number.

"In Lower Canada, until of late, volunteer corps have been chiefly organised in the cities, but within the last six months a considerable number of volunteers have been organised in the rural parts, and now evidences are not wanting that ere long applications will be received at this department for permission to increase this number considerably.

"The present volunteer force comprises field batteries, troops of cavalry, foot companies of artillery, engineer companies, rifle companies, companies of infantry, and naval and marine companies, and is divided properly into three classes, viz.: Class A, and two divisions of Class B.

"Corps in Class A are those who have furnished their own uniforms, and who have been paid $6.00, for each man uniformed, for 12 days' drill performed in 1862.

"First corps in Class B who have furnished their own uniforms, and who have been paid $6.00 in lieu of clothing, after 12 days' drill performed in 1862.

"Second corps in Class B who have been organised upon the understanding that they receive no pay for the 12 days' drill, but that the Government will provide them with uniforms and drill instruction.

"Of the corps in Class A, 6 field batteries, 11 troops of cavalry, 2 companies of foot artillery, and 33 rifle companies have certified to the performance of 12 days' drill in accordance with the General Order of the 4th November last, and have received from the Government $22,672 therefor.

"Of the corps in Class B, 3 troops of cavalry, 8 foot companies of artillery, 2 engineer corps, 49 rifle companies, 15 companies of infantry and one naval company have certified to the performance of 12 days' drill in accordance with the General Order of the 4th November last, and have received from the Government $20,952 therefor."

In the twenty-one districts there were recorded 468 battalions of sedentary militia. Seventy-six drill associations, composed of the officers and non-commissioned officers, had been formed, and were to be supplied with arms and instructors, to which number considerable additions have since been made. The total number of militia men in Lower Canada was estimated at 190,000; in Upper Canada, at 280,000. In the former, 63,000 first-class service men; in the latter, only 33,000 first-class service men. Second-class, 58,000 and 83,000 respectively. Reserve, 20,000 and 25,000 respectively. The cities of Upper Canada gave 29 volunteers for every 1000—the rural districts only 9 volunteers for every 1000. In three counties containing 50,000 people there was no volunteer or volunteer corps. In thirteen counties the average number of volunteers was 250, and in sixteen counties it was only 125.

In Lower Canada, however, the zeal of the people for militia volunteering was by no means remarkable. Thirty counties, with a population of 450,000, had not a single volunteer corps, nor one volunteer. The towns gave 36 volunteers per 1000, the rural districts only 5 per 1000. In fact, the people of French descent appeared to consider militia volunteering a sort of playing at soldiers, which had no particular attractions for them. England had taken them in charge, and might do as she liked with them.

By degrees, a great change occurred in the sentiments if not in the actions of the people. A little more address in dealing with their prejudices; a little more of a conciliatory tone; somewhat greater tact in legislative business, produced beneficial results. The foundation, at all events, was laid of a sound militia bill. The Commissioners who reported in 1862, including Mr. Cartier, Mr. John A. Macdonald, Mr. Galt, and Colonel Lysons, proposed a scheme which was very comprehensive and ably conceived; but it was not considered suitable to the means of the country by the politicians, and the debates which arose on the Militia Bill prepared in accordance with its recommendations, were characterised by an acrimony and party spirit which flavoured the subsequent discussions on the same subject. They recommended complete battalions as the base of the system, for reasons which are in the abstract irrefutable. They then recommended that the Province should be divided into military districts, as the Commander-in-Chief might direct, and that each military district should be divided into regimental divisions. They further recommended as follows:—

"That in order to facilitate the enrolment, relief and reinforcement of an active force, each regimental division be divided into 'sedentary battalion divisions,' and be sub-divided into 'sedentary company divisions.'

"That each regimental division shall furnish one active and one reserve battalion, to be taken as nearly as practicable in equal proportions from the male population of such division, between the ages of 18 and 45.

"That each company of an active battalion, together with its corresponding reserve company, be taken from within the limits of a defined territorial division, the boundary of which shall be identical with that of a sedentary battalion division, or of a distinct portion of such division.

"That in order to accommodate the sedentary battalion divisions to the organisation of the active battalions, the limits of the former be, where necessary, re-arranged.

"We recommend that each of the principal cities of the Province, namely — Quebec, Montreal, Ottawa, Kingston, Toronto, Hamilton, and London, with such portions of the surrounding country as may, from time to time, be added to them by the Commander-in-Chief, shall constitute a military district, to be divided into regimental and sedentary battalion divisions, as hereinbefore detailed; that they be allowed to furnish volunteer militia of the three arms in the proportions hereinafter detailed in lieu of active battalions of regular militia. In the event of these cities failing to furnish their full complement of volunteers, they shall in part, or altogether, fall under the general regulations of the regular militia, in such manner as the Commander-in-Chief shall direct."

The recommendations of the Commissioners were to some extent acted upon; and since the foregoing pages were written the first-fruits of the volunteer organisation have been witnessed, in the actual appearance on service of a number of companies, which have been dispatched to guard the frontiers of Canada from being made the base of offensive operations against the Northern States by Confederate partisans sheltered for the time under the British banner. These are but the advance guard of the 80,000 men who have been ordered to hold themselves in readiness for active service.

The summons of the Governor-General has been heard and obeyed in the best spirit. The people of Canada have answered to the call with an honourable alacrity, and have displayed a temper which gives the fairest guarantee of their services; but they have not indulged in threats or offensive language, and the most irritable of Federal Republicans must admit that the cause which has called them from their homes is entitled to consideration and respect.

CHAPTER XIII.

Possible Dangers—The Future Danger—Open to Attack—Canals and Railways—Probable Lines of Invasion—Lines of Attack and Defence—London—Toronto—Defences of Kingston—Defences of Quebec.

THE return of able-bodied males fit for military service in Montcalm's time, exceeded the whole number of volunteers now actually enrolled; but the present force is possessed of seven field batteries, of several squadrons of cavalry, and of 15,000 men armed with rifled muskets. There must be at this moment in Canada at least 50,000 rifles of the best kind. There were four 18-pound batteries, two 20-pound Armstrong batteries, a large number of howitzers, and an immense accumulation of stores last year, which have received constant accessions ever since, as the threats of the New York press have produced to us in increased expense some of the evil results of war. There are also in the stores great quantities of old-fashioned brass and iron field and siege guns, of shot and shell, of mortars, and of ammunition.

The Americans can find no fault with us for taking steps, in view of contingencies which they have threatened, to obviate, as far as possible, the disadvantages to which distance from the mother country exposes the Provinces. It was enough that before the days of steam, which has greatly increased the disparity between us, Great Britain submitted to conditions in regard to the Lakes which could only be justified by the supposition that Canada was the western shore of Great Britain. By the articles of the Treaty of 1817, the United States of America and Great Britain are limited to one vessel with one 18-pounder and a crew of one hundred men each on Lake Ontario, Lake Champlain, and the upper lakes. No other vessels of war are to be built or armed, and six months' notice is required to terminate the treaty obligations.

It will have been observed that the Americans of the Northern States are spoken of as the only enemies whom Canada has to fear. They are the only people who threaten from time to time the conquest and annexation of the Provinces, and who have declared by the mouths of their statesmen, that they intend to insist, when they are strong enough, on the fulfilment of the doctrine that the whole continent is theirs; for the natural basis of the Monroe dogma is, the right of the Americans to lay down the doctrine at all, and if they can say to the nations of Europe, "You shall make no further settlements on this soil," they can say, when it pleases them, with just as much right, "You who are now occupying this soil must either leave it or own allegiance to the Union." The Union is now, what it never was before, a sovereignty, and Americans in its name fancy that they can do what they please. The Canadians are by no means well-disposed towards their neighbours' institutions, manners, and customs, and do not desire to be incorporated with them. The annexation must, therefore, be effected by force, sufficiently great to overpower the resistance of the inhabitants, whether singly, or supported by the British army and navy.

It fortunately happens that the freedom of speech and writing prevalent in the United States are safety-valves for the popular steam, and that words are not always indicative of immediate or even of remote action. It would be difficult to estimate the nature of the influences which shall prevail when the American civil war is over. If the North succeeds in overcoming the South, no great danger of war with Great Britain or of invasion of Canada will exist. It will need every man of the Federal army to occupy the Southern States. If, on the other hand, the North should be obliged to abandon her project of forcing the carcase of the South back into the Union by the sword, she will suddenly find herself with a large army on her hands, with a ruined exchequer, and an immense fund of mortified ambition and angry passion to discount.

It is possible that the sober and just-minded men who form a large part of American society may be able to avert a conflict, if the American soldiery and statesmen entertain the views attributed to them; but that is just the point on which no information exists. It is not easy to ascertain the actual weight of the classes who would naturally oppose the press and the populace in a crusade against Great Britain. My own experience, limited and imperfect as it is, leads me to think that there is in the States a very great number, if not an actual majority, of people whose views are not much influenced by violent journals or intemperate politicians, who rarely take part in public affairs, but exercise, nevertheless, their influence on those who do. There is not a community in the Northern States which does not contain a large proportion of educated, intelligent, and upright men, who shrink from participation in party struggles and intrigue; and I regret that they are not more largely known. Their existence is marked by no outward sign which foreign nations can recognise. It is on them, however, that the safety and reputation of the Federal Government depends; it will be on them that their country's reliance must be placed when the legions return home.

If the war were over in 1865 there would probably be 600,000 men under arms, and there would be at least 200,000 more men in the States who had served, and would take up arms against England with alacrity. A considerable proportion of that army would indeed seek their discharge, and go quietly back to their avocations; but the Irish, Germans, &c., to whom the license of war was agreeable, would not be unwilling to invade Canada, and a per centage of Americans would doubtless eagerly seek for an opportunity of gaining against a foreign enemy the laurels they had not found whilst contending with their fellow countrymen. Commerce indeed would suffer—the Americans would find for the first time what it was to enter upon a quarrel single-handed with the British nation. They have hitherto met only the side blows and stray shots of the old mother country—and they believe they have encountered the full weight of her arm, and the utmost extent of her energies. The wicked men who are striving to engage the two States in a quarrel which would cover the seas of the world with blood and wreck, cannot be deterred from their horrible work by any appeals to fear or conscience; but the influence of the past, and of the Christian and civilised people of the ex-United States will, it is to be hoped, defeat their efforts, seconded though they may be by the prejudice, religious animosity, and national dislike of a portion of the people. If the war party prevail they will have no want of pretexts—the San Juan question alone would suffice them if they had not a whole series of imaginary wrongs to resent arising from the incidents of the present war, and a multitude of claims to prefer to which England can never listen.

At some day, near or remote, Canada must become either independent in whole or in part, or a portion of a foreign state. It will be of no small moment for those then living in Great Britain whether they have alienated the affections or have won the hearts of the newly-created power. Those who doubt this may consider how a Gaul now rules over the ruler of Rome, and how all that remains of an evidence of the occupancy of this Island by the masters of the world for four hundred years, are tumuli, ruined walls, stratified roads, and bits of tile and pottery. The climate of Canada is not more severe than that of Russia—her natural advantages are much greater—her inland seas are never frozen—her communications with Europe are easy—she offers a route to all the world from the Atlantic to the Pacific. The United States will be no longer a country for the poor man to live in; the load of taxation will force emigration to Canada, and the States lying on the left banks of the lakes and of the St. Lawrence will be enriched by the demands of America for her produce, in proportion as the waste lands are occupied, and the Union is filled with a tax-paying swarming population. It is astonishing how soon a man liberates himself from the traditions and allegiance of his native country in the land of his adoption, when his interests and his pride are touched. The attitude of our immediate colonies in face of the transportation question will at once satisfy us that the mother country has little to expect from old associations, whenever her interests are made to appear antagonistic to those of her colonies. Canada has the most liberal institutions in the world—her municipal freedom is without parallel—education is widely disseminated—religious toleration restrains the violence of factions. The cold is by no means as great as that which is borne by the inhabitants of the greater part of northern Europe, and is far less dangerous to health than the more temperate climates of lower latitudes, where rain and tempest are substituted for snow and hard frosts.

The frontier of Canada is assailable at all points. In some places it is constituted by a line only visible on a map, in others it is a navigable inland sea, in others a line drawn in water, in others the bank of a river or the shore of a lake. Coincident with it runs the frontier of the United States.

The best guarantee against invasion would be, complete naval supremacy on the lakes and rivers, because they constitute the most accessible roads for the invaders, and the most serviceable barriers for defenders if they have the proper means of defence. To give any chance of successful resistance, some equality of naval force on the part of the invaded is almost indispensable. The question arises, who shall provide this naval force? Canada cannot. She is prevented by Imperial treaties, by want of means, and even if she had them, she is forbidden to use the means, by the principle which forbids a dependency equipping ships of war in times of peace. Great Britain has no doubt a powerful fleet, but the far inferior navy of the United States, close at hand, contains more vessels suitable for warlike operations in inland waters and canals than we possess, 4000 miles away. In fact we ought to have a very great preponderance of small vessels to give us a fair start, and even then it would be difficult to begin hostilities on equal terms. Lake Michigan, with the enormous resources of Chicago, is entirely American, and the possession of such a base is an advantage which is by no means counterbalanced by our position on Lake Huron. To prevent the enemy clearing all before them on the lakes, by an energetic naval sortie from their ports, it would be necessary to have the means of furnishing a flotilla as soon as hostilities became imminent, and to watch every point, particularly such as that of Sorel, where communication from Richelieu to the St. Lawrence might be interrupted. But it is thought we cannot hope to cope with the Americans on equal terms in all the lakes, and that we must be content with concentrating our strength on Lake Ontario and in the St. Lawrence. All our waterways are very much exposed. Whilst Great Britain retains her supremacy, the St. Lawrence is open during the summer, and can be kept free by iron-plated vessels as far up as Montreal. The day of wooden gunboats has passed, and it becomes requisite for the Government to take immediate steps to secure an adequate supply of armoured vessels on the spot as soon as hostilities become probable. It is gratifying to know that the Canadian Legislature is about to fortify the harbour and arsenal at Kingston, so as to cover the infant naval force. Under any circumstances, it is not possible to defend a canal by guarding the locks, or by placing forts at particular places, and yet the canals are of vital importance to us. The Beauharnais Canal runs on the right bank of the St. Lawrence, and is peculiarly unfortunate in its military position. The Welland Canal is of consequence, but it would be better to destroy it than permit an enemy to hold it. The Rideau Canal, which runs from Lake Huron to Kingston, is a very valuable communication, but it needs to be deepened and enlarged at the Rapids. All the canals require to be enlarged and improved, but they are far better placed, bad as their state and position are, than the roads and railways. The Grand Trunk Railway is open to attack for many miles at different parts of its course, and in some places trains could be fired upon from American territory! Our reinforcements last winter were sent through New Brunswick and Nova Scotia, in sleighs, along a route which for miles could be cut across at any time by the enemy from Maine, and it would be necessary, to make all safe, for us to follow the Metapodliac road, or to construct the intercolonial railway.

The harbours of Halifax and of St. John's are not closed in winter, and the mode which was adopted of sending troops into Canada by those points would no doubt be reverted to till some better means shall be provided. From St. Andrew's, in New Brunswick, there is a railroad to Woodstock, which lies near the state boundary of Maine. Here the route from St. John's meets the St. Andrew road, and united the line follows the course of the St. John River, and may be divided into four days' marches—to Florenceville, 1; to Tobique, 2; to Grand Falls, 3; to Little Falls, 4. All this route lies close to the American frontier, and is therefore quite unfit for the march of troops in detachments. The St. John's route also takes four days to Woodstock. Even with the advantages afforded by the line of railroad, it must be remembered that the snows of winter may often mar all combinations;—our first detachments suffered considerably from cold in the railway carriages, and it may be readily conceived that the course of an army in sleighs to Rivière du Loup on the St. Lawrence, where the Grand Trunk Railway begins or terminates, might be rendered very unsafe by no more formidable agencies than violent snow storms alone.

Our military authorities do not, it is said, fear a winter campaign, but the Americans have already shown that they are not to be deterred by frost and snow from moving troops into Canada. To ensure moderate security the Metis road, notwithstanding its greater length, should be improved and adapted for military purposes, and the railway should be constructed to complete the work. In considering the three modes of invasion of which I shall speak, it may be inferred that Montreal will be the most likely point of attack, and that Quebec will be comparatively safe at first, but it would not be wise to act on the hypothesis as if it were an absolute certainty.

In the State of New York, at its capital of Albany,

the Americans possess an admirable base of operations against us. Except in winter, the Hudson is an open highway between Albany and New York, and the sea and railways connect it with the shores of the lakes and with the vast centres of American resource and industry. Albany is specially capable of serving as a base against the very places most likely to be assailed, Montreal and Quebec. There is no necessity for any argument to show that the loss of these places would be equivalent to the overthrow of the British in Canada. From the Hudson there is a canal to Lake Champlain, on the upper extremity of which, and almost on the railroad connecting Montreal with New York, is situated a casemated work popularly known as Rouse's Point, about two days' march from the commercial capital of Canada. Rouse's Point would serve as an immediate base for the collection of supplies and the concentration of an army, whilst Albany would become the great dépôt for the war. It is probable that the Americans would try to strike several blows at once. They might direct one expeditionary force from Rouse's Point against Montreal, and others from Albany and Rouse's Point against Quebec. They might also menace, or actually attack, the frontier at Detroit or at Niagara. As a war with Great Britain would be popular, and no lack of men would be found, it would also be practicable for them to direct from either of those points an expedition to attack Ottawa, or the towns west of the river Ottawa.

Kingston would also be a point of attack, as much from its importance to us as from its value to the enemy, who would, by the possession of it, command the Rideau Canal, which connects the river Ottawa with Lake Ontario. It is plain that if the points liable to attack were left in their present state, there would be little hope of our ability to defend them by fighting in the open field. United, the Americans are to the Canadians as about eight to one. The State of New York alone is as populous, and is richer, than the Canadas. Great Britain, thousands of miles away, could not hope, by any expenditure of money, or by any display of military skill, to equalise the conditions of the assailants and the defenders of her sovereignty. The engineers are right, therefore, in the argument, that the only way of enabling the Canadians and their British allies to make way against the Republicans, is to establish fortified works supported by or supporting a naval force. The Americans have an idea that it is possible to carry on operations during winter. Our engineers start with the assumption that it is impossible to do so on any large scale, and that it is out of the question for some five months of the year in Canada. The obstructions to siege operations might not be so serious, but they would be so considerable as to render the undertaking of them exceedingly hazardous, and little likely to succeed. The question, then, presents itself whether Canada can be defended for the time in each year during which operations are practicable, and if so, in what manner the defence is to be conducted. Our military authorities are of opinion that Canada can be defended. The Americans, as far as I could judge from their remarks on the subject, and from conversations with several of their officers, conceive that Canada lies at their mercy whenever they choose to attack it. As a chain of great frontier fortresses could not be established or maintained, the means suggested for the purposes of defence are principally of a provisional

LINES OF ATTACK AND DEFENCE. 233

character. To meet the flood of invasion, it is proposed to cover the approaches to the vulnerable points. Ottawa, Montreal, and Quebec would be defended by forces posted in earthworks, and covered by entrenched camps at Prescott and Richmond, and other suitable places.

If we examine the modes of proceeding to which the enemy would probably resort, we shall find them classified under five heads. First, a naval descent on Goderich. Second, the descent of a force between Detroit and London. Thirdly, the descent of a force on Niagara. Fourthly, the passage of a force between the St. Lawrence and Ogdensburg. Fifthly, an attack by several columns converging in concert on a point between Derby and Huntingdon, with a view of concentrating on Montreal, and cutting the communications with Kingston as well as with Quebec. Let us take a glance at the present state of the principal points, and consider what is needed to improve their condition.

If we look at the map of Upper Canada, the position of Paris at once attracts the eye as a favourable site for the main body of the defensive force; whilst Stratford and London, being points of railway junction, would naturally be held as long as possible. Guelph would serve as a point of concentration for troops obliged to fall back from London or from Stratford, according to the direction from which the enemy came. Toronto would become the natural point of concentration for troops obliged to retire from Guelph, and under the conditions necessitating such a retreat the force defending the Niagara frontier would be obliged to fall back upon Hamilton to the entrenched position covering that town. If the Americans attack the western settlements near Georgian Bay, it seems impossible to oppose them with assured advantage. A calm consideration of the subject has led the best authorities to the conclusion that we cannot hope at present to establish a naval force on either Lake Huron or Lake Erie. The Welland Canal is, in its present state, unsuited to the purposes of modern naval warfare, and a canal is at all times, and under the most favourable circumstances, very little to be depended upon. With the aid of fortified harbours there is, however, no reason to fear for our naval supremacy on Lake Ontario, and it is to that object our best efforts should be directed. It would of course be impolitic to leave Toronto and Hamilton open to naval demonstrations, but the principal efforts of the authorities should be directed to establish permanent works to protect Ottawa, Montreal, Kingston, and Quebec, and to prepare positions for entrenched camps and earthworks on the points most likely to be assailed.

It is plain that a navy alone can prevent descents on the land line of such extensive waters, and that the possession of Rouse's Point enables the Americans to turn the line of the Richelieu and threaten Montreal. Let us run rapidly over the positions, beginning with the west. If works were thrown up at Goderich and Sydenham on points there which are suitable for defensive positions, it might be possible to check any adventurous force intent on speedy victory and conquest; but no fortifications could be maintained on those remote points for permanent occupation, as the enemy could operate on the flanks and rear and turn them from Huron or Georgian Bay.

A permanent work on Point Edward Sarnia, to command the St. Clair River, has been suggested, and it has been recommended that the defences of Fort Maldon and Bar Island should be made permanent works, but other engineers have considered it unwise to erect fortifications at Sarnia or Amherstburg, and contend that the Niagara and Detroit frontiers are too much exposed to be tenable by any works. Guelph should also be rendered worthy of its important position. London, being a railway station, is, in event of a war, an important point to hold for the carriage of troops; and although there is no ground close at hand admitting of tenacious grip, there is a tolerably good line of defence at Konoska, which the spade could convert into a fair position.

When we come to consider the condition of the Toronto district it becomes apparent that two points require especial attention—Fort Dalhousie and Port Colborne. It is unwise to leave these places without defences to cover the garrisons, and to enable them to protect the shore against desultory operations and isolated detachments. Domville and Maitland are open to predatory attacks which might be prevented by ordinary fortifications or earthworks on eligible sites. It is impossible to defend a canal; but much good might be done by enlisting the employés on the Welland as a sort of guard, whose local knowledge would be available in time of danger. Although, as I have said, strong reasons are urged against any outlay for the defence of the Niagara frontier, on the ground of its exposure, there are distinguished authorities who insist that a permanent work is required at Fort Erie; and who contend that another fort should be erected at

Niagara, in support of an entrenched camp, which would exercise a most powerful influence over the movements of an invading force, particularly if there were gunboats placed on the Chippewa. One of the painful necessities of war between the United States and Great Britain would be the destruction of the suspension bridges over the river. Hamilton is generally considered as incapable of defence, but it lies in a district which presents two lines of hills capable of being adapted to defensive purposes, and earthworks there might be stiffly held, in case of attack, by the troops of the district, to enable the forces to concentrate and retire along routes previously determined. Toronto itself may be regarded as an open place equally incapable of defence by ordinary works; but it should not be left open to such a *coup* by a single cruiser, as might be obviated by the erection of a fort on the site of the new barracks: and it would be necessary to construct a strong entrenched camp to cover it and protect the troops retiring before the enemy. A chain of earthworks might be placed on the elevated ridges which run from the Don River towards Humber Bay. A casemated fort on the island is also most desirable. Toronto has something more than its mere strategical importance to recommend it. It has special claims to consideration as an important centre of civilised life, commerce, enterprise, and learning.

The defences of Kingston are more worthy of its ancient importance. In fact, the only works in Canada suited to modern warfare are those at Kingston and Quebec. The latter are capable of much improvement, as has been already pointed out. Both need to be strengthened, and to be extended. If the

Americans have beaten us by treaty, why should we not at all events have iron-plated vessels sent up the St. Lawrence as far as treaty will allow them to go, and prepare naval establishments and encourage naval volunteers for times of danger at Kingston? Fort Henry, Fort Frederick, an earthen work, and the Market Battery, are in good condition, but much must be done before the place can be regarded as being in a satisfactory state. The Shoal Tower, the Cedar Island Tower, and the Murney Tower, constructed of stone, are placed on points covering the water approaches to Kingston. But all the guns in these works, with one exception, are *en barbette*, and to render Kingston safe it would be necessary to erect strong works to resist the advance of an enemy landing either above or below the town. It is estimated that £390,000 would be sufficient for the purpose of erecting the permanent forts absolutely indispensable for the safety of the harbour and dockyard establishment. The position of these works should be chosen with a due regard to all possible conditions of attack. Wolfe Island, Abraham's Head, Snake Island, Simcoe Island, and Garden Island, should be provided with adequate forts to support the new scheme of defence. The Navy Yard should be removed, and the points now open to attack at once fortified. Belleville and Prescott both afford admirable ground for works of great importance: the former possesses a most advantageous site for temporary works and for a line of defence; and the latter has such a commanding situation that a permanent work, with casemates, should be constructed there to guard what is, according to some of our engineers, one of the most valuable positions in the province.

When we come to consider the actual state of Montreal, its importance, its liability to attack and the difficulty of offering an adequate defence, the best means to adopt are not very obvious. The best method of defence would doubtless be to construct an entrenched position, consisting of a parapet strengthened by redoubts, to cover the approach from the south side. A *tête de pont* should be built to cover the approaches now so open and exposed to attack.

The enlargement of the Ottawa and Rideau canals is of obvious importance, and outlying works might be traced which could be used in case of invasion to hold the enemy in check; but still, as a precautionary measure, it would be desirable to remove the more important stores at Montreal to Quebec and Ottawa, if it is in contemplation to make this valuable position subsidiary to any other place in Canada.

Permanent works might be erected at St. John's, the Isle aux Noix and St. Helen's Island, where forts should be reconstructed on improved principles. But the most obvious measure, in the opinion of some engineers, the fortification of the hill over the city, and the erection of a Citadel upon it, which would render the mere occupation of the town below valueless to an enemy, is not approved of by more recent authorities.

Gunboats on Lake St. Louis would prove most valuable in defending the works at Vaudrueuil.

Quebec is however the key of Canada; and that key can be wrested from our own grasp at any moment by a determined enemy, unless the recommendations so strongly urged from time to time by all military authorities meet with consideration. The old enceinte should be removed, and the French works restored, according to the suggestions of scientific officers, and of the ablest engineers we possess. An entrenched camp might be marked out to the west of the Citadel, with a line of parapet and redoubts extending from the St. Lawrence to the St. Charles river. In order to cover the city from an attack on the south side, it would be necessary to occupy Point Levi, and to construct a strong entrenched line, with redoubts at such a distance as would prevent the enemy from coming near the river to shell the city and citadel. But it is evident that they are *nil ad rem*, unless behind these works, and in support of them in the open, can be assembled a force of sufficient strength to prevent an investment, or to attack the investing armies, and at the same time to hold front against them in the field. It is estimated that 150,000 men might hold the whole of the Canadas, East and West, against twice that number of the enemy. If we are to judge by what has passed, it is not probable the United States will be inclined or able for such an effort. Quebec might be held with 10,000 men against all comers. From 25,000 to 30,000 men would make Montreal safe. Kingston would require 20,000 men, and Ottawa would need 5000. The greater part, if not all of them, might be composed of militia, and volunteers trained to gunnery and the use of small arms. For the protection of the open country, and to meet the enemy in the field, an army of from 25,000 to 35,000 men would be needed from Lake Ontario to Quebec. The western district on Lake Erie could not be protected by less than 60,000 men.

Thus, in case of a great invasion from the United

States, Canada, with any assistance Great Britain could afford her, must have 150,000 men ready for action. What prospect there is of this, may best be learned from a consideration, not so much of the resources of Canada, as of the willingness of the people to use them.

CHAPTER XIV.

Rapid Increase of Population—Mineral Wealth—Cereals—Imports and Exports—Climate—Agriculture—A Settler's Life—Reciprocity Treaty—Report of the Committee of the Executive Council—Mr. Galt—Senator Douglas—A Zollverein—Terms of the Convention—Free Trade, and what is meant by it—Mr. Galt's opinion on the subject—Canadian Imports and Exports.

THE rapid increase of population and settlements in Canada, and the growth of cities and towns, are among the great marvels of the last and of the present century, so rich in wonders of the kind. It is not too much to say, that any approximation to a similar rate of increase will make British North America a great power in the world. The direction of emigration has not been favourable. The Germans and the Irish have rather sought the United States. The emigrating powers of Scotland are rapidly decreasing, and the few English who emigrate prefer Australia, New Zealand, even the States of the Union, to a country which suffers from the early neglect of the home government, the studied aspersions and misrepresentations of powerful agencies, and the ignorance of the poorer classes who seek to improve their condition by going forth in search of new homes.

Mr. Sheridan Hogan, the writer of a prize essay on

Canada of no ordinary excellence, has devoted some of his pages to show that the growth of Canada in population has been overlooked in the scope of the wondering gaze which Europe has fixed on the development of the United States, although, in fact, the increase of Canadians in the land has been quite as astonishing as that of Americans south of the St. Lawrence. In 1800, he says the population of the United States was 5,305,925. In 1850 it was 20,250,000. The increase was therefore 300 per cent. nearly. In 1811 the population of Upper Canada was 77,000, and in 1851 it was 952,000, an increase of over 1100 per cent. in forty years. Within the decade up to 1855 the rate of increase in the United States was 13·20 per cent. In Upper Canada it was 104 per cent. from 1841 to 1851. Upper Canada exhibited in forty years nearly four times the increase of the United States in fifty years. Even the population of Lower Canada increased 90 per cent. from 1829 to 1854. In a table in the same work it appears that the Irish in Lower Canada were more than double the English and Scotch together, and that they equalled both in Upper Canada. The writer says:—

"The 'World's Progress,' published by Putnam, of New York,—a reliable authority,—gives the population and increase of the principal cities in the United States. Boston, between 1840 and 1850, increased forty-five per cent. Toronto, within the same period, increased *ninety-five* per cent. New York, the great emporium of the United States, and regarded as the most prosperous city in the world, increased, in the same time, sixty-six per cent., about thirty less than Toronto.

"The cities of St. Louis and Cincinnati, which have also experienced extraordinary prosperity, do not compare with Canada any better. In the thirty years preceding 1850, the population of St. Louis increased fifteen times. In the thirty-three years preceding the same year, Toronto increased *eighteen times*. And Cincinnati increased, in the same period given to St. Louis, but twelve times.

"Hamilton, a beautiful Canadian city at the head of Lake Ontario, and founded much more recently than Toronto, has also had almost unexampled prosperity. In 1836 its population was but 2,846, in 1854 it was upwards of 20,000.

"London, still farther west in Upper Canada, and a yet more recently-founded city than Hamilton, being surveyed as a wilderness little more than twenty-five years ago, has now upwards of ten thousand inhabitants.

"The City of Ottawa, recently called after the magnificent river of that name, and upon which it is situated, has now above 10,000 inhabitants, although in 1830 it had but 140 houses, including mere sheds and shanties; and the property upon which it is built was purchased, not many years before, for *eighty pounds*.

"The Town of Bradford, situated between Hamilton and London, and whose site was an absolute wilderness twenty-five years ago, has now a population of 6,000, and has increased, in ten years, upwards of *three hundred per cent.;* and this without any other stimulant or cause save the business arising from the settlement of a fine country adjacent to it.

"The Towns of Belleville, Cobourg, Woodstock, Goderich, St. Catherine's, Paris, Stratford, Port Hope, and Dundas, in Upper Canada, show similar prosperity, some of them having increased in a ratio even greater than that of Toronto, and all of them but so many evidences of the improvement of the country, and the growth of business and population around them.

"That some of the smaller towns in the United States have enjoyed equal prosperity I can readily believe, from the circumstance of a large population suddenly filling up the country contiguous to them. Buffalo and Chicago, too, as cities, are magnificent and unparalleled examples of the business, the energy, and the progress, of the United States. But that Toronto should have quietly and unostentatiously increased in population in a greater ratio than New York, St. Louis, and Cincinnati, and that the other cities and towns of Upper Canada should have kept pace with the Capital, is a fact creditable alike to the steady industry and the noiseless enterprise of the Canadian people.

"Although Lower Canada, from the circumstance already alluded to of the tide of emigration flowing westward, has not advanced so rapidly as her sister Province, yet some of her counties and cities have recently made great progress. In the seven years preceding 1851, the fine County of Megantic, on the south side of the St. Lawrence, and through which the Quebec and Richmond Railroad passes, increased a hundred and sixteen per cent.; the County of Ottawa, eighty-five; the County of Drummond, seventy-eight; and the County of Sherbrooke, fifty. The City of Montreal, probably the most substantially-built city in America, and certainly one of the most beautiful, has trebled her population in thirty-four years. The ancient City of Quebec has more than doubled her population in the same time, and Sorel, at the mouth of the Richelieu, has increased upwards of four times; showing that Lower Canada, with all the disadvantages of a feudal tenure, and of being generally looked upon as less desirable for settlement than the West, has quietly but justly put in her claim to a portion of the honour awarded to America for her progress."

Save and except coal, the want of which is to a considerable extent compensated by the vast stores of forest, of bog and of mineral oils in the Provinces, Canada is very rich in many minerals of the first importance. Iron is deposited in exceeding abundance in the Laurentian System—lead, plumbago, phosphate of lime, sulphate of barytes, and marbles are found in the same wide-spread formation of gneiss and limestone.

The Huron System of slate, &c., contains copper, silver, and nickel, jaspers and agates. The Quebec group in the East promises to be equally valuable. The bases of metallic and ochreous pigments, every description of marble and slate, minerals, and substances useful in chemistry, in arts, in agriculture, in architecture, are scattered throughout the land, from Lake Superior to Gaspé. Notwithstanding the long winter, Upper Canada yielded, according to late averages, 21 bushels of winter wheat and $18\frac{1}{2}$ bushels of spring wheat to the acre; Lower Canada, where agriculture has not received the same development, yields a smaller proportion to the acre, but the wheat is of excellent quality. In Upper Canada the yield of oats is about 30 bushels to the acre; in Lower Canada it is 23 bushels. Barley is a little less in Upper, and about the same as oats in Lower Canada, and Indian corn is about as much as oats. The potato yields from 125 to 176 bushels per acre. All these crops, as well as those of roots of every description, are increasing rapidly, and it is calculated that the value of the farms of Upper Canada is no less than 60,000,000*l.* sterling, whilst the live stock in the same Province was estimated to be worth nearly 9,000,000*l.* In 1860 the value of the timber exported was, 1,750,000*l.*, and the forest yielded altogether just 2,000,000*l.* sterling. As there is reason to know that in 1851 the value of agricultural exports was 6,000,000*l.*, it may be assumed with some degree of certainty as a near approximation that Canada sends abroad about ten millions' worth of forest and farm produce. It is estimated that the imports of the same year were worth eighteen millions sterling.

There are many other illustrations of the rapidity of Canadian increase, but the foregoing must suffice for the purposes of this volume. It is only surprising that the Provinces should have advanced at all, considering the misrepresentations which have been circulated concerning their climate, condition, and prospects, and the attractions held forth to emigrants by the United States.

The popular idea as to the barrenness and cold of Canada would be most effectually dispelled by a glance at garden products and cereals in autumn only, or by the experience of a winter in New York and a winter in London or Hamilton. The author of a pamphlet, published by authority of the Bureau of Agriculture, observes:—

"The most erroneous opinions have prevailed abroad respecting the climate of Canada. The so-called rigour of Canadian winters is often advanced as a serious objection to the country by many who have not the courage to encounter them, who prefer sleet and fog to brilliant skies and bracing cold, and who have yet to learn the value and extent of the blessings conferred upon Canada by her world-renowned 'snows.'

"It will scarcely be believed by many who shudder at the idea of the thermometer falling to zero, that the gradual annual diminution in the fall of snow, in certain localities, is a subject of lamentation to the farmers in Western Canada. Their desire is for the old-fashioned winters, with sleighing for four months, and spring bursting upon them with marvellous beauty at the beginning of April. A bountiful fall of snow, with hard frost, is equivalent to the construction of the best macadamised roads all over the country. The absence of a sufficient quantity of snow in winter for sleighing, is a calamity as much to be feared and deplored as the want of rain in spring. Happily neither of these deprivations is of frequent occurrence.

"The climate of Canada is in some measure exceptional, especially that of the Peninsular portion. The influence of the great Lakes is very strikingly felt in the elevation of winter temperatures and in the reduction of summer heats. East and West of Canada, beyond the influence of the Lakes, as in the middle of the states of New York and Iowa, the greatest extremes prevail,—intense cold in winter, intense heat in summer, and to these features may be added their usual attendant, drought.

"Perhaps the popular standard of the adaptation of climate to the purposes of agriculture is more suitable for the present occasion than a reference to monthly and annual means of temperature. Much information is conveyed in the simple narration of facts bearing upon fruit culture. From the head of Lake Ontario, round by the Niagara frontier, and all along the Canadian shores of Lake Erie, the grape and peach grow with luxuriance, and ripen to perfection in the open air, without the slightest artificial aid. The island of Montreal is distinguished everywhere for the fine quality of its apples, and the island of Orleans, below Quebec, is equally celebrated for its plums. Over the whole of Canada the melon and tomato acquire large dimensions, and ripen fully in the open air, the seeds being planted in the soil towards the latter end of April, and the fruit gathered in September. Pumpkins and squashes attain gigantic dimensions; they have exceeded 300 pounds in weight in the neighbourhood of Toronto. Indian corn, hops, and tobacco, are common crops and yield fair returns. Hemp and flax are indigenous plants, and can be cultivated to any extent in many parts of the Province. With a proper expenditure of capital, England could be made quite independent of Russia, or any other country, for her supply of these valuable products.

"The most striking illustration of the influence of the great Lakes in ameliorating the climate of Canada, especially of the western peninsula, is to be found in the natural limits to which certain trees are restricted by climate. That valuable wood, the black walnut, for which Canada is so celebrated, ceases to grow north of latitude 41° on the Atlantic coast, but under the influence of the comparatively mild Lake-climate of Peninsular Canada it is found in the greatest profusion, and of the largest dimensions, as far north as latitude 43°."

This subject is well illustrated by the subjoined table, showing the mean temperature and rainfall at Toronto from 1840 to 1859 :—

TABLE of Mean Monthly and Annual Temperature at Toronto, Canada West, from 1840 to 1859, taken from the Records of the Provincial Magnetic Observatory, by Professor Kingston.

						MONTHS.							
	Jan.	Feb.	March.	April.	May.	June.	July.	Aug.	Sept.	Oct.	Nov.	Dec.	Mean Annual
1840 } 1859 }	°23.72	°22.83	°30.07	°41.00	°51.33	°61.27	°67.06	°66.12	°57.98	°45.27	°36.65	°25.97	°44.11

MEAN Monthly and Annual Fall of Rain at Toronto, from 1840 to 1859.

						MONTHS.							
	Jan.	Feb.	March.	April.	May.	June.	July.	Aug.	Sept.	Oct.	Nov.	Dec.	Mean Annual
	In.	In.	In.	In.	In.	In.	In.	In.	In.	In.	In.	In.	In.
1840 } 1859 }	1.480	1.043	1.553	2.492	3.305	3.198	3.490	2.927	4.099	2.557	3.109	1.606	30.859

The Rev. Mr. Hope, who has been indefatigable in his efforts to promote the interest of his adopted country, quotes the following passage from the Toronto *Globe* of September 21st, 1860, to show that people at home are much mistaken in considering Canada a region of frost and snow.

"The display of fruit, in quantity and quality, surpassed what has been shown at any previous Exhibition. The results in this department were very satisfactory, proving that the climate of Canada admirably adapts it for the raising of many of the most valuable kinds of fruit. One of the principal exhibitors was Mr. Beadle of St. Catharine's nurseries. On one side of the central stand in the Crystal Palace, he had 115 plates of apples, pears, peaches, &c., and 30 jars of cherries, currants, raspberries, blackberries, &c. Mr. Beadle exhibited ten varieties of peaches grown in the open air. Several of these varieties were of very large dimensions, and were much admired for the delicate richness of their tints. He exhibited also numerous varieties of apples; 41 in one collection of three of each sort, and 20 in another collection of six of each sort. He had also a large show of pears, comprising a large number of varieties. Among the varieties of open-air grapes shown by Mr. Beadle, were the Bloodblacks, the Delaware, the Diana, the Northern Muscadine, the Perkins, Sage's Mammoth, and the Wild Fox."

In 1828, when the whole population of Upper Canada amounted to 185,500 inhabitants, the number of acres under agricultural improvement was 570,000, or about $3\frac{1}{14}$ for each individual; in 1851 the average for each inhabitant was very nearly four acres. The comparative progress of Upper and Lower Canada, in bringing the forest-clad wilderness into cultivation, may be inferred from the following table:—

Year.	LOWER CANADA. No. acres cultivated.	UPPER CANADA. No. acres cultivated.
1831	2,065,913	818,432
1844	2,802,317	2,166,101
1851	3,605,376	3,695,763

Hence, in a period of twenty years, Lower Canada increased her cultivated acres by ·75, and Upper Canada by 3·5. Before proceeding to describe in detail the progress of agriculture in Upper Canada, it will be advisable to glance at the efforts made by societies and the Government of the Province to elevate the condition of husbandry in all its departments, and to induce the people at large to join hand in hand in the march of improvement.

The Board of Agriculture for Lower Canada took decisive steps during the year 1862 to secure the proper disbursements of the provincial grant, and to devote liberal awards of public money to the promotion of agricultural industry in all its important branches. The Lower Canadian Provincial Shows had previously partaken more of the character of an agricultural festival than of a meeting for the purpose of securing the progress of the Science and Art of Agriculture by fair and open competition and peaceful rivalry. In this respect they differed materially from the same annual expositions in Upper Canada, where astonishing advances in the proper direction had been made. The Board determined to establish an Agricultural Museum, and to give assistance to county societies towards the importation of improved breeds of horses, cattle and sheep. The Board is willing to advance to any society funds for the purchase of stock, retaining one-third of the annual government allowance for three successive years to discharge the debt thus incurred. If this new spirit of enterprise should continue, the progress of agriculture in Lower Canada will be much accelerated. Although it must be acknowledged that in the face of many difficulties, national prejudices, and peculiarities of character, a very marked improvement has taken place in many departments of husbandry, and in many parts of the Lower Province, much, very much, remains to be done. The influence exercised by the Agricultural School at St. Anne is already favourably felt, and this establishment appears likely to work a beneficial change in Lower Canadian husbandry. The details of its operations show its great utility.

The indirect assistance given by the Imperial Government to Agriculture in Upper Canada dates from a much earlier period than the encouragement given to Agricultural Societies by the Provincial Government; for we find among the donations of George III. to the U. E. Loyalists the old English plough. It consisted of a small piece of iron fixed to the coulter, having the shape of the letter L, the shank of which went through the wooden beam, the foot forming the point, which was sharpened for use. One handle, and a plank split from a curved piece of timber, which did the duty of a mold-board, completed the rude implement. At that time the traces and leading lines were made of the bark of the elm or bass-wood, which was manufactured by the early settlers into a strong rope. About the year 1808 the "hog-plough" was imported from the United States; and in 1815 a plough with a cast iron share and mold-board, all in one piece, was one of the first implements, requiring more than an ordinary degree of mechanical skill, which was manufactured in the province. The seeds of improvement were then sown, and while in the address of the President at the Frontenac Cattle Show in 1833, we observe attention called to the necessity for further improvement in the ploughs common throughout the country, we witness, in 1855, splendid fruit at the Paris Exhibition. In a notice of the trial of ploughs at Trappes, the *Journal d'Agriculture Pratique* makes the following reference to a Canadian plough: "The ploughing tests were brought to a close by a trial of two ploughs equally remarkable— to wit, the plough of Ransome and Sims, of Suffolk, England, and that of Bingham, of Norwich, Upper Canada. The first is of wood and iron, like all the English ploughs, and the results which it produced seemed most satisfactory, but it appeared to require a little more draught than the Howard plough. Bingham's plough very much resembles the English plough; it is very fine and light in its build; the handles are longer than ordinary, which makes the plough much more easy to manage. The opinion of the French labourers and workmen who were there, appeared, on the whole, very favourable to this plough."

The following extracts from Mr. Hogan's book are as truthful as they are eloquent:—

" Great as has been the prosperity of America, and of the settlements which mark the magnificent country just described, yet nature has not been wooed in them without trials, nor have her treasures been won without a struggle worthy of their worth. Those who have been in the habit of passing *early clearings* in Upper Canada must have been struck with the cheerless and lonely, even desolate appearance of the first settler's little log hut. In the midst of a dense forest, and with a 'patch of clearing' scarcely large enough to let the sun shine in upon him, he looks not unlike a person struggling for existence on a single plank in the middle of an ocean. For weeks, often for months, he sees not the face of a stranger. The same still, and wild, and boundless forest every morning rises up to his view; and his only hope against its shutting him in for life rests in the axe upon his shoulder. A few blades of corn, peeping up betwen stumps whose very roots interlace, they are so close together, are his sole safeguards against want; whilst the few potato plants, in little far-between 'hills,' and which struggle for existence against the briar bush and luxuriant underwood, are to form the seeds of his future plenty. Tall pine trees, girdled and blackened by the fires, stand out as grim monuments of the prevailing loneliness, whilst the forest itself, like an immense wall round a fortress, seems to say to the settler,—'how can poverty ever expect to escape from such a prison house.'

" That little clearing—for I describe a reality—which to others might afford such slender guarantee for bare subsistence, was nevertheless a source of bright and cheering dreams to that lonely settler. He looked at it, and instead of thinking of its littleness, it was the foundation of great hopes of a large farm and rich cornfields to him. And this very dream, or poetry, or what you will, cheered him at his lonely toil, and made him contented with his rude fire-side. The blades of corn, which you might regard as conveying but a tantalising idea of human comforts, were associated by him with large stacks and full granaries; and the very thought nerved his arm, and made him happy.

"Seven years afterwards I passed that same settler's cottage—it was in the valley of the Grand River in Upper Canada, not far from the present village of Caledonia. The little log hut was used as a back kitchen to a neat two story frame house, painted white. A large barn stood near by, with stock of every description in its yard. The stumps, round which the blades of corn, when I last saw the place, had so much difficulty in springing up, had nearly all disappeared. Luxuriant Indian corn had sole possession of the place where the potatoes had so hard a struggle against the briar bushes and the underwood. The forest—dense, impenetrable though it seemed—had been pushed far back by the energetic arm of man. A garden, bright with flowers, and enclosed in a neat picket fence, fronted the house; a young orchard spread out in rear. I met a farmer as I was quitting the scene, returning from church with his wife and family. It was on a Sunday, and there was nothing in their appearance, save perhaps a healthy brown colour in their faces, to distinguish them from persons of wealth in cities. The waggon they were in, their horses, harness, dresses, everything about them, in short, indicated comfort and easy circumstances. I enquired of the man—who was the owner of the property I have just been describing? 'It is mine, sir,' he replied; 'I settled on it nine years ago, and have, thank God, had tolerable success.'

"There is, perhaps, no class in the world who live

better—I mean who have a greater abundance of the comforts of life—than men having cleared farms, and who know how to make a proper use of them, in Upper Canada. The imports of the country show that they dress not only well, but in many things expensively. You go into a church or meeting-house in any part of the province which has been settled for fifteen or twenty years, and you are struck at once with the fabrics, as well as the style of the dresses worn by both sexes, but especially by the young. The same shawls, and bonnets, and gowns which you see in cities, are worn by the women, whilst the coats of the men are undistinguishable from those worn by professional men and merchants in towns. A circumstance which I witnessed some years ago, in travelling from Simcoe to Brantford—two towns in the interior of the province—will serve to convey an idea of the taste as well as the means of enjoyment of these people. At an ordinary Methodist meeting-house, in the centre of a rural settlement, and ten miles from a village or town, there were *twenty-three pleasure carriages,* double and single, standing in waiting. The occasion was a quarterly meeting, and these were the conveyances of the farmers who came to attend it. Yet twenty years before, and this was a wilderness; twenty years before, and many of these people were working as labourers, and were not possessed of a pair of oxen; twenty years before, and these things exceeded even their brightest dreams of prosperity.

"The settler who nobly pushes back the giant wilderness, and hews out for himself a home upon the conquered territory, has necessarily but a bony hand and a rough visage to present to advancing civilisation.

His children, too, are timid, and wild, and uncouth. But a stranger comes in; buys the little improvement on the next lot to him; has children who are educated, and a wife with refined tastes,—for such people mark, in greater or less numbers, every settlement in Upper Canada. The necessities of the new comer soon bring about an acquaintance with the old pioneer. Their families meet—timid and awkward enough at first, perhaps; but children know not the conventionalities of society, and, happily, are governed by their innocence in their friendships. So they play together, go to school in company; and thus, imperceptibly to themselves, are the tastes and manners of the educated imparted to the rude, and the energy and fortitude of the latter are infused into their more effeminate companions. Manly but ill-tutored success is thus taught how to enjoy its gains, whilst respectable poverty is instructed how to better its condition. That pride occasionally puts itself to inconvenience to prevent these pleasant results, my experience of Canada forces me to admit; and that the jealousy and vanity of mere success sometimes views with unkindness the manner and habit of reduced respectability—never perhaps more exacting than when it is poorest—I must also acknowledge. But that the great law of progress, and the influence of free institutions, break down these exceptional feelings and prejudices, is patent to every close observer of Canadian society. Where the educated and refined undergo the changes incident to laborious occupations—for the constant use of the axe and the plough alters men's feelings as well as their appearances,—and where rude industry is also changed by the success which gives it the benefit of education, it is impossible for the two classes not to meet. As the one goes down—at least in its occupations,—it meets the other coming up by reason of its successes, and both eventually occupy the same pedestal. I have seen this social problem worked out over and over again in Upper Canada, and have never known the result different. Pride, in America, must 'stoop to conquer;' rude industry rises always.

"The manner of living of the Upper Canadian farmer may be summed up in few words. He has plenty, and he enjoys it. The native Canadians almost universally, and a large proportion of the old country people, sit at the same table with their servants or labourers. They eat meat twice, and many of them thrice a day: it being apparently more a matter of taste than of economy as to the number of times. Pork is what they chiefly consume. There being a great abundance of fruit, scarcely a cleared farm is without an orchard; and it is to be found preserved in various ways on every farmer's table. Milk is in great abundance, even in the early settler's houses, for where there is little pasture there are sure to be large woods, and 'brouse,' or the tops of the branches of trees, supply the place of hay. The sweetest bread I have eaten in America I have eaten in the farmers' houses of Upper Canada. They usually grind the 'shorts' with the flour for home consumption, and as their wheat is among the finest in the world, the bread is at once wholesome and exceedingly delicious. Were I asked what is the characteristic of Canadian farmers, I would unhesitatingly answer 'Plenty!'"

CHAPTER XV.

Reciprocal Rights—American Ideas of Reciprocity—The Ad Valorem System—Commercial Improvements—Trade with America—The Ottawa Route—The Saskatchewan—Fertility of the Country—Water Communication—The Maritime Provinces—Area and Population.

THE absence of a winter port is an evil to Canada, for which no energy and no advantages can compensate. Although Halifax has a magnificent harbour, New Brunswick and Nova Scotia offer but small facilities for winter navigation; and the day seems distant when the great railroad of which so much has been spoken and written shall open the communication between England and the remotest portions of the vast empire which reaches from the Atlantic to the Pacific.

The position of Canada threw her into close relations with the United States, and the result of her geographical condition was the Reciprocity Treaty, which has caused so much discussion and discontent on both sides of the St. Lawrence, and which the Government of the Federal States has now given notice to terminate.

In March, 1862, the report of the Committee of the Executive Council, to which an able paper of Mr. Galt, then Finance Minister, had been referred, advised that the views and suggestions therein expressed by Mr. Galt should be adopted, and that report was approved by Lord Monck. Mr. Galt's Report was founded on a reference made to him of the report of the Committee on Commerce of the House of Representatives at Washington respecting the Reciprocity Treaty, and of a memorial from the Chamber of Commerce of Minnesota.

The House of Representatives reported in favour of a system resembling that of the "Zollverein" as the only means of securing the benefits of reciprocal trade, and recommended as desirable a uniform system of lighthouses, copyrights, postage, patents, telegraphs, weights and measures, and coinage.

This was a favourite scheme of the late Senator Douglas; and if the American Government had exhibited any desire to diminish the rigours of Morrill Tariffs and of State protective enactments, we might applaud the liberality of their views and the noble candour of their conclusions. They believed that "free commercial intercourse between the United States and the British North-American Provinces, developing the natural, geographical, and other advantages of each for the good of all, is conducive to the present interests of each, and is the proper basis of our intercourse for all time to come"—sentiments certainly noble, if somewhat vaguely expressed. We will see presently how Mr. Galt deals with the practical rendering of them by the Federal Government. The Reciprocity Treaty, negotiated between Lord Elgin and Mr. Marcey in June, 1854, was entered into to avoid further misunderstanding in regard to the extent of the right of fishing on the coasts of British North America, and to regulate the commerce and navigation between the respective territories and people in such a manner as to render the same reciprocally beneficial and satisfactory.

The Convention secured to American fishermen the liberty of taking, curing, and drying fish on the British North-American coast generally; the Treaty extended to them the liberty to take fish of every kind (except shell-fish) along the coast of Canada, New Brunswick, Prince Edward's Island, &c., with permission to land, to dry nets, and cure fish, without any restrictions as to distance from shore—reserving only the right of private property and the salmon and shad-fishings in the rivers; and the same rights were conceded to British subjects on the eastern sea-coasts of the United States north of the 36th parallel of latitude. It provided that the following articles should be admitted duty-free reciprocally:—Grain, flour and breadstuffs, animals, fresh and salt meat, cotton seed and vegetables, fruit, fish, poultry, hides and skins, butter, cheese, tallow, lard, horns, manure, ores, coal, stone, slate, pitch, turpentine, timber and lumber, plants, firs, gypsum, grindstones, dye-stuffs, flax, rags, and unmanufactured tobacco. It gave to Americans the right to navigate the St. Lawrence and the Canadian canals, subject to the tolls, and it gave to British subjects the right to navigate Lake Michigan; but it reserved to the British Government the right of suspending, on due notice, the privileges of Canadian navigation, in which event the right of British subjects to navigate Lake Michigan should also cease and determine, and the United States should have the right of suspending the free import and export of the articles specified. But here, it will be observed, there was a one-sided reciprocity. The Americans received, absolutely, the right of using all the canals in Canada from the British Government; the Government of the United States conferred no such privilege reciprocally on British subjects. All they did—perhaps all they could do in consonance with the doctrine of States Rights they are so busily engaged at present in destroying—was to engage to urge on the State Governments to secure to the subjects of Her Britannic Majesty the use of the several ship-canals on terms of equality with the inhabitants of the United States. It was also provided that "American lumber floated down to St. John and shipped to the United States from New Brunswick should be free of duty." This treaty was to remain in force for ten years from the date at which it came into operation, and further until the expiration of twelve months after either of the contracting parties gave notice to the other of its wish to terminate the same—each of them being at liberty to give notice at the end of the ten years, or at any time afterwards. This treaty expired on the 11th September, 1864, since which time the United States and Great Britain have been free to give notice of the termination of its provisions, to take effect in twelve months after the date of the notice. Of this power, as already stated, the United States Government has availed itself. An exception to the operation of the treaty is made in the case of Newfoundland, in respect to which its provisions hold good till December 12th, 1865. The State of New York, by its Legislature, urged Congress to protect the United States from what they denounced as an "unequal and unjust system of commerce." They asserted that nearly all the articles which Canada has to sell are admitted into the United States free of duty, whilst heavy duties are imposed on many articles of American manufacture, with the intention of excluding them from the Canadian market; and that discriminating tolls and duties, in favour of an isolating and exclusive policy against American merchants and forwarders, to destroy the effect of the treaty and in opposition to its spirit, have been adopted by Canada; and on these grounds they demanded a change in the system of commerce now existing, to protect the interests of the United States in the manner intended by the treaty.

The Canadian Minister, in reply, observed that the treaty made no mention whatever of the matters complained of, and, in a very lucid argument, charges against the Legislature of the United States the very same grounds of complaint as the Committee alleged against Canada. No accusation of an infraction of the treaty is made, and therefore the subjects treated of in the Report affect the commercial relations and not the good faith of the contracting parties. The Committee accuse Canada of violating the spirit and intent of the treaty, by an increase of duties on manufactured articles, by a change in the mode of levying duties, and by abolishing tolls on the St. Lawrence canals and river; but Mr. Galt contends that the treaty had nothing to do with manufactures, but was expressly limited to the growth and produce of the two countries mentioned in the schedule. Those articles not enumerated in it are necessarily excluded from its operations, and must be made the subject of special legislation between the two States before any act of either respecting the mode of their admission can be made ground of remonstrance.

As a proof of the narrow spirit in which these fine declaimers about " liberty of commerce and reciprocity of trading advantages" have dealt with the treaty, it may be mentioned that they imposed duties on planks in part planed, tongued, or grooved, and on flour ground in Canada from American wheat, and on lumber made in Canada out of American logs. The Canadian Government, however, have maintained, both against the Americans and the mother country, their right to decide for themselves both as to the mode and the extent to which taxation should be imposed. Declamations against a policy of Protection come indeed with a bad grace from the United States; and Mr. Galt, in suppressed sarcasm and irony, shows that their doctrine of Free Trade with Canada really means an exclusive protection for themselves against the manufactures of Great Britain.

If the gentlemen who composed the elaborate Report, bristling all over with generous sentiments and with the expression of the most enlightened and liberal doctrines, could blush, they might well perform that interesting operation when reading Mr. Galt's reply. Canada admits the registration of foreign vessels without charge; the United States do not. Canada has sought admission to the great lakes for coasters; the United States refuse. Canada allows American vessels to pass free through her canals; not a Canadian vessel is allowed, even on payment of toll, to enter an American canal. The promise in the treaty, that the Government of Washington would urge on the States the concession of a right to navigate their canals on equal terms with American subjects, has not been kept; at least, there is no trace of any effort having been made to induce the State Legislatures to relax their present extreme policy, which is in strong contrast with the professions of their Committee-men. Canada permits foreign goods bought in the United States to be imported on the payment of duty on the original invoice; the United States will not permit similar purchases to be made in Canada. Tea imported from Canada is weighted with duty of ten per cent., while the duties under the Canadian tariff are very much lower than those levied in America. The permission to pass goods under bond through the States conferred an obvious advantage on American railroads; but, indeed, the Committee were fain to admit that the United States had not established a fair reciprocity, inasmuch as they recommend that reciprocity should be made complete. Duties have been imposed in the United States for purposes of Protection, and they can scarcely bring accusations against Canada until they have established a system of duties as low as those of Canada. The *ad valorem* system of Canada, against which the Committee protest, is the system of the United States; for tea and sugar there is a discriminating duty in favour of American vessels of twenty per cent. Duty is levied in Canada solely for purposes of revenue: and though this policy, which has led the late Minister and his predecessors to reduce tolls and customs-dues to a minimum, has alarmed the canal and ship-owners and railway-directors of New York, it is viewed with approbation by the great Western States.

"It is," says Mr. Galt, "a singular charge to make of discrimination on our part against them, that we do not permit one section of our public works to be used for purposes exclusively beneficial to them, when they absolutely, and contrary to the engagements of the treaty, debar any Canadian vessel from entering their waters, if we except Lake Michigan, specially mentioned in the treaty. Surely Canada does enough for them when she places them precisely on the same footing as she does her own vessels; and it is a novel doctrine that because the whole St. Lawrence is made free, therefore an injury is done to the New York route. The remedy is simple, and in their own hands: let them do as Canada has done—repeal the tolls on their canals, and admit Canadian vessels to ply upon them—and then the desired state of 'fair competition' will have arisen. But the Committee must have formed but a low estimate of the intelligence of their own people in the West, when they make it a subject of complaint against Canada that she has opened the St. Lawrence freely to their trade. The undersigned apprehends that the inhabitants of those great States will be much more likely to demand from their own Government an equitable application of their own customs-laws, so as to permit them to import direct *viâ* the St. Lawrence, and to buy in the Canadian market, rather than to join with the Committee in requiring a return to a system by which the entire West has hitherto been held in vassalage to the State of New York."

Mr. Galt argues that an increase of customs-duties does not, necessarily, injuriously affect foreign trade within certain limits, and that those limits have not been exceeded in Canada. Formerly the cost of British goods in Canada was much enhanced, owing to natural causes, whilst Canadian producers obtained a minimum price for their exports. The duty was then generally 2½ per cent., but the price was enormous; and the Canadian suffered, *pro tanto,* in his means to purchase them. Suppose the duties, increased five per cent., were to produce a reduction of ten per cent. on other charges, "the benefit," says Mr. Galt, "would accrue equally to the British manufacturer and to the consumer; the consumer would pay five per cent. more to the Government, but ten per cent. less to the merchant and forwarder." As Mr. Galt considers the principle of Canadian finance and customs to be misapprehended in England as well as in the United States, it may be as well to give his own words:—

"The Government has increased the duties for the purpose of enabling them to meet the interest on the public works necessary to reduce all the various charges upon the imports and exports of the country. Lighthouses have been built, and steamships subsidised, to reduce the charges for freight and insurance; the St. Lawrence has been deepened, and the canals constructed, to reduce the cost of inland navigation to a minimum; railways have been assisted, to give speed, safety, and permanency to trade interrupted by the severity of winter. All these improvements have been undertaken with the twofold object of diminishing the cost to the consumer of what he imports, and of increasing the *net* result of the labour of the country when finally realised in Great Britain. These great improvements could not be effected without large outlays; and the burthen necessarily had to be put either through direct taxation, or by customs-duties on the goods imported, or upon the trade by excessive tolls corresponding with the rates previously charged. Direct taxation was the medium employed, through the local municipalities, for the construction of all minor local works—roads, court-houses and gaols, education, and the vast variety of objects required in a newly-settled country; and this source of taxation has thus been used to the full extent which is believed practicable without producing serious discontent. No one can, for a moment, argue that, in an enlightened age, any Government could adopt such a clumsy mode of raising money as to maintain excessive rates of tolls; nor would it have attained the object, as American channels of trade were created simultaneously, that would then have defied competition. The only effect, therefore, of attempting such course would have been to give the United States the complete control of our markets, and virtually to exclude British goods. The only other course was therefore adopted, and the producer has been required to pay, through increased customs-duties, for the vastly greater deductions he secured through the improvements referred to. What, then, has been the result to the British manufacturer? His goods are, it is true, in many cases subjected to 20 per cent. instead of $2\frac{1}{2}$ per cent., but the cost to the consumer has been diminished in a very much greater degree; and the aggregate of cost, original price, duty, freight, and charges are now very much less than when the duty was $2\frac{1}{2}$ per cent., and consequently the *legitimate protection* to the home-manufacturer is to this extent diminished. Nor is this all: the interest of the British manufacturer is not merely that he shall be able to lay down his goods at the least cost to the consumer, but equally is he interested in the ability of the consumer to buy. Now, this latter point is attained precisely through the same means which have cheapened the goods. The produce of Canada is now increased in value exactly in proportion to the saving on the cost of delivering it in the market of consumption.

"If the aggregate of cost to the consumer remained the same now as it was before the era of canals and railroads in Canada, what possible difference would it make to the British manufacturers whether the excess over the cost in Great Britain were paid to the Government or to merchants and forwarders? It would certainly not in any way affect the question of the protection to home-manufacturers : but when it can be clearly shown that by the action of the Government, in raising funds through increased customs-duties, the cost to the consumer is now very much less, upon what ground can the British manufacturer complain that these duties have been restrictive on his trade ?

"The undersigned might truly point to the rapid increase in the population and wealth of Canada, arising from its policy of improvement, whereby its ability of consumption has been so largely increased. He might also show that these improvements have, in a great degree, also tended to the rapid advance of the Western States, and to their increased ability to purchase British goods. He might point to the fact that the grain supplied from the Western States and Canada keeps down prices in Great Britain, and therefore enables the British manufacturer to produce still cheaper. But he prefers resting his case, as to the propriety of imposing increased customs-duties, solely on the one point, that through that increase the cost of British manufactured goods, including duty, has been reduced to the Canadian consumer, and that consequently the increase has in its results, viewing the whole trade, tended to an augmentation of the market for British goods."

In a tabular statement it is shown that the average amount of duty levied on imports from the United States in 1861 is the same as the average of the previous twelve years, that the variations have been very slight, and that the rate per cent. was less than half what it had been a few years before, whilst American trade has been steadily increasing. Under the operation of the treaty, the imports from the United States, in 1861, were nearly trebled, and the exports from Canada to the United States were nearly quadrupled; the whole amount of trade in 1851 being, in round numbers, 12,500,000 dollars, which was increased to 24,000,000 dollars in 1854, and to 35,500,000 dollars in 1861. These advantages may be still further extended without injury to either nation or to the just claims of Great Britain to an equality in the Canadian market; and Mr. Galt professed himself quite ready for the abolition of the coasting laws on inland waters—of all discrimination as to nationality in respect of vessels —the free import of wooden wares, agricultural implements, machinery, and books—the assimilation of the patent-laws: but he totally opposes the project of a Zollverein, on the ground that it would be inconsistent with the maintenance of connexion with Great Britain, inasmuch as Canada would be called upon to tax goods of British manufacture, while she admitted those of the United States free.

"Great Britain is," he observes, "the market for Canadian produce to a far greater extent than the United States." The United States would necessarily impose her views on the Zollverein, and "the result would be," says Mr. Galt, "a tariff not, as now, based on the simple wants of Canada, but upon those of a country engaged in a colossal war." It must be regretted, notwithstanding Mr. Galt's arguments, that the Canadian tariff is so high; but if she be called upon to incur a fresh debt for the purposes of defence, it is more likely that it will be increased rather than diminished. In connection with the relations of Canada and the West to the United States, the opening of new water-ways and roads becomes of paramount interest and importance.

In March, 1863, a Select Committee was appointed by the Legislative Assembly to investigate the subject of a navigable line between Montreal and Lake Huron, by the Ottawa and Matawan Rivers, Lake Nipissing, and French River. That Committee reported that there were no engineering difficulties to interfere with the opening of this route for vessels of every class up to the draught of twelve feet, and that it would shorten the line to Chicago 350 miles, the exact difference in favour of the Ottawa communication from Montreal to Mackinaw being 68 miles. In point of time there would be a reduction of 47 hours. The trade between the Western States and the sea has increased to such an extent during the last four years, that 120,000,000 of bushels of wheat and grain stood in need of transport, according to the last calculation; and even with its present communications, Montreal is second only to New York as a grain-exporting port, the quantity shipped last year from it being over 15,000,000 of bushels. The Ottawa route would actually be the shortest line of communication between the ports on Lake Michigan and New York itself by 150 miles, when the Champlain Canal shall have been made, and the Northern Canal enlarged.

The tract through which the proposed line would pass, exceeding in area the whole of the five New England States, is covered with a wealth of timber surpassing belief; and the forestless prairies would furnish a market valuable as gold itself to the lumberer. Vessels going down and discharging their cargoes would return with cargoes of timber, the demand for which in the West is so great, that the city of Chicago consumes alone 100,000*l.* worth in the year. Canadian pines would be in demand to construct the new cities which are rising in the Prairie State, and to keep the hearth fires alight through their rigid winters. The effect of such a line in developing local traffic, agricultural improvement, commercial enterprise, and the spread of civilisation, cannot be over-estimated. In reference to the military advantages to be derived from its construction, the Committee makes but a meagre reference; but it is obvious that by securing such a route, far removed from a foreign frontier, between the sea and the western lakes, the means of defence and of transport in war would be very much strengthened and improved.

The St. Lawrence canals can be destroyed, as Mr. Chamley observes, by the Americans, without their being obliged to land a man in Canada; whilst by the Ottawa route gunboats could proceed from the St. Lawrence to Lake Huron in less time than they would now require to get to Lake Erie. It is not to be overlooked, however, that the higher latitudes through which the canal would run, expose the waters to a longer frost and necessary cessation of traffic. The advantages of the route to New York and to other North-Eastern States of America, can only be gained by completing the proposed Cooknawoogo Canal, between the St. Lawrence and Lake Champlain, and it is doubtful whether the jealousy of the Americans would not prevent their furthering a project which would confer great benefits on the Provinces, even though their refusing to do so might deprive them of certain advantages. This line would, in fact, give us or the Canadians an admirable interior communication, and at the same time confer military, political, and commercial benefits on the Provinces, the extent of which cannot be easily foreseen.

Mr. Galt admits that there may be jealousies, though he protests there should not be, and calls to mind the opposition of Mohawk Dutchmen, the Frenchmen of Detroit, and others, to the Erie Canal. If the plans for improving the communications which have been suggested should ever be developed, the valley of Red River would be reached without much difficulty, and land as good as that in the unsettled portions of Iowa and Minnesota would be opened to the British emigrant.

In the valleys of the Saskatchewan and Assiniboine, Canada possesses a vast north-west of her own, enjoying a mild climate, which contains, according to one of the witnesses whose opinion is cited by the Committee, 500,000 square miles of fertile land, capable of sustaining a population of nearly 30,000,000 of people.

It has been ascertained beyond doubt, that the tract between the North and South Saskatchewan on the east is exceedingly fertile, and that no intense cold prevails throughout an enormous region of rich prairies on cretaceous and tertiary deposits. It is scarcely possible for us to conceive what an enormous expanse of fertile land lies to the east of the Rocky Mountains, about the sources of those rivers; but there are too many witnesses of unmistakeable veracity to render us sceptical concerning the beauty and capabilities of these regions. Could the poor emigrant be carried to these fertile districts, instead of sinking into the rowdyism of American cities, or beating down the rate of wages by competition, he would find at least a comfortable subsistence, even if he were unable at once to obtain a profitable market for his labours.

Father de Smet, the missionary, a man whose name is a tower of strength and faith, describes a district which makes us wonder that poverty should ever be known in Europe, and corroborates the glowing picture of Sir George Simpson:—a soil and climate better suited for agriculture than that of Toronto—a region abounding in game of all kinds, rivers and lakes swarming with fish, plains covered with buffaloes—seams of coal —delicious wild fruits—forests of pine, cypress, poplar, and aspen. Even at Edmonton, potatoes, wheat and barley, corn and beans, are produced in abundance. "Are these vast and innumerable fields of hay," asks Father de Smet, "for ever destined to be consumed by fire, or perish in wintry snows? How long shall these superb forests be the haunts of wild beasts? Are these abundant mines of coal, lead, sulphur, iron, copper, and saltpetre doomed to remain for ever valueless? No; the day must come when the hand of labour shall give them value, and stirring and enterprising people are destined ere long to fill this void; the wild beasts will give place to domestic animals; flocks and herds will graze on the beautiful meadows, and the mountain-sides and valleys will swarm with life."

Before this picture, however, be realised, some communication must be opened east or west between the community and the outer world; and if the British Government does not take some steps to secure a settlement of these regions by its own subjects, the irresistible agency of American emigration will erase mere lines upon the map, and determine the question of nationality beyond the power of appeal or alteration. It is agreeable to admit that the inhabitants of the State of Minnesota have not hitherto evinced any design of raising difficulties as to jurisdiction, or of disturbing the relations between the two Governments. In fact, the St. Paul Chamber of Commerce, in 1862, presented a strong memorial against the proposal to suspend or abrogate the provisions of the Reciprocity Treaty. This memorial says :—

"Central British America, including an inhabitable area of 300,000 square miles, and extending north-west of Minnesota to the Rocky Mountains, will probably be organised as a crown colony of England, with the seat of government at Selkirk. There is good reason to believe that a bill for this purpose will become an Act of Parliament at the session now impending. British Columbia, on the Pacific coast, having received a similar organisation in 1858, the establishment of the province of Central British America will go far to realise the hope so gracefully expressed three years since from the throne of England: 'That her Majesty's dominions in North America may ultimately be peopled in an unbroken chain from the Atlantic to the Pacific, by a loyal and industrious population of subjects of the British crown.'

"Minnesota, with the co-operation of the Government at Washington, has relied with confidence upon the probability of such a colonisation of the fertile valleys which stretch beyond the international boundary, from the lakes of Superior and Winnepeg, or the western limits of Canada, to the Pacific colony of British Columbia. Our mails, our trains of regular transportation, and our steam-vessels on the Red River of the North, are already provided as important links of international communication from Toronto to St. Paul, and thence to Fort Garry. The projected railroads of Minnesota, with extensive grants of land from Congress in behalf of their construction, harmonise in a north-western trend to the valleys of the Red River of the North, and the still more remote Saskatchewan. Our whole commercial future has been projected in concert with the victories of peace, even more renowned than war, of which we still hope to witness the achievement in north-west America, irrespective of the imaginary line of an international frontier.

"Animated by these expectations, which the march of events has hitherto justified, we invoke the 'sober second thought' of the country upon the subject of our continental policy. With the suppression of the Southern rebellion; with dispassionate discussions by all the parties interested; with the happy accord of minds like Cobden in England and Chase in America upon the best methods of revenue; and lastly, with the lessons and suggestions of the next three years, a treaty, eminently deserving the designation of a reciprocity treaty, will probably be submitted to the Congress of 1864."

When the Committee of Commerce, to which the Legislature of New York referred its petition against the Reciprocity Treaty, made their report, they gave expression to very different sentiments; and enlarged on the magnitude of the present possessions of the British Crown on the American continent, and the probable grandeur of their future, in a manner which indicated certainly the existence of a feeling not far removed from jealousy. With great truth they say, that the value of the British North-American possessions is seldom appreciated: stretching from the Atlantic to the Pacific, they contain an area of at least 3,478,380 miles. The isothermal line of 60 degrees for summer rises on the interior plains of this continent as high as the 61st parallel,—its average position in Europe. And a favourable comparison may also be traced for winter and other seasons in the year. Then, elevated by the subject, and warming by degrees, the Committee draw a glowing picture of this enormous empire. "Spring opens simultaneously," they say, "on the plains, which stretch for 1200 miles, from St. Paul's to the McKenzie River. Westward are countries of still milder climate, now scarcely inhabited, but of incalculable value in the future. Eastward are the small settlements, yet distant from the other abodes of civilisation, enjoying the rich lands and pleasant climate of the Red River." It may well surprise the inhabitants of these isles, who have not got 100 miles of natural navigable rivers in the three kingdoms, to learn that this same Red River is capable of steamboat navigation for 400 miles.

The following extract from this Report gives perhaps the best idea of the British Possessions in a few words which can be presented to the reader:

"It is asserted by those who add personal knowledge of the subject to scientific investigation, that the habitable but undeveloped area of the British Possessions westerly from Lake Superior and Hudson's Bay, comprises sufficient territory to make twenty-five States equal in size to Illinois. Bold as this assertion is, it meets with confirmation in the isothermal charts of Blodgett, the testimony of Richardson, Simpson, Mackenzie, the maps published by the Government of Canada, and the recent explorations of Professor Hind, of Toronto.

"North of a line drawn from the northern limit of Lake Superior to the coast at the southern limit of Labrador exists a vast region, possessing in its best parts a climate barely endurable, and reaching into the Arctic regions. This country, even more cold, desolate, and barren on the Atlantic coast than in the interior latitudes, becoming first known to travellers, has given character in public estimation to the whole north.

"Another line, drawn from the northern limit of Minnesota to that of Maine, includes nearly all the inhabited portion of Canada, a province extending opposite the Territory of Dakota and States of Minnesota, Wisconsin, Michigan, Ohio, Pennsylvania, New York, Vermont, New Hampshire, and Maine, possessing a climate identical with that of our Northern States.

"The 'Maritime Provinces' on the Atlantic coast include New Brunswick, Nova Scotia, Prince Edward's Island, and Newfoundland. Geographically they may be regarded as a north-easterly prolongation of the New England system. Unitedly they include an area of at least 86,000 square miles, and are capable of supporting a larger population than that at present existing in the United States or Great Britain. They are equal in extent to the united territory of Holland, Greece, Belgium, Portugal, and Switzerland.

"New Brunswick is 190 miles in length and 150 in breadth. Its interests are inseparably connected with those of the adjacent State of Maine. It has an area of 22,000,000 acres, and a seacoast 400 miles in extent, and abounding in harbours. Its population some years ago numbered 210,000, whose chief occupations are connected with shipbuilding, the fisheries, and the timber trade. Commissioners appointed by the Government of Great Britain affirm that it is impossible to speak too highly of its climate, soil, and capabilities. Few countries are so well wooded and watered. On its unreclaimed surface is an abundant stock of the finest timber; beneath are coal fields. The rivers, lakes, and seacoast abound with fish.

"Nova Scotia, a long peninsula, united to the American continent by an isthmus only fifteen miles wide, is 280 miles in length. The numerous indentations on its coast form harbours unsurpassed in any part of the world. Including Cape Breton, it has an area of 12,000,000 acres. Wheat, and the usual cereals and fruits of the Northern States, flourish in many parts of it. Its population in 1851 was declared by the census to be 276,117. Besides possessing productive fisheries and agricultural resources, it is rich in mineral wealth, having beneath its surface coal, iron, manganese, gypsum, and gold.

"The province of Prince Edward's Island is separated from New Brunswick and Nova Scotia by straits only nine miles in width. It is crescent-shaped, 130 miles in length, and at its broadest part is 34 miles wide. It is a level region, of a more moderate temperature than that of Lower Canada, and well adapted to agricultural purposes. Its population in 1848 was 62,678.

"The island of Newfoundland has a seacoast 1000 miles in extent. It has an area of 23,040,000 acres, of which only a small portion is cultivated. Its spring is late, its summer short, but the frost of winter is less severe than in many parts of our own Northern States and Territories. It is only 1665 miles distant from Ireland. It possesses a large trade with various countries, including Spain, Portugal, Italy, the West Indies, and the Brazils.

"The chief wealth of Newfoundland and of the Labrador coast is to be found in their extensive and inexhaustible fisheries, in which the other Provinces also partake. The future products of these, when properly developed by human ingenuity and industry, defy human calculation. The Gulf Stream is met near the shores of Newfoundland by a current from the Polar basin, vast deposits are formed by the meeting of the opposing waters, the great submarine islands, known as 'The Banks,' are formed; and the rich pastures created in Ireland by the warm and humid influences of the Gulf Stream are compensated by the 'rich sea-pastures of Newfoundland.' The fishes of warm or tropical waters, inferior in quality and scarcely capable of preservation, cannot form an article of commerce like those produced in inexhaustible quantities in these cold and shallow seas. The abundance of these marine resources is unequalled in any portion of the globe.

"Canada, rather a nation than a province in any common acceptation of the term, includes not less than 346,863 square miles of territory, independently of its North-western Possessions not yet open for settlement.

It is three times as large as Great Britain and Ireland, and more than three times as large as Prussia. It intervenes between the Great North-west and the Maritime Provinces, and consists chiefly of a vast territorial projection into the territory of the United States, although it possesses a coast of nearly 1000 miles on the river and gulf of the St. Lawrence, where fisheries of cod, herring, mackerel, and salmon are carried on successfully. Valuable fisheries exist also in its lakes. It is rich in metallic ore and in the resources of its forests. Large portions of its territory are peculiarly favourable to the growth of wheat, barley, and the other cereals of the north. During the life of the present generation, or the last quarter of a century, its population has increased more than fourfold, or from 582,000 to 2,500,000.

"The population of all the provinces may be fairly estimated as numbering 3,500,000. Many of the inhabitants are of French extraction, and a few German settlements exist; but two-thirds of the people of the provinces owe their origin either to the United States or to the British Islands, whose language we speak, and who 'people the world with men industrious and free.'

"The climate and soil of these Provinces and Possessions, seemingly less indulgent than those of tropical regions, are precisely those by which the skill, energy, and virtues of the human race are best developed. Nature there demands thought and labour from man as conditions of his existence, but yields abundant rewards to wise industry. Those causes which, in our age of the world, determine the wealth of nations are those which render man most active; and it cannot be too often or too closely remembered in discussing subjects so vast as these, where the human mind may be misled if it attempts to comprehend them in their boundless variety of detail, that sure and safe guides in the application of political economy, and to our own prosperity, are to be found in the simple principles of morality and justice, because they alone are true alike in minute and great affairs, at all times and in every place."

CHAPTER XVI.

The "Ashburton Capitulation"—Boundaries of Quebec—Arbitration in 1831—Lord Ashburton's Mission—The Questions in Dispute—"The Sea" v. "The Atlantic"—American Diplomatists—Franklin's Red Line—Compromise—The Maps—Maine—Damage to Canada—Mr. Webster's Defence—His Opinion of the Road—Value of the Heights—Our Share of Equivalents—Value of Rouse's Point—Vermont—New Hampshire.

It was by the celebrated Treaty of Washington, August 9th, 1842, that the boundary line between the British possessions in Canada and the State of Maine in the territories of the United States, was settled and determined. That treaty has been sometimes spoken of as the "Ashburton Capitulation." The story of the two maps which played so distinguished a part in the negotiations, is tolerably well known, and has formed a subject of many discussions which have now settled down into fixed convictions. By many, if not by most Americans, acquainted with the subject, it is believed that Mr. Webster did a very smart thing. Englishmen, similarly instructed, believe their country to have been cheated by the great American elocutionist. Canadians are of opinion that they have suffered an irreparable injury at the hands of, or through the weakness of, those appointed to guard their interests by the Imperial Government. The Treaty of Paris, in 1783, did not define the north-eastern boundary of the United States; it merely declared that the boundary was drawn along the highlands which divide the rivers that empty themselves into the river St. Lawrence from those which fall into the Atlantic Ocean. If we had had at that time the knowledge of geography and geology, with respect to the basin of the St. Lawrence, which, thanks to the labours of the United States' engineers and of Sir William Logan, we now possess, there would not have been much difficulty in fixing on the real line, as there could not well be any dispute respecting the exact line of highlands from which the rivers flowing into the St. Lawrence came, and from the other side of which the water-shed was towards the Atlantic Ocean. Tons of pamphlets, years of controversy, and thousands of pounds might have been spared, not to speak of much national animosity.

It may be remarked here, that the difficulty of reconciling States' rights with Imperial Federal policy was fore-shadowed in the original disputes which took place at the time of the treaty adjustment. The Treaty speaks of the " boundaries between the possessions of Her Britannic Majesty in North America and the territories of the United States ;" but the State of Maine in its vehement protest against the line of the King of the Netherlands, assumed the language and the port of an independent Power. Mr. Thomas Colley Grattan, in his work, " Civilised America," has collected an immense amount of information, and has drawn up an argument on the subject, which prove beyond a doubt, even without collateral aid, that the line yielded by Lord Ashburton was not that which was meant by the framers of the Treaty of 1783. Let us consider how the case stood.

In 1763 the French possessions in North America

were ceded to Great Britain, and in the October of that year a royal proclamation defined the boundaries of the government of Quebec, "bounded on the Labrador coast by the river St. John, which falls into the mouth of the St. Lawrence, and from there by a line drawn from the head of that river through the Lake of St. John to the south end of the Lake Nipissing, from whence the said line, crossing the river St. Lawrence and Lake Champlain in 45 degrees of north latitude, passes along the highlands which divide the rivers that empty themselves into the said river St. Lawrence from those which fall into the sea, and also along the north coast of the Bay of Chaleurs and the coast of the Gulf of St. Lawrence to Cape Rosière, and from thence crossing the mouth of the river St. Lawrence by the west end of the island of Anticosti, terminates in the aforesaid Lake of St. John." It is fortunate enough that we have no neighbours to raise any question about "the line drawn through the Lake of St. John to the south end of the Lake Nipissing."

Previous to the Treaty of Independence only one Act was passed bearing upon the southern boundary of Canada. The Quebec Act of 1774 draws its boundaries between the province of Quebec and the colonies of Nova Scotia and Massachusetts, in words nearly the same as those of the Proclamation of 1763. When the State of Massachusetts and the State of Maine were acknowledged to be "free, sovereign, and independent," by the Treaty of 1783, the contracting parties appeared to have defined the boundary-line with tolerable exactitude. They wished to prevent disputes between the United States and the colonies, and therefore the boundaries were constituted "from the north-west angle of Nova Scotia,— viz., that angle which is formed by a line drawn due north from the source of the St. Croix river to the highlands, along the said highlands which divide those rivers that empty themselves into the St. Lawrence from those which fall into the Atlantic Ocean,—to the north-westernmost head of Connecticut river east, by a line to be drawn along the middle of the river St. Croix from its mouth in the Bay of Fundy to its source, and from its source directly north to the aforesaid highlands which divide the rivers which fall into the Atlantic Ocean from those which fall into the river St. Lawrence, comprehending all highlands within twenty leagues of any harbour of the United States, and lying between lines to be drawn due east from the points where the aforesaid boundaries between Nova Scotia on the one part, and East Florida on the other, shall respectively touch the Bay of Fundy and the Atlantic Ocean, except such highlands as now are, or heretofore have been, within the limits of the said province of Nova Scotia."

The north-west angle of Nova Scotia thus becomes a point of consequence—upon the determination of it rests the true line. The British maintain that the angle is contained at the point " where the line due north from the river St. Croix touches the highlands at a point about 100 miles south of the point claimed by the United States." The Americans argue that the north-west angle was " considerably nearer to the St. Lawrence, at a spot 145 miles north of the source of the St. Croix." In 1794 Commissioners were appointed to determine " where a line drawn due north from the St. Croix would intersect a line of highlands corresponding with those mentioned in the Treaty of 1783." The umpire called in by the Commissioners fixed on the most northern point of the river as the place from which the line to the highlands was to be drawn, and the result was that the line so drawn did not strike the highlands which we held to be those meant by the treaty, but passing them at a distance of twenty miles on the west, came to an isolated mountain called Mars Hill, from which the Americans desired to prolong it northwards beyond the river St. John to the highlands above the source of the Restegouche; but the British Commissioners insisted that the line should not proceed further north, and that the highlands which ran west from near that point to the head of the Connecticut river should form the next boundary-line.

Events of greater importance for a time prevented any attempt to adjust a question, which promised, however, no slight difficulty in time to come. Then war broke out between the United States and Great Britain; but the Peace of 1814 rendered it necessary to renew the attempt to define the boundaries of the two States. The Commissioners appointed by the Treaty of Ghent were not more fortunate than their predecessors; and it was thirteen years after the signing of that treaty before the Governments of the two countries arranged a convention, to carry out the provision made by an article in the Treaty for the appointment of a referee in case of disagreement. The King of the Netherlands, who accepted the office of arbiter in 1831, delivered his award, which, taking the line drawn north from the St. Croix to Mars Hill, passed beyond it to the river St. John, whence it took the course of the river westward, inside the line claimed by the United States to the head of the Connecticut River. This compromise was identical with the actual line established by the Treaty of 1842, except on the western side, where the line fixed by the King and that claimed by the United States are the same. The King's line approximates much more closely to the United States' line than it does to that which we claim : however, the Americans refused to accept it, on the grounds that the King had no right to go beyond the matter referred to him of determining which of the two lines was right, and that he had exceeded his province in proposing a line which had not been referred to him by either of the parties.

Eleven years passed in unavailing endeavours to adjust a question which rose into the highest rank of diplomatic difficulties. Lord Ashburton, the head of the commercial house of Baring, whose relations with American commerce were supposed to be likely to recommend him to American statesmen, was dispatched in 1842 to determine the boundary, in concert with Mr. Webster. These gentlemen were assisted by seven Commissioners from Maine and Massachusetts. The author of a pamphlet of very great ability, quoted by Mr. Grattan, arrived at the conclusion that the line designated in the Proclamation of 1763, is identical with that claimed by the United States, and that the line indicated in the treaty of 1783 is almost the same as that claimed by Great Britain. He argued that it was clearly intended to create a new boundary, because Mr. Townsend said so, and Lord North repeated the statement in Parliament. He maintained that the variations in the wording of the treaty from that of the proclamation, were specially introduced to show that a new boundary was intended, and that if it had not been so, the description in the treaty would have been the same as it was in the proclamation; and he then proceeded further to contend, with greater force of reasoning, that the proclamation boundary, although it might have adequately defined the limits of a province, would have been obviously unsuitable as between two independent nations, because it would cut off communication between two portions of the territory of one of the Powers, and give it to another independent State. He further asserted, that all negotiations and projects for peace on the part of the United States were based on the supposition that England would demand a new line, and that Congress never contemplated an adherence to the Proclamation of 1763. All the reasoning of the pamphleteer in support of these propositions is distinguished by acuteness, and inclines the mind to accept them with confidence; and he is not less happy in his argument that the Madawaska river is distinct from the river St. John—that it is a tributary, not a branch, of that stream.

The question as to the range of highlands meant by the treaties can only be settled by analytical reasoning, which, in relation to matters of fact of the kind under dispute, is satisfactory only to those who direct their own course of argument. There are two ranges of highlands dividing the rivers which flow into the St. Lawrence and those which empty themselves into the Atlantic; the first, running from the sources of the Connecticut towards the Bay of Chaleurs, certainly separates rivers emptying into the St. Lawrence from those emptying into the sea; but the second line starting from the same mountainous germ at the sources of the Connecticut, branching off from the first range at a point about eighty miles from its commencement, takes a southern course towards the head of the St. Croix, and divides the rivers which empty themselves into the St. Lawrence from those which flow into the Atlantic Ocean. It is contended on one side, with much force of reasoning and probability, that the highlands specified in the Treaty of 1783 are those of the southern range. It was necessary of course to fix upon some great natural features in a district vast in extent and unknown to all but the Red men and the hunter. Rivers and the summit level between two great watersheds would be obviously selected. It was the object of England to secure free communication between all parts of her American territory, and, of course, between Canada and Nova Scotia. The Americans proposed the line of the St. John, which was at once rejected. That being the case, it is difficult to conceive how they could go back and propose, as a line more likely to meet the views of England, the highlands of the northern range close to the St. Lawrence, which would throw the greatest difficulties in the way of the communication which it was a vital point for England to secure. It will have been observed that the words "the Sea" and the "Atlantic Ocean" are used in the treaties, and it certainly is not easy to comprehend how the Americans can maintain that these terms have an identical meaning, if the description of the maps which they had before them at the time is correct. The Connecticut, the Penobscot, and the Kennebeck, can be considered as flowing into the Atlantic Ocean from one range of highlands only, and it is equally plain that the other, or northern, range was that which was meant as the highlands from which rivers flowed into the "sea."

It has been urged, ingeniously and truly, that the words "The Sea," give a larger range of boundary than the words "The Atlantic;" and that therefore the boundary which depended on a reference to the Atlantic, was intended to have a smaller extent than that which was made to depend upon the Sea. The Atlantic was certainly substituted for the Sea, not only in the treaty, but in the Commissions of the Governors of Quebec, showing an alteration of the boundary of their jurisdiction, whilst no change was made in the Commissions of the Governors of New Brunswick, because the boundary of their province depended upon that of Quebec. The highlands separating rivers that empty into the Atlantic Ocean, are by no means identical with the highlands separating the rivers that empty into the Sea. The Americans have urged that the northern range divides the rivers of the St. Lawrence from the Atlantic rivers, but it certainly does not separate the Penobscot branches north and east which flow into the Atlantic from the southern range; and the term "The rivers," of course means all the rivers, because, otherwise, such a considerable stream as the Penobscot would have been excepted specially. The southern range separated all the rivers which flow into the Atlantic, from all the rivers which flow into the St. Lawrence.

Had the Commissioners drawn the due north line from the western branch of the St. Croix, which formed the ancient boundary of Nova Scotia, instead of from the northern branch, the whole of the complicated and vexatious questions might have been evaded, and the claim urged by the United States might never have been heard. It was the doctrine of State rights alone which justified the rejection of the Netherlands compromise. The tract in dispute was indeed but seven million acres of river, mountain, and forest, but the northern boundary of this tract overlooked the course of the St. Lawrence, and carried American territory within a day's march of its stream, whilst the direct roads and communications between the Provinces east and west, would be placed inside American territory. To the Maine lumberers, however, this tract was not uninviting, and it became a debateable land, in which British colonists from New Brunswick, and American squatters, carried on a series of inroads and forcible settlements, which were fortunately unattended by actual bloodshed. Lord Palmerston, who in 1835 notified the refusal of the British Government to accept the Netherlands compromise, appointed Commissioners in 1839 to inquire into the state of the question upon the spot, and their report, which was handed to the United States Government in 1840, in the most absolute terms laid it down that the southern range was that intended by the treaty of 1783. Mr. Grattan, who was by no means unduly disposed to favour American pretensions, describes with terse propriety the disputes which now arose. "All on our side," he says, "was supercilious pride; on that of the United States, aggressive coarseness."

To Sir Robert Peel is due the praise of having taken a decided step to settle the north-eastern boundary. Lord Ashburton, received with considerable enthusiasm in the United States, was at once accepted by President Tyler, and for the better adjustment of the difficulty, it was arranged that he should be met by Mr. Webster in a spirit of perfect candour; that memoranda and despatches were to be dispensed with, and that every honest, straightforward exertion should be made on both sides to come to a satisfactory settlement of the vexed question. Lord Ashburton had, however, to encounter not only the Secretary of State, but the Commissioners of Maine and Massachusetts, among whom were Mr. Abbott Lawrence and Mr. Preble.

Mr. Grattan, who was actually invited to assist at the negotiations by the American Commissioners, and went to Washington as *amicus curiæ*, gives a most minute and interesting account of the whole of the proceedings, and states positively that Mr. Webster sent a confidential agent to the Commissioners, proposing a line far south of the St. John's River, before they had got further than New York, which gave great offence to Mr. Preble, by whose influence it was rejected. His pertinacity and the pomposity of Lawrence, with which we are well acquainted in England, were obstacles in the way of a calm discussion of adverse claims, but the other Commissioners are described as exceedingly forbearing, unassuming, and well-behaved.

At first Lord Ashburton seemed to make way with Mr. Webster, and to be on the point of obtaining a more favourable line than that proposed by the Netherlands compromise, but the British Commissioner had no special proof or absolute document to show that the highlands south of St. John indicated the boundary meant by the treaty of 1783. It was known that Dr. Franklin sent from Paris to Washington, at the time of making the treaty, a map on which was drawn a red ink line to show the boundary to Mr. Jefferson.

It is strange enough that, in the state of confusion caused by conflicting statements and contradictory documents, it should not have occurred to Lord Ashburton or to Mr. Grattan, who records his own anxious searches after Dr. Franklin's map, that a counterpart might have been readily found in Paris in the archives of the Foreign Office; but the fact was, Franklin's map could nowhere be found in the State Paper Department of Washington.

The production of that map with the red ink line must have placed the boundary question beyond the reach of controversy; in fact, the map of De Vergènnes could have been consulted at Paris, and the same red line might have been seen on it as that which was seen in Franklin's. Lord Aberdeen had for some inscrutable reason resolved that the boundary should be drawn so as to include the settlement of Madawaska on the St. John, within the British possessions, whilst the Commissioners were equally resolute not to except an inch south of the St. John itself; and the arrangement proposed by a small European monarch was regarded by the Americans as a proof that they were entitled to all that they had asked, and that the compromise was suggested to propitiate England.

The expectations which had been entertained of an immediate adjustment were followed by a renewal of angry feeling and political commotion. Lord Ashburton, after an unequal struggle with Webster and the Commissioners, in a controversial correspondence on which he had not very wisely entered, yielded in a spirit of honourable concession the claim of

Great Britain to the southern line of highlands. He was impressed somewhat, no doubt, by the vehemence and force of unanimous public opinion in America respecting the justice of their claim, the strong and general conviction felt that the country was in the right. Extended and accessible on every side, his mind could not resist the constant pressure of the audacious and penetrating weight of Webster's intellect, and he gradually gave way like a crumbling wall to the flood-tide of intense determination by which he was assailed. The middle of the St. John was accepted as the boundary, but instead of following the highlands overlooking the valley of the St. Lawrence, a line was determined upon sixty miles more to the south, which thus removes the United States frontier to a tolerable distance from the navigation of the river and the military control of the banks.

On both sides of the Atlantic this compromise was received with expressions of disgust and anger. The Americans, knowing themselves very well and Englishmen very little, declared that Daniel Webster had been bought.

In the land of liberty it is the custom of the representatives of the people to conduct their debates in secret whenever any question of public interest arises, and the Senate ratified the treaty by a large majority, after a long debate carried on with closed doors for several days.

Some time after the treaty had been signed, it turned out that Mr. Webster had all the time possessed a map on which Franklin's red line, tracing the boundary of 1783 south of the St. John, was distinctly marked.

The map in question was an authentic copy of one which was given to De Vergènes by Dr. Franklin himself when the treaty was made. Its existence had been made known to the President, to the Senate, and to all the Americans engaged in the negotiation. This map was no doubt the same as that which had disappeared from the State Department. Its existence was known to many people. It appears that Mr. Jared Sparkes, of Boston, found in the archives at Paris the following letter.

"*Paissey, Decr. 6th,* 1782.

"SIR,—I have the honour of returning herewith the map your Excellency sent me yesterday. I have marked with a strong red line, according to your desire, the limits of the United States as settled in the preliminaries between the British and American Plenipotentiaries.

"With great respect,
"I am, &c.,
"B. FRANKLIN."

This letter was addressed to the Count De Vergènnes, the French Minister. Mr. Sparkes, in fact, discovered the actual map of North America of 1746, and on it was drawn a strong red line throughout the entire boundary of the United States, answering exactly to Franklin's description. "Imagine," says Mr. Sparkes, "my surprise on discovering that this line runs wholly south of the St. John's, and between the head waters of that river and those of the Penobscot and Kennebec; in short, it is exactly the line contended for by **Great Britain**, except that it concedes more than is claimed."

When the secret debates of the Senate were published, it was seen that Mr. Rives, the Chairman of the Committee on Foreign Affairs, had fortified his argument against the rejection of this Ashburton line by quoting the existence of this map, and warning them of the risk and danger of a further search into the archives of Europe. In the debate that followed, Mr. Benton, eager to overthrow the value of Mr. Sparkes' discovery and of Mr. Rives's argument, produced a map from the Jefferson collection in the library of Congress, which contained a dotted line marking the boundary of the Government of Quebec under the proclamation of 1763, but strange to say, he overlooked the fact which was at once visible to every eye, that a strong red line, indicating the limits of the United States according to the Treaty of Peace, was traced across it, which coincided minutely and exactly with the boundary on Mr. Sparkes' map.

Those who wish for the most minute details respecting this map, may be referred to Mr. Grattan's work. The map of Baron Steiben, and that of Faden, coincide in a most remarkable manner in marking the limits of the United States.

It is worthy of note that Mr. Buchanan, the last President of the United States, did his very best to maintain the propriety of the deceit. Mr. Calhoun is supposed to have appreciated the importance of the discoveries, and to have felt the injury to American diplomacy which Mr. Webster's suppressions of truth might create on future occasions. The Americans actually made use of the weakness of the English Minister as an argument that they had been cheated themselves, and Mr. Webster's ability in concealing the truth was considered evidence that he had not gone far enough in the same line, and his reputation as a skilful and successful negotiator was considered not to stand very high. The action of Sir Robert Peel, however, prevented any endeavour to obtain the legitimate advantages which the discovery of these maps ought to have produced.

The decision arrived at affected the State of Maine and the pretensions of its people, but it had little to do with the prosperity or military strength of the whole of the Union: whilst it weakened Canada in its weakest point, and conferred most signal advantage on the only enemy it had to fear: it bit in to the substance of the Provinces, and at the same time cut the vein of communication with the sea for five long winter months. Strange that a line drawn upon a piece of paper by the hand of a man gathered to his fathers for so many years, should for a time at least decide so much of a nation's happiness and prosperity—for a time only, because it must soon be that the increasing power or failing resources of the United States, or of Canada, will cause a modification of the present frontier, more in accordance with the commercial and military exigencies of the two States. The Canadians feel that Imperial diplomacy has done them a great wrong, possibly very much as France feels in respect to her Rhenish boundary; but in a military point of view, perhaps the cession of Rouse's Point has been the most serious of all the circumstances affecting the relations for aggressive purposes of the United States with the Provinces.

In order that we may appreciate the importance of Mr. Webster's achievement, let us quote his own description of it in the great debate which took place in the Senate on the Washington Treaty. Mr. Webster, in noticing some of the many charges made against him in reference to the treaty, dealt with the question of military concession in the following manner:—

"Lord Palmerston (if he be the author of certain publications ascribed to him) says that all the important points were given up by Lord Ashburton to the United States. I might here state, too, that Lord Palmerston called the whole treaty 'the Ashburton capitulation,' declaring that it yielded everything that was of importance to Great Britain, and that all its stipulations were to the advantage of the United States, and to the sacrifice of the interests of England. But it is not on such general, and, I may add, such unjust statements, nor on any off-hand expressions used in debate, though in the roundest terms, that this question must turn. He speaks of this military road, but he entirely misplaces it. The road which runs from New Brunswick to Canada follows the north side of the St. John to the mouth of the Madawaska, and then, turning northwest, follows that stream to Lake Temiscoata, and thence proceeds over a depressed part of the highlands till it strikes the St. Lawrence 117 miles below Quebec. This is the road which has been always used, and there is no other.

"I admit that it is very convenient for the British Government to possess territory through which they may enjoy a road; it is of great value as an avenue of communication in time of peace; but as a military communication it is of no value at all. What business can an army ever have there? Besides, it is no gorge, no pass, no narrow defile, to be defended by a fort. If a fort should be built there, an army could, at pleasure, make a *détour* so as to keep out of the reach of its guns. It is very useful, I admit, in time of peace. But does not everybody know, military man or not, that unless there is a defile, or some narrow place through which troops must pass, and which a fortification will command, that a mere open road must, in time of war, be in the power of the strongest? If we retained by treaty the territory over which the road is to be constructed, and war came, would not the English take possession of it if they could? Would they be restrained by a regard to the treaty of Washington? I have never yet heard a reason adduced why this communication should be regarded as of the slightest possible advantage in a military point of view.

"But the circumstance to which I allude is, that, by a map published with the speech of the honourable member from Missouri, made in the Senate, on the question of ratifying the treaty, this well-known and long-used road is laid down, probably from the same source of error which misled Lord Palmerston, as following the St. John, on its south side, to the mouth of the St. Francis; thence along that river to its source, and thence, by a single bound, over the highlands to the St. Lawrence, near Quebec. This is all imagination. It is called the 'Valley Road.' Valley Road, indeed! Why, Sir, it is represented as running over the very ridge of the most inaccessible part of the highlands! It is made to cross abrupt and broken precipices, 2000 feet high! It is, at different points of its imaginary course, from fifty to a hundred miles distant from the real road.

"So much, Mr. President, for the great boon of military communication conceded to England. It is nothing more nor less than a common road, along streams and lakes, and over a country in great part rather flat. It then passes the heights to the St. Lawrence. If war breaks out, we shall take it if we can, and if we need it, of which there is not the slightest probability. It will never be protected by fortifications, and never can be. It will be just as easy to take it from England, in case of war, as it would be to keep possession of it, if it were our own.

"In regard to the defence of the heights, I shall dispose of that subject in a few words. There is a ridge of highlands which does approach the river St. Lawrence, although it is not true that it overlooks Quebec; on the contrary, the ridge is at the distance of thirty or forty miles.

"It is very natural that military men in England, or indeed in any part of Europe, should have attached great importance to these mountains. The great military authority of England, perhaps the highest living military authority, had served in India and on the European continent, and it was natural enough that he should apply European ideas of military defences to America. But they are quite inapplicable. Highlands such as these are not ordinarily found on the great battle-fields of Europe. They are neither Alps nor Pyrenees; they have no passes through them, nor roads over them, and never will have.

"Then there was another cause of misconception on this subject in England. In 1839 an *ex parte* survey was made, as I have said, by Colonel Mudge and Mr. Featherstonhaugh, if survey it could be called, of the region in the North of Maine, for the use of the British Government. I dare say Colonel Mudge is an intelligent and respectable officer; how much personal attention he gave the subject I do not know. As to Mr. Featherstonhaugh, he has been in our service, and his authority is not worth a straw. These two persons made a report, containing this very singular statement: That in the ridge of highlands nearest to the St. Lawrence, there was a great *hiatus* in one particular place, a gap of thirty or forty miles, in which the elevation did not exceed fifty feet. This is certainly the strangest statement that ever was made. Their whole report gave but one measurement by the barometer, and that measurement stated the height of 1200 feet. A survey and map were made the following year by our own commissioners, Messrs. Graham and Talcott, of the Corps of Topographical Engineers, and Professor Renwick, of Columbia College. On this map, the very spot where this gap was said to be situated is dotted over thickly with figures, showing heights varying from 1200 to 2000 feet, and forming one rough and lofty ridge, marked by abrupt and almost perpendicular precipices. When this map and report of Messrs. Mudge and Featherstonhaugh were published, the British authorities saw that this alleged gap was laid down as an indefensible point, and it was probably on that ground alone that they desired a line east of that ridge, in order that they might guard against access of a hostile power from the United States. But in truth there is no such gap; our engineers proved this, and we quite well understood it when agreeing to the boundary. Any man of common sense, military or not, must therefore now see, that nothing can be more imaginary or unfounded than the idea that any importance attaches to the possession of these heights.

"Sir, there are two old and well-known roads to Canada; one by way of Lake Champlain and the Richelieu, to Montreal — this is the route which armies have traversed so often, in different periods of our history. The other leads from the Kennebec river to the sources of the Chaudière and the Du Loup, and so to Quebec—this last was the track of Arnold's march. East of this, there is no practicable communication for troops between Maine and Canada, till we get to the Madawaska. We had before us a report from General Wool, while this treaty was under negotiation, in which that intelligent officer declares that it is perfectly idle to think of fortifying any point east of this road. East of Arnold's track it is a mountain region, through which no army can possibly pass into Canada. With General Wool was associated, in this examination, Major Graham, whom I have already mentioned. His report to General Wool, made in the year 1838, clearly points out the Kennebec and Chaudière road as the only practicable route for an army between Maine and Quebec. He was subsequently employed as a commissioner in the *ex parte* surveys of the United States. Being an engineer officer of high character for military knowledge and scientific accuracy, his opinion had the weight it ought to have, and which will be readily given to it by all who know him. His subsequent and still more thorough acquaintance with this mountain range, in its whole extent, has only confirmed the judgment which he had previously formed. And, Sir, this avenue to Canada, this practicable avenue, and only practicable avenue east of that by way of Lake Champlain, is left now just as it was found by the treaty. The treaty does not touch it, nor in any manner affect it.

"But I must go further. I said that the treaty of Washington was a treaty of equivalents, in which it was expected that each party should give something and receive something. I am now willing to meet any gentleman, be he a military man or not, who will make the assertion, that, in a military point of view, the greatest advantages derived from that treaty are on the side of Great Britain. It was on this point that I wished to say something in reply to an honourable member from New York, who will have it that in this treaty England supposes that she got the advantage of us. Sir, I do not think the military advantages she obtained by it are worth a rush. But even if they were, if she had obtained advantages of the greatest value, would it not have been fair in the member from New York to state, nevertheless, whether there were not equivalent military advantages obtained on our side, in other parts of the line? Would it not have been candid and proper in him, when adverting to the military advantages obtained by England, in a communication between New Brunswick and Canada, if such advantages there were, to have stated, on the other hand, and at the same time, our recovery of Rouse's Point, at the outlet of Lake Champlain? an advantage which overbalanced all others, forty times told. I must be allowed to say, that I certainly never expected that a member from New York, above all other men, should speak of this treaty as conferring military advantages on Great Britain without full equivalents.

I listened to it, I confess, with utter astonishment. A distinguished senator from that State saw at the time, very clearly, the advantage gained by this treaty to the United States and to New York. He voted willingly for its ratification, and he never will say that Great Britain obtained a balance of advantages in a military point of view.

"Why, how is the State of New York affected by this treaty? Sir, is not Rouse's Point perfectly well-known, and admitted, by every military man, to be the key of Lake Champlain? It commands every vessel passing up or down the lake, between New York and Canada. It had always been supposed that this point lay some distance south of the parallel of 45°, which was our boundary line with Canada, and therefore was within the United States; and, under this supposition, the United States purchased the land, and commenced the erection of a strong fortress. But a more accurate survey having been made in 1818, by astronomers on both sides, it was found that the parallel of 45° ran south of this fortress, and thus Rouse's Point, with the fort upon it, was found to be in the British dominions. This discovery created, as well it might, a great sensation here. None knows this better than the honourable member from South Carolina, who was then at the head of the Department of War. As Rouse's Point was no longer ours, we sent our engineers to examine the shores of the lake, to find some other place or places which we might fortify. They made a report on their return, saying that there were two other points some distance south of Rouse's Point, one called Windmill Point, on the east side of the lake, and the other called Stony

Point, on the west side, which it became necessary now to fortify, and they gave an estimate of the probable expense. When this treaty was in process of negotiation, we called for the opinion of military men respecting the value of Rouse's Point, in order to see whether it was highly desirable to obtain it. We had their report before us, in which it was stated that the natural and best point for the defence of the outlet of Lake Champlain was Rouse's Point. In fact, anybody might see that this was the case who would look at the map. The point projects into the narrowest passage by which the waters of the lake pass into the Richelieu. Any vessel passing into or out of the lake, must come within point-blank range of the guns of a fortress erected on this point; and it ran out so far that any such vessel must approach the fort, head on, for several miles, so as to be exposed to a raking fire from the battery, before she could possibly bring her broadside to bear upon the fort at all. It was very different with the points farther south. Between them the passage was much wider; so much so, indeed, that a vessel might pass directly between the two, and not be in reach of point-blank shot from either."

Mr. Dickinson, of New York, here interposed, to ask whether the Dutch line did not give us Rouse's Point.

"Certainly not. It gave us a semicircular line, running round the fort, but not including what we had possessed before. And besides, we had rejected the Dutch line, and the whole point now clearly belonged to England. It was all within the British territory.

"I was saying that a vessel might pass between Windmill Point and Stony Point, and be without the range of both, till her broadside could be brought to bear upon either of them. The forts would be entirely independent of each other, and, having no communication, could not render each other the least assistance in case of attack. But the military men told us there was no sort of question that Rouse's Point was extremely desirable as a point of military defence. This is plain enough, and I need not spend time to prove it. Of one thing I am certain, that the true road to Canada is by the way of Lake Champlain. That is the old path. I take to myself the credit of having said here, thirty years ago, speaking of the mode of taking Canada, that, when an American woodsman undertakes to fell a tree, he does not begin by lopping off the branches, but strikes his axe at once into the trunk. The trunk, in relation to Canada, is Montreal, and the River St. Lawrence down to Quebec; and so we found in the last war. It is not my purpose to scan the propriety of military measures then adopted, but I suppose it to have been rather accidental and unfortunate that we began the attack in Upper Canada. It would have been better military policy, as I suppose, to have pushed our whole force by the way of Lake Champlain, and made a direct movement on Montreal; and though we might thereby have lost the glories of the battles of the Thames and of Lundy's Lane, and of the sortie from Fort Erie, yet we should have won other laurels of equal, and perhaps greater value, at Montreal. Once successful in this movement, the whole country above would have fallen into our power. Is not this evident to every gentleman?

"Rouse's Point is the best means of defending both the ingress into the lake, and the exit from it. And I say now, that on the whole frontier of the State of New York, with the single exception of the Narrows below the city, there is not a point of equal importance. I hope this government will last for ever; but if it does not, and if, in the judgment of Heaven, so great a calamity shall befall us as the rupture of this Union, and the State of New York shall thereby be thrown upon her own defences, I ask, is there a single point, except the Narrows, the possession of which she will so much desire? No, there is not one. And how did we obtain this advantage for her? The parallel of 45° north was established by the treaty of 1783 as our boundary with Canada in that part of the line. But, as I have stated, that line was found to run south of Rouse's Point. And how did we get back this precious possession? By running a semicircle like that of the King of the Netherlands? No; we went back to the old line, which had always been supposed to be the true line, and the establishment of which gave us not only Rouse's Point, but a strip of land containing some thirty or forty thousand acres between the parallel of 45° and the old line.

"The same arrangement gave us a similar advantage in Vermont; and I have never heard that the constituents of my friend near me made any complaint of the treaty. That State got about sixty or seventy thousand acres, including several villages, which would otherwise have been left on the British side of the line. We received Rouse's Point, and this additional land, as one of the equivalents for the cession of territory made in Maine. And what did we do for New Hampshire? There was an ancient dispute as to which was the north-westernmost head of the Connecticut River. Several streams were found, either of which might be insisted on as the true boundary. But we claimed that which is called Hall's Stream. This had not formerly been allowed; the Dutch award did not give to New Hampshire what she claimed; and Mr. Van Ness, our commissioner, appointed under the Treaty of Ghent, after examining the ground, came to the conclusion that we were not entitled to Hall's Stream. I thought that we were so entitled, although I admit that Hall's Stream does not join the Connecticut River till after it has passed the parallel of 45°. By the Treaty of Washington this demand was agreed to, and it gave New Hampshire 100,000 acres of land. I do not say that we obtained this wrongfully; but I do say that we got that which Mr. Van Ness had doubted our right to. I thought the claim just, however, and the line was established accordingly. And here let me say, once for all, that, if we had gone for arbitration, we should inevitably have lost what the treaty gave to Vermont and New York; because all that was clear matter of cession, and not adjustment of doubtful boundary."

Unfortunately Mr. Webster but too well described our share of the advantages obtained by this "treaty of equivalents." The consequences to us in a war might be more disastrous than those he indicated.

CHAPTER XVII.

The Acadian Confederation — Union is Strength—The Provinces—New Brunswick—The Temperature—Trade of St John—Climate and Agriculture of Nova Scotia—Prince Edward Island—Newfoundland—The Red River District—Assiniboia—The Red River Valley—Minnesota and the West—The Hudson's Bay Company—Their Territory—The North-West Regions—Climate of Winnipeg Basin — Its Area — Finances of the Confederation — Imports, Exports, and Tonnage—Proposed Federal Constitution—Lessons from the American Struggle.

WE have now seen the dangers which threaten Canada, we have to some extent examined the means of resisting them, and have followed the process by which a severe injury was inflicted on her powers of defence. Mr. Webster was a grand specimen of unscrupulous intelligence—he was a colossal " Yankee." It will be observed that he regarded the acquisitions so dexterously made—*quocunque modo rem*—as valuable on account of their military capabilities—that he took the highest point accessible to the American mind when he showed that his work could be made available for the annoyance and injury of Great Britain. In so far he betrayed—if indeed there is any deception in the matter—the animating principle of American political life. Let any public man prove that he has hurt the English power or affronted it—that he has damnified its commerce and lowered its prestige, and the popular sentiment will applaud him, no matter the agency by which his purpose was effected. Recent events have greatly inflamed the spirit which always burned against us. The very events which have broken up the Union may resolve its fragments into a new combination more formidable and more aggressive.

The course open to Canada, which may feel once more the force of that permanent principle in the American mind, is plain. Great Britain may be too far off. She may be too much engaged to be able to aid Canada efficiently and fully. But on the borders of Canada there are provinces with great resources and a great future, which have hitherto been prevented by various considerations from welding themselves into a Confederation. The time has come now in the white heat of American strife for the adoption of the process. The Confederation of States with divers interests under a weak executive has fallen to pieces. All the more reason for a Confederation of States with common interests and with one governing principle. If we accept the common governing principle of all the Colonies and Provinces to be their attachment to Monarchical institutions, any pressure from the influences of Republican institutions can but consolidate their union.

Under the circumstances in which the various distinct dependencies of the British Crown in the Continent of North America find themselves placed, it is not surprising that the idea of a Confederation for the purposes of common defence and military corroboration should have arisen. It is surprising that it should have floated about so long, and have stirred men to action so feebly. I think it is the first notion that occurs to a stranger visiting Canada and casting about for a something to put in place of the strength which distant England cannot, and Canadians will not, afford.

At least, there is no sign as yet that the Canadians will quite arouse from a sleep which no fears disturb, although they hear the noise of robbers. They will not prepare for war, because they wish for peace, and it is plain enough that if war should come instead of peace, England would be too late to save them, because she would be too far. Now, let it not be supposed that any confederation of the Canadas and British North American provinces would yield such an increase of force as would enable the collective or several members of it to resist the force of the Republic of the Northern American United States—at least, not just now. But in the very conflict in which the Northern and Southern Confederations are engaged, we see the vast energy and resources of a union of States in war time as compared with the action of States not so joined:—France, Great Britain, Turkey, and Sardinia were associated in the war with Russia, but their power would have been much greater had they acted under a common head. There is in every association of the States the danger of ultimate convulsions, and of death itself, whenever the Constitution and ideas of one State differ from those of another: for the difference of constitution and ideas is sure to produce soon a conflict of interests and opinions which the bond of Federation cannot compress. In the two Canadas there are certain opposing principles at work which have interfered with harmonious action at times. These might receive greater vitality and power on each side if the cohesion of the British dependencies were not complete. The religious questions which now are mixed with questions of race would perhaps acquire development, and become more active and more mischievous. But the actual positive visible dangers of non-Confederation are more weighty than those which may come by-and-by from the adoption of a common central government subject to the Crown. Setting out with the principle of submission to the Throne—with the recognition of the sovereignty of the monarch of Great Britain and Ireland—with the full acknowledgment of the rights and prerogatives pertaining to the Crown—with the charters of their several and collective liberties in their possession, the only great schism to be apprehended is one which might arise from the exercise of Parliamentary control over the action of the Confederation, because colonists will never admit that the Parliament can stand in the place of the Crown. Let us take a glance at the vast area, and consider the importance of the various colonies which own now no bond of connection, except a common obedience to the Queen, in order that we may appreciate their strength as a Confederation.

The Province of New Brunswick contains just 28,000 square miles; it lies between 45° and 48° lat. (north), and 63° 45' and 67° 50' long. (west), washed on the east by the waters of the Gulf of St. Lawrence, and on the south by those of the Bay of Fundy. It has a very extensive seaboard, not less than two-thirds being maritime; whilst on the west it is bounded by the frontier of the State of Maine, and on the north by Lower Canada. The population in 1851 was 193,000, and it probably is not less now than 225,000 souls. The boastfulness of the Americans, and more especially of New Englanders, in all that relates to their country, causes us to overlook the progress of our own colonies, and we shall be surprised to find the increase of people in New Brunswick has been greater than that of Vermont, Maine, or New Hampshire, by an average of 10 per cent. within the decade up to 1851. The Government is vice-monarchical and parliamentary; the Lieutenant-Governor of the Province being Commander-in-Chief, Admiral, and Chancellor. His ministers are the Executive Council, consisting of nine members, whose tenure of office depends on the will of the people, inasmuch as they must retire on a vote of want of confidence. The Parliament consists of the Legislative Council, which is somewhat analogous to the House of Peers. It is composed of 21 members, who are appointed by the Crown *durante placito*, but who usually hold office for life. Although the Peers of Parliament are in one sense nominated by the Crown, they are legislators *durante vitâ*, and cannot be removed from their functions by the Crown, and in other respects there are defects in an analogy between them and the House of Lords. The House of Assembly, consisting of 41 members, is elected every four years by the people of the fourteen counties, and of the city of St. John. The House levies taxes and duties, and regulates the expenditure and internal affairs of the Province; but the Legislative Council may reject all its measures except those relating to money matters, and the assent of the Governor-General is needed to all measures whatever. But it does not follow that the consent of Council, Assembly, and Lieutenant-Governor will do more than stamp the measure with the popular and official *imprimatur* in the eyes of the Home Government, because Her Majesty in Council may reject any law whatever. It is rather in theory than in practice, however, that such an exercise of prerogative exists;

but in case of any marked difference of opinion between the Home Government and the Colonial Legislature, it is obvious that such a power, however consonant with monarchical right and tradition, might cause serious antagonism and create wide breaches. The risk of such disturbing influences would, of course, be diminished by the action of a general government.

It is little more than 100 years since a number of English settlers and colonists, then loyal, coming from Massachusetts, sailed from Newbury Fort to the coast of New Brunswick, which had been ceded by France to the British in 1713. Constantly menaced by the French Canadians, the few English who represented the Crown could scarcely be considered to hold the most attenuated possession of the Province, until the French were obliged finally to cede all claims to the possession of an acknowledged nationality in British North America. The English maintained that the whole tract of country now known as Nova Scotia and New Brunswick belonged to the Crown by virtue of the discoveries of Sebastian Cabot; but the French were the first to found permanent settlements, and certainly gave good reason why Acadia, as they termed the district, despite its frosts and snows and long lugubrious winters, should belong to the *fleur-de-lys*. As soon as Wolfe's victory had established the power of England, the enterprising spirit of the New Englanders led them to undertake settlements in these neglected regions. They carried with them what they had derived from the old country—a love of law, not of litigation; the forms of justice in the courts which administered its substance:—a magistracy, a police, a moral life and social liberty; these were possessed by the settlers at a time when the vast majority of the people of Ireland was deprived of any semblance of such rights; and when Scotland, unsuccessful in her last effort for legitimacy and the Divine right of kings, was just recovering from the swoon into which she had fallen as the last volleys rolled away from Culloden.

The New Englanders who settled Maugerville and civilised Sunbury were loyal to the Crown in the revolt of the colonies; they formed a nucleus round which gathered many of the New England Tories and their families, so that in 1783 it was considered expedient by the Government to locate those who were called loyalists, and who shook the dust off their feet at the door of the New Republic, along the cleared settlements adjoining the Bay of Fundy and the water of St. John. It is strange that the first newspaper should have been printed by these outcasts at a time when there were scarcely half-a-dozen journals known in the mother country; but the peculiar circumstances under which these immigrants were placed no doubt developed the energies of a press which was not shackled by any political censorship. The wealth of the people lay around them; their mines were in the forest, and the axe provided them with currency. To Sir Guy Carlton, the first Governor, when New Brunswick received a distinct Charter and a new Constitution and was separated from Nova Scotia, in 1788, must be conceded the credit of having nursed for twenty years, with singular care and success, the infancy of the colony :—a succession of Presidents or Governors and Councillors, whose names are reproduced in the history of the American colonies,—such men as Beverley, Robinson, Putman, Winslow, and Ludlow,—succeeded in the charge, and gradually developed the resources of the rising community.

Fire has wrought more than one great wrong to this land of frost and snow. Yet it would not be just to describe New Brunswick as a Siberia. From Christmas to March the country is tolerably well provided with a coating of snow. From April to May ploughing and seed time last, and before October the harvests are generally gathered in. A glorious autumn yields to the rainfalls of November, and these in their turn harden to sleet and snow in December; but, after all, nearly seven months give space for sowing, ploughing, reaping, and saving. The New Brunswickers, indeed, believe that the very severity of the frost in winter tends to render the cultivation of the land more easy than it is in Britain; and certainly rainfalls, and all the variableness of climate, do more injury in England than they do in New Brunswick. The greatest ranges of temperature are in the Gulf of St. Lawrence, where they reach from 20° below zero to 90° above it; the highest temperature at St. John may be reckoned at 86°, the lowest at 14°. There are about 180 clear days and 120 cloudy days in the year, and the snow-storms rarely last more than two days at a time. Now here is a region to which one would think the bedrenched Highlander, the betaxed Englishman, and much-vexed Irishman would resort in myriads. And there is land for many. At least 6,000,000 acres of land suited for crops and wood settlements are still to be disposed of. For half-a-crown a man may buy an acre of land, but of that sum only $7\frac{1}{2}d.$ is demanded on sale, and the remainder may be paid in instalments extending over three years. The sales of the country lands are monthly. If the settler likes to pay on the spot he can have his land for 2s. an acre. Think of that, conacre men of Tipperary and Leitrim! Think of that, farmers of the Lothians, or tenants of the Highland straths! Shall I ask the men of Dorsetshire and East Gloucester to think of it too? Nor need they fear to change their mode of life, except it be for the better, after the first rude work of labour is done; nor need they fear to suffer from climate or disease. Typhus will cease to kill—fever and dysentery to decimate. And if the settler has kinsmen and friends willing to join with him, he can claim for himself and each of them 100 acres of land, and pay for it by the work of road-making in the new country, so that in four years, if the work set by the Commissioners be executed, each man who has been one year resident and has brought ten acres into cultivation, becomes, *ipso facto*, owner of the whole lot of 100 acres. Now this is in a country which has been described by no incompetent witness, not as the peer of any region on earth in the beauty of wood and water, but as the superior of the best. The St. John flows in all its grandeur through the midst of the province, and the Restigouché gives a charm of scenery to the forest not to be surpassed. Lakes and streams open up dell, valley, and mountain pass. Every creek in the much-indented coast swarms with fish. The Bay of Fundy abounds with codfish and pollock, hake, haddock, shad, herring, halibut, mackerel, eels, skate, and many other kinds of fish. The mouths of the rivers swarm with salmon, trout, striped basse, gaspereaux, shad, and white trout. The Gulf of St. Lawrence and the Bay of

Chaleurs yield nearly every description of valuable fish, as well as lobsters, crabs, oysters, and other shellfish. The Province receives nearly 100,000*l.* a year in exchange for the fish packed in ice, or cured and exported to foreign countries. Its wealth in timber is incalculable, because the value rises gradually with the demand for the produce of its forests all over the world, and, with prudent management, these forests may be considered as inexhaustible. Coal of a bituminous character has been worked for some years past in several districts; iron, manganese, lead, and copper, also exist in considerable quantities, and the mineral produce of the Province will no doubt add much to its importance as the works receive greater development.

Although the trade of shipbuilding does not show a regular increase, the size of the vessels built at St. John and Miramichi has been increasing. Upwards of 100 ships were launched at these ports in 1860, with a measurement of 41,000 tons, and were worth upwards of 320,000*l.* Various branches of trade have obtained respectable dimensions and are growing steadily. Fredericton, the capital of the Province, is situated on the St. John, eighty-two miles from the sea, where the navigation for sea-going ships may be regarded as at an end. The number of great lakes which are available for internal commerce and transport complete the facilities offered by the river system and by the main roads, the latter of which have been liberally promoted by the Province. The water power of the colony is boundless. Education is provided by the Legislature, so that the poorest man can give his children the advantage of a sound instruction almost without cost. Religion is free, and the voluntary system mitigates the animosity of sects. Emigrants from the South of Ireland have found here all the conditions of prosperity, and have turned them to good account. Scotch and English thrive exceedingly. Indeed, if it were not that the greater clamour and bustle of the United States had succeeded in overpowering the appeals of New Brunswick to the favour of the emigrant, many thousands of our countrymen would have there found the ease and comfort which they have sought in vain under the rule of the Republic. The very name, New Brunswick, has no doubt repelled settlers. A New Brunswick ship they know nothing of even if they see one, and the name itself rarely reaches their ears.

Nova Scotia formerly comprised the Province of New Brunswick, but is now reduced to the length of 256 miles, and the breadth of 100 miles. The island of Cape Breton, which belongs to it, is 100 miles long, and 72 broad. The area of Nova Scotia and Cape Breton is over 18,000 square miles. The population is estimated at 370,000, the Census of 1861 having given 330,860 and the ratio of increase having been on an average of four per cent. per annum; but emigrants are rarely attracted to the colony. In 1861, of the people, 294,000 were native Nova Scotians, 16,000 were of Scottish, 9,000 of Irish, 3,000 of English origin; France, which founded the colony, had only 88 representatives on land. The English Church had 48,000 members, the Scotch Church numbered 88,000, the Church of Rome 80,000; there were 56,000 Baptists, 34,000 Wesleyans, and, wonderful to say, only 3 Deists. When it is considered that the coal-fields of Nova

Scotia are the finest in the world, that her mining wealth is extraordinary, that her seas, lakes, and rivers teem with fish, that her forests yield the finest timber, that the soil gives an ample return to the farmer, and the earth is full of mineral resources, it is surprising that emigrants of limited means have not been tempted to try their fortune, in spite of the threatening skies and somewhat rigid winters. Nearly five millions and a half acres of land are still in the hands of the Crown, of which upwards of four million acres are open for settlement, and the average price is about 1s. 8d. an acre. From a very trustworthy work prepared by Messrs. Hind, Keefer, Hodgins, Robb, Perley, and the Rev. Wm. Murray, to which I am indebted for much valuable information, it would appear that the climate of Nova Scotia is by no means so severe as it is reported to be, both in Great Britain and the United States. Though, at some seasons, the weather is very severe, as compared with England, Ireland, the South of Scotland, and a great portion of the United States of America, still it is more conducive to health than the milder but more humid corresponding seasons in those countries. The length and severity of Nova Scotia winters are greatly compensated by the mildness and beauty of autumn—which is protracted, not unfrequently, into the middle of December—as well as by the months of steady sleighing which follow. The extreme of cold is 24° Fahr. below zero; the extreme of heat, 95° above, in the shade. These extremes have not been often attained to of late years. The mean temperature of the year is 43°. There are about 100 days in which the temperature is above 70° in summer. There are about twenty nights in the year in which the temperature is below zero. The coldest season is from the last week of December till the first week of March. The following table exhibits the annual mean temperature of several European cities, as compared with Halifax, Nova Scotia, and Toronto, C.W.:—

Latitude.		Fahrenheit.
44° 40′ . . .	Halifax . . .	43·8
43 39 . . .	Toronto . . .	44·4
52 31 . . .	Berlin . . .	47·5
53 23 . . .	Dublin . . .	49·1
50 7 . . .	Frankfort . .	49·5
49 39 . . .	Cherbourg . . .	52·1

MEAN SUMMER TEMPERATURE.

	Fahrenheit.
Halifax	62·0
Toronto	64·5
Greenwich	60·9
Berlin	63·2
Cherbourg	61·9

The annual quantity of rain which falls is about forty-one inches. Of this quantity about six and a half inches fall in the form of snow. The annual depth of snow is eight and a half feet. Much of this quantity of snow is not allowed to rest long in its solid form. There are about 114 days of rain on the average in each year; much of this occurs in winter. The average number of days of snow in each year is about sixty. Violent tempests are not of frequent occurrence in Nova Scotia. The prevailing winds are the south-west, west, and north-west. In summer the north, north-west, and west winds are cool and dry. In winter they are cold and piercing. The south and south-west are mild—agreeable—delightful. The north-east brings the greatest snow-storms; the east and south-east the most disagreeable rain-storms. Spring commences in

Nova Scotia with the beginning of April. Seed-time and planting continue till the middle of June. Summer begins with the latter part of June, and embraces July and August. Vegetation is very rapid in the middle and western parts of the province, where the hay crop, and usually nearly all the grain crops, are harvested by the last week of August or first week of September. Autumn is the finest season in Nova Scotia. It is mild, serene, and cool enough to be bracing, and the atmosphere is of a purity that renders it peculiarly exhilarating and health-giving. The "Indian summer" occurs sometimes as late as the middle of November, and lasts from three to ten days. The winter in Nova Scotia may be said to comprise about four months. It begins, some seasons, with the 1st of December, and runs into the month of April. In other seasons it begins in the middle of December and ends with the last of March. The mean temperature of spring is 49°; of summer, 62°; of autumn, 35°; of winter, 22°. Similarity in agricultural productions furnishes a very fair criterion for the comparison of the climates of different countries. Wheat, rye, oats, barley, buckwheat, Indian corn, potatoes, turnips, mangel-wurzel, tomatoes, and other roots and grains grow in abundance and perfection in Nova Scotia. Apples, pears, plums, cherries, and a multitude of smaller garden-fruits attain the utmost perfection. In some sections of the country peaches and grapes ripen in the open air. The climate of Nova Scotia is highly favourable both to health and length of days. Men and women frequently attain to the age of eighty years with the full possession of their mental faculties, and in excellent bodily health. It is not unusual to find men enjoying good health at ninety;

and not a few reach one hundred years, while some pass that extreme boundary. Let the proportion of deaths to population in Nova Scotia be compared with that in Great Britain and the State of Rhode Island :—

  Nova Scotia, 1 in 70·71, or less than 1½ per cent.
  Rhode Island, 1 in 46·11, or more than 2 „
  Great Britain, 1 in 44·75, or more than 2 „

The climate of Nova Scotia is not noted for the generation of any disease peculiar to itself. Diphtheria has, of late years, been its most terrible scourge.

Prince Edward Island—called so after the father of Queen Victoria—is another member of the great group of British colonies and dependencies. This island, which is about 130 miles long and 30 miles broad, has less than 100,000 inhabitants. It contained less than 5,000 souls in 1770, when it was separated from the government of Nova Scotia, and was erected into an independent province under unfavourable circumstances, arising out of the unfortunate conditions which were made when the land was allotted to the original proprietors. The early history of the colony afforded a remarkable exemplification of wrong-doing with good intentions, and the errors of the first English rulers who regulated the settlement of the province were not atoned for till many years of patient effort on the part of the people had been devoted to a removal of abuses. The island is under a Governor named by the Crown, whose Cabinet consists of an Executive Council of nine, selected from the Legislative Council and from the House of Assembly, the former consisting of twelve, the latter of thirty members, elected by the people.

Newfoundland is 420 miles long, and has an extreme breadth of 300 miles. The population is now about 130,000. Notwithstanding its name, there is reason to believe that it was known to Icelanders and Norwegians, to Vikings and Danes, four centuries before Cabot came upon his Bonavista. The early history of our connection with this great island is not creditable to those who had influence with the home authorities. In 1832, following the principle of universal suffrage, which was considered applicable to a colony, though it was rejected at home, a Legislative system was erected on the basis of manhood franchise, the only qualification being that the voter should have been a year in the same house. The Governor, who is of course a representative and nominee of the Crown, is assisted by an Executive Council of five members, and the Parliament consists of a Legislative Council of twelve and a House of Assembly of thirty members.

There exists on the west of Canada a vast region which may, perhaps, become great and flourishing in less time than the districts which, inhabited by red men and wild beasts in 1776, now form some of the most important of the North and South American States.

It is one of the very greatest of the evils connected with our parliamentary system, that small or local interests at home are likely to receive attention in preference to the largest general interests of dependencies. The Colonial Office is a sort of buffer between Parliament and the shocks of colonial aggressions and demands; and the Chancellor of the Exchequer can at any time find easy means of squelching any tendency in the chancellor of a barbarian administration "to dip his finger" into the Imperial purse. Now, when "the People of Red River settlement" address a memorial to the British and Canadian Governments with the view of obtaining a road to open up the wonderfully fine country they inhabit to British subjects and to commerce, without dependency on the United States, it may so happen that at the period in question the smallest claim of a metropolitan borough shall be considered of far greater preponderance; nor will the Government or the Colonial Office at any time be much disposed to irritate a friendly member who is inimical to colonies, or to provoke the animosity of economists, for an object which is as intangible and incomprehensible to the mass of Parliament as a project to run a railway to Eutopia, or to connect Timbuctoo with China. Mr. Sandford Fleming, who has been selected as the agent of these very settlers, has set forth their case with much ability; but he will scarce become the Lesseps of this overland Suez, unless some members of the House, who really look beyond the interests of the day, and take heed for the future of the Empire, can be induced to listen to his facts and arguments. In 1863 a statement was submitted by that gentleman to Lord Monck in elucidation of the memorial of the settlers, which contains most interesting facts and some valuable arguments. Among the works of good Governments the making of roads and securing of easy means of intercommunication among the people subject to them must ever be of paramount importance. The people of Red River ask for the opening of the Lake Superior route to British Columbia, and to have a telegraphic line established, to both of which objects they will contribute to the best of their ability. The point of British territory nearest to the Red River settlement by water is on the northern shore of Lake Superior, 400 miles distant; and the intervening distance can only be traversed by a combined system of "portages" and canoe voyages so difficult and tedious as in effect to bar the access of commercial enterprise, and to chill any spirit but that of adventurous geography, amateur travel, or the search after gold and game—thus, in fact, constituting obstacles which are well described as "practically exiling the settlers for the last two generations." The route proposed for the links which are to connect the exiles with the world would be a part of the great project to connect the shores of the Atlantic and Pacific within the British possessions; and it is maintained that the favourable character of the Red River district for such a road removes the objections which might be formed on the ground of distance and difficulty. The Hudson's Bay Company used the Pigeon River route, which runs along by the boundary of the United States, and is therefore not desirable in case of hostilities, and the Kaministiguia route, called so from the river of that name. Mr. Fleming, taking up the suggestions of Mr. Dawson in his report to the Canadian Government, recommends the creation of a territorial road from some point in connection with the railway system, such as Ottawa, to Nipigon Bay on Lake Superior, which would be ample as a trading port, whence a stage and steamboat communication could be established by making 197 miles of roads and two dams—one at the outlet of Dog Lake, and the other at Little Falls; or, by making 232 miles of road, and a couple of locks at Fort Francis, and a dam, the route might be reduced to 273 miles of water, if the road were pushed on to Savanne River. It must be remembered that the Americans have already established a route by Chicago; but an examination of the distances from Toronto shows that the Lake Superior route would save no less than 715 miles of rail, 35 of water, and 58 of road. The American route, however, possesses the advantage of having already 820 miles of rail, of which 514 carry the traveller to Chicago from Toronto, and 306 convey him from Chicago to Prairie La Crosse; whereas there is only a length of 95 miles open in Canada, from Toronto westwards to Collingwood. There is also an American route by Detroit, Milwaukee, and La Crosse to Fort Garry, 1696 miles long, but that is still 646 miles longer than the communication which could be made by means of 232 miles of road, the construction of a dam and the locks in question. Labour might be tempted by offering, as is suggested, blocks of 100 acres to settlers on condition of their giving ten days' work in each year for ten years on the road, and thus preparing it for a railway track; but the settlers must be more patient and easily satisfied than their language now indicates, if they are content with the prospect of such a tedious fulfilment of their wishes. They are willing to open a road 100 miles long to the Lake of Woods if England or Canada will guarantee the rest of the road to Lake Superior; and they believe such a road would rapidly fill Central British America with an industrious loyal people, and counteract the influence of the North American Republics. Whether the grand confederation which they foresee of flourishing provinces from Vancouver's Island to Nova Scotia, commanding the Atlantic and the Pacific, and keeping in line the boundaries of the Republicans, be ever realised in our day, it is plain that the people will neither be British nor loyal if they are neglected. The Americans have long been turning their eyes in the direction of these regions. Mr. Sibley, the last Governor of Minnesota, ordered Mr. James W. Taylor to obtain reliable information relative to the physical aspects and other facts connected with the British possessions on the line of the overland route from Pembina, viâ the Red River settlement and the Saskatchewan Valley, to Frazer's River. That gentleman's report was presented by Governor Ramsay to the Legislature of the State in 1860, with a recommendation to their attention as "relating to matters which concern in a great degree the future growth and development of our State." Mr. Taylor was received by Mr. McTavish at the Selkirk settlement with every respect and consideration. He found the British colony of Assiniboia prosperous and flourishing. Respecting that colony he says:—

"Of the present community of ten thousand souls, about five thousand are competent, at this moment, to assume any civil or social responsibility which may be imposed upon them. The accumulations from the fur trade during fifty years, with few excitements or opportunities of expenditure, have secured general prosperity, with frequent instances of affluence; while the numerous churches and schools sustain a high standard of morality and intelligence.

"The people of Selkirk fully appreciate the advantages of communication with the Mississippi River and Lake Superior through the State of Minnesota. They are anxious for the utmost facilities of trade and intercourse. The navigation of the Red River by a steamboat during the summer of 1859 was universally recognised as marking a new era in their annals. This public sentiment was pithily expressed by the remark: 'In 1851 the Governor of Minnesota visited us; in 1859 comes a steamboat; and ten years more will bring the railroad!'"

The persons who expressed that sentiment differed entirely from the memorialists already mentioned; but it must be that the Selkirk people, if neglected, will incline towards the hand which is stretched out to them across the waste, no matter whence it comes. "Most amicable relations" do no doubt "exist between the trading post at Port Garry and Kitson's Station at St. Boniface;" but long as they may endure—and I trust they may be perpetual—they will not amount to a preference for Republican institutions, if the mother country seeks to secure the settlers by the most tender or subtle link of interest or regard. What change may be made in respect to the jurisdiction and powers of the Hudson's Bay Company by the home authorities must depend for the time on circumstances; but the actual settlers seem to hope that the rumours which attributed to Lord Derby's Government the intention of organising a colony, bounded by Lakes Superior and Winnipeg on the east, by the Rocky Mountains on the west, by the American frontier on the south, and by lat. 55 deg. on the north, may yet be justified. The Canadian Government, Palliser's expedition, Noble's explorations, Mr. J. W. Hamilton's surveys, and a considerable number of public and private investigations conducted in the interests of politics, commerce, religion, and geographical science, have all contributed their share to our knowledge of this vast territory; and the more we know of it the more eligible it seems as a field for individual enterprise, and an area for the exercise of legitimate Imperial ambition.

From Lake Winnipeg to the highest navigable point of Red River, which flows into the lake with a course from north to south, there is a distance of 575 miles, only interrupted by some very insignificant shoals at the mouth of Goose River and the Shayenne. Red Lake River and the Assiniboina extend the area of "coast" navigable by steamers in the Red River Valley to 900 miles—much more than is enjoyed internally by the United Kingdom and France together. Throughout the districts thus permeated by navigable rivers, rye, oats, barley, potatoes, grass, and wheat, grow as well as they do in Minnesota; and to these wild regions must be added the country along the great north Saskatchewan, and even the region which lies between it and the Rocky Mountains in a northerly direction. When Mr. Taylor wrote his Report, there was no reason to believe that "an adjustment of the future relations of the British Provinces and of the American States on a basis of mutual good-will and interest" might not be practicable; but Fort Sumter changed all that, we fear, and there seems little chance of such an international compact as he anticipates for a customs and postal union. In reference to such an adjustment he says:—

"It should, at all events, stipulate that the Reciprocity Treaty, enlarged in its provisions and renewed for a long period of years, shall be extended to the Pacific Ocean, and, in connection therewith, all laws discriminating between American and foreign built vessels should be abolished, establishing freedom of navigation on all the intermediate rivers and lakes of the respective territories. Such a policy of free trade and navigation with British America would give to the United States, and especially to the western States, all the commercial advantages, without the political embarrassments, of annexation, and would, in the sure progress of events, relieve our extended northern frontier from the horrors and injuries of war between fraternal communities."

It is little to be doubted that the people of Minnesota are very well disposed to remain on friendly terms with their neighbours; but the Federal Government at Washington, no matter for what party or section it acts, must, by the very necessity of its being and conditions of power, conduct the policy of the United States in a very different spirit. It is true, our friends have, even so early, given some indications that they are prepared for eventualities.

Whilst they have not been indifferent to the erection of a military post at Pembina, some of their politicians, with a ludicrous pretence of fear from the colonists, in case of war, have called for the creation of frontier forts; and the Indians in the north-west of Minnesota, who had a reservation, are to be treated with the usual measure of justice used by the white skin in dealing with the red skin, and to be exterminated or driven into space as soon as convenient or practicable. Mr. Taylor, in reference to the existence of coal near the sources of the Saskatchewan, which is undoubted, admits the uncertainty of carboniferous strata in the ridges between the Minnesota and the Red River north of the Mississippi and Saskatchewan, though there are geological reasons to hold that they will be found there. In justice to the spirit in which this Report is conceived, I quote the concluding passages :—

"The allusion just made to the exploring expedition conducted under the authority of Canada, justifies a tribute to the zeal and intelligence with which the enterprise of an emigration and transportation route, from Fort William on the north shore of Lake Superior, to Fort Garry, is prosecuted. With the civil organisation of Central British America, a waggon road between those points, to be followed by a railroad, will receive all requisite encouragement, certainly from the Canadian Treasury, perhaps by the efficient co-operation of the Home Government. The North-west Transit Company, acting under a Canadian charter, but understood to have enlisted London capitalists, is expected to resume operations during the summer of 1860. These movements of our provincial neighbours cannot fail to influence the policy of Minnesota in favour of more satisfactory communications than we now possess between Lake Superior and the channels of the Upper Mississippi and the Red River of the north.

"I desire, in conclusion, to express my obligations to the late Executive of Minnesota, for the confidence implied by the commission, to which the foregoing is a response. Believing firmly that the prosperity and development of this State is intimately associated with the destiny of North-west British America, I am gratified to record the rapid concurrence of events which indicate that the frontier, hitherto resting upon the sources of the St. Lawrence and the Mississippi, is soon to be pushed far beyond the international frontier by the march of Anglo-Saxon civilisation."

It is indeed "a country worth fighting for;" and whether the contest be carried on by the slow processes of immigration or by the ruder agencies of neglect, the conqueror and the conquered will have reason to regard the result with very decided sentiments of joy or sorrow at no distant time. In the language of the report of the New York Chamber of Commerce—" There is in the heart of North America a distinct sub-division, of which Lake Winnipeg may be regarded as the centre. This sub-division, like the valley of the Mississippi, is distinguished for the fertility of its soil, and for the extent and gentle slope of its great plains, watered by rivers of great length, and admirably adapted for steam navigation. It has a climate not exceeding in severity that of many portions of Canada and the eastern States. It will, in all respects, compare favourably with some of the most densely peopled portions of the continent of Europe. In other words, it is admirably fitted to become the seat of a numerous, hardy, and prosperous community. It has an area equal to eight or ten first-class American States. Its great river, the Saskatchewan, carries a navigable water-line to the very base of the Rocky Mountains. It is not at all improbable that the valley of this river may yet offer the best route for a railroad to the Pacific. The navigable waters of this great sub-division interlock with those of the Mississippi. The Red River of the north, in connection with Lake Winnipeg, into which it falls, forms a navigable water-line, extending directly north and south nearly eight hundred miles. The Red River is one of the best adapted to the use of steam in the world, and waters one of the finest regions on the continent.

Between the highest point at which it is navigable, and St. Paul, on the Mississippi, a railroad is in process of construction; and when this road is completed, another grand division of the continent, comprising half a million square miles, will be open to settlement."

It would be unjust to the Hudson's Bay Company to refuse them the praise due to the efforts of their servants in exploring the vast region over which they ruled, and to the constancy with which they have resisted aggression; but as the privileges of that body have now become part of the stock-in-trade of a great mercantile association, there can be no reason for doubting that a change of policy, in consonance with the tone of the governing sentiment of the age, will take place, and that the interests of free trade, and the more extensive interests connected with Imperial and Colonial progress and with colonisation itself, will be found not incompatible. When the ichthyophilists of London betake themselves, in the leafy month of June, to Gravesend, in search of the placid turtle or the strenuous shrimp, they may be startled by the booming of guns from the bosom of the river, and by certain loud cheers from two strict-rigged craft anchored in the stream. A gaily-decked river-steamer, from the flag-staff of which flutters a hieroglyph in blue and white, with the motto, "*Pro pelle cutem,*" is lying alongside the larger of the two. On board the steamer are many sorts and conditions of men — the friends of directors, outlying members of both Houses, old salts and older commercial personages, and men wearing the bright, crisp, clean look of prosperous clerkdom. These circulate from the deck of the steamer to the broader expanse of the vessel alongside, where a stout weather-beaten crew are drawn up, listening to the recital of articles. Dipping down the companion it is probable that the visitor will find in the captain's cabin an assemblage of gentlemen, eating biscuit and drinking sherry to the health of the skipper, whilst others are peering into compartments and berths 'twixt bulkheads filled with odd merchandise, from gas-pipe-barrelled guns to needles, anchors, blankets, crinoline, and artificial flowers. They are people whom we might meet in any place in London from west to east, wearing the indescribable air of men "out for the day." On deck are some old-fashioned brass-bound boxes, inscribed " Hudson's Bay Company," guarded by very ancient and fishlike attendants, in a red and blue livery. The steamer leaves the bluff double-cased sides of the vessel for a visit to her consort, for the two ships now-a-days form the sum total of the fleet sailing annually to the Hudson's Bay settlements, where once there was a flotilla of smaller craft, dressed in all their bravery of flags, and making old Gravesend re-echo to their salvos as they went forth on that which was then a dubious and adventurous voyage. Then, after much leave-taking, and drinking of anchor cups, the steamer starts, amid the cheers of the outward-bound crew, for the Nore, to enjoy a little fresh air before she comes back to the Falcon at Gravesend, where the annual dinner is held, and where many good speeches are made and friendly sentiments expressed in support of the Hudson's Bay Company. The sagacious face of old Edward Ellice, seamed with the fine graver of thought, and plastic still as in youth, for many a long year fixed men's eyes with kindly regard; and the *mitis sapientia* of his counsels, his unrivalled tact, albeit the exquisite touch lay inside a shagreen glove, and his great ability in the conduct of affairs, gave the Company that which Rupert's charters, Charles's parchments, or prescriptive rights, never could have secured so long.

It was under Sir E. L. Bulwer's administration of foreign affairs that the most strenuous attempt was made by the Government to adjust the conflicting claims of Canada and Great Britain with those of the Hudson's Bay Company, by the decision of the Judicial Committee of Privy Council; but the Company, though always willing to enter into an arrangement with the Government for the adjustment of contending interests, uniformly and not unwisely refused to accept any arbitration or judgment involving the question of the validity of their charters. The refusal of Parliament to renew the exclusive right of trading, in 1859, and the assumption of the control of Vancouver's Island by the Crown on the expiration of the lease in the same year, were heavy blows at the vested interests of the Company, which deprived its *cessio bonorum* to the English Credit Mobilier, in 1863, of great political importance, though enormous commercial results may still be obtained from the extension of trading and from settling and gold-exploring operations. When the speedy colonisation and rapid rise of British Columbia caused some attention to be directed towards the means of getting there, and of cultivating an acquaintance promising such great advantages, and it was found that from east to west two routes were practicable, it was not surprising if jealousy and alarm were aroused because the Americans, by further representations, unhappily baseless, respecting the energy of the initiative taken by Canada and England, had first started to clear the way to the west, and to open communications with the Red River settlement, *en route*. Fort Garry, in the Selkirk settlement, was first visited by a steamer from the American post of Fort Abercrombie, in 1859. Minnesota was a State which had the advantage of a continental existence on the soil of the Great Republic. " Organised as a territory in 1849, a single decade had brought the population, the resources, and the public recognition of an American State. A railroad system, connecting the lines of the Lake States and Provinces at La Crosse with the international frontier on the Red River at Pembina, was not only projected, but had secured in aid of its construction a grant by the Congress of the United States of three thousand eight hundred and forty acres a mile, and a loan of State credit to the amount of twenty thousand dollars a mile, not exceeding an aggregate of five million dollars. Different sections of this important extension of the Canadian and American railways were under contract and in process of construction. In addition, the land surveys of the Federal Government had reached the navigable channel of the Red River; and the line of frontier settlement, attended by a weekly mail, had advanced to the same point. Thus the Government of the United States, no less than the people and authorities of Minnesota, were represented in the north-west movement."

No matter how prosperous a colony of Great Britain may be, a colony it must be so long as it is not independent. The first result of the prosperity of an American colony is its independence as a State, and its incorporation as a member of the common sovereignty.

The distinction arises from geographical considerations, but it is not the less potent—I shall not yet say, more to be regretted. The retention of Canada would be of little value to us if there were to the west of it a great and populous community, absorbing its capital, labour, and enterprise for the benefit of aliens, and if to the south there were a series of States animated by an intense *political* dislike to the mother country. But there is, as they say in Ireland, " the makings " of four free and independent States, on the American model of Ohio, in that district between the valleys of the North and South Saskatchewan. In 1858 an American writer again described the region which the British Government, the Colonial Office, and the Imperialism of bureaux, inclined to cast away without even a mess of pottage. That writer says :—

" Here is the great fact of the north-western areas of this continent. An area not inferior in size to the whole United States east of the Mississippi, which is perfectly adapted to the fullest occupation by cultivated nations, yet is almost wholly unoccupied, lies west of the 98th meridian, and above the 43rd parallel, that is, north of the latitude of Milwaukee, and west of the longitude of Red River, Fort Kearney, and Corpus Christi; or, to state the fact in another way, east of the Rocky Mountains, and west of the 98th meridian, and between the 43rd and 60th parallels, there is a productive, cultivable area of 500,000 square miles. West of the Rocky Mountains and between the same parallels, there is an area of 300,000 square miles.

" It is a great mistake to suppose that the temperature of the Atlantic coast is carried straight across the continent to the Pacific. The isothermals deflect greatly to the north, and the temperatures of the Northern Pacific are paralleled in the high temperatures in high latitudes of Western and Central Europe. The latitudes which inclose the plateaus of the Missouri and Saskatchewan, in Europe inclose the rich central plains of the Continent. The great grain growing districts of Russia lie between the 45th and 60th parallel, that is, north of the latitude of St. Paul, Minnesota, or Eastport, Maine. Indeed, the temperature in some instances is higher for the same latitudes here than in Central Europe. The isothermal of 70 deg. for the summer, which on our plateau ranges from along latitude 50 deg. to 52 deg., in Europe skirts through Vienna and Odessa in about parallel 46 deg. The isothermal of 55 deg. for the year runs along the coast of British Columbia, and does not go far from New York, London, and Sebastopol. Furthermore, dry areas are not found above 47 deg., and there are no barren tracts of consequence north of the Bad Lands and the Coteau of the Missouri; the land grows grain finely, and is well wooded. All the grains of the temperate districts are here produced abundantly, and Indian corn may be grown as high as the Saskatchewan.

"The buffalo winters as safely on the upper Athabasca as in the latitude of St. Paul, and the spring opens at nearly the same time along the immense line of plains from St. Paul to Mackenzie's River. To these facts, for which there is the authority of Blodgett's Treatise on the Climatology of the United States, may be added this, that to the region bordering the Northern Pacific, the finest maritime positions belong throughout its entire extent, and no part of the west of Europe exceeds it in the advantages of equable climate, fertile soil, and commercial accessibility of coast. We have the same excellent authority for the statement that in every condition forming the basis of national wealth, the continental mass lying westward and northward from Lake Superior is far more valuable than the interior in lower latitudes, of which Salt Lake and Upper New Mexico are the prominent known districts. In short, its commercial and industrial capacity is gigantic. Its occupation was coeval with the Spanish occupation of New Mexico and California."

The climate of this district is at least as favourable to the agriculturist as that of Kingston, Upper Canada, and is quite salubrious. Special science thus describes it:—

Professor Hind, who spent two summers in the country in charge of an expedition sent out by the Canadian Government, writes: "The basin of Lake Winnipeg extends over twenty-eight degrees of longitude, and ten degrees of latitude. The elevation of its eastern boundary, at the Prairie Portage, 104 miles west of Lake Superior, is 1480 feet above the sea, and the height of land at the Vermillion Pass is less than 5000 feet above the same level. The mean length of this great inland basin is about 920 English miles, and its mean breadth 380 miles; hence its area is approximately 360,000 square miles, or a little more than that of Canada.

"Lake Winnipeg, at an altitude of 628 feet above the sea, occupies the lowest depression of this great inland basin, covering with its associated lakes, Manitobah, Winnipegosis, Dauphin, and St. Martin, an area slightly exceeding 13,000 square miles, or nearly half as much of the earth's surface as is occupied by Ireland.

"The outlet of Lake Winnipeg is through the contracted and rocky channel of Nelson River, which flows into Hudson's Bay.

"The country, possessing a mean elevation of 100 feet above Lake Winnipeg, is very closely represented by the outline of Pembina Mountain, forming part of the eastern limit of the cretaceous series in the northwest of America.

"The area occupied by this low country, which includes a large part of the valley of Red River, the Assiniboine, and the main Saskatchewan, may be estimated at 70,000 square miles, of which nine-tenths are lakes, marsh, or surface rock of Silurian or Devonian age, and, generally so thinly covered with soil as to be unfit for cultivation, except in small isolated areas.

"Succeeding this low region there are the narrow terraces of the Pembina Mountain, which rise in abrupt steps, except in the valleys of the Assiniboine, Valley River, Swan River, and Red Deer's River, to the level of a higher plateau, whose eastern limit is formed by the precipitous escarpments of the Riding, Duck, and Porcupine Mountains, with the detached outliers, Turtle, Thunder, and Pasquia Mountains. This is the great *prairie plateau* of Rupert's Land; it is bounded towards the south-west and west by the Grand Coteau de Missouri, and the extension of the tableland between the two branches of the Saskatchewan, which forms the eastern limit of the *plains* of the north-west. The area of the prairie plateau, in the basin of Lake Winnipeg, is about 120,000 square miles; it possesses a mean elevation of 1100 feet above the sea.

"The plains rise gently as the Rocky Mountains are approached, and at their western limit have an altitude of 4000 feet above the sea level. With only a very narrow belt of intervening country, the mountains rise abruptly from the plains, and present lofty precipices that frown like battlements over the level country to the eastward. The average altitude of the highest part of the Rocky Mountains is 12,000 feet (about lat. 51 deg). The forest extends to the altitude of 7000 feet, or 2000 feet above the lowest pass.

"The *fertile belt* of arable soil, partly in the form of rich, open prairie, partly covered with groves of aspen, which stretches from the Lake of the Woods to the foot of the Rocky Mountains, averages 80 to 100 miles in breadth."

Dr. James Hector, and all the explorers, agree in their descriptions of this region. It is difficult to reach; but is it so difficult to reach as the shores of America itself were, 300, or 200, or 100 years ago? We cannot conceive what a century has done in America, or at home. How little, then, can we conjecture what the next fifty years will effect in these distant lands! The map, which now is crowded with the names of cities where red men roamed *in terra incognita* so recently as the beginning of this century, should reprove any incredulity. The nations are like water. When a country is filled above its capacity, its surplus overflows. As soon as all the eligible districts of Canada are occupied, the streams of settlers will pour westwards; tracks and roads will be made; and, if the land be good, it will soon be filled with people. As to the great regions which lie to the west, and open on the Pacific, it can only be said that they are to us what California was to the United States on the first discovery of gold; and that after fifty years they may be less than California is now, if steps be not taken to bind them up with British interests, and to oppose the Americanisation with which they are threatened. Without reference to the Far West, or the Far North-West,—without regard to the Red River and Assiniboia or to British Columbia, there is before us the great fact, that out of the Canadas, and the British North American Provinces and dependencies, can be created a powerful Confederation attached to this country, and capable of the grandest development in spite of climatic influences. We have already given a slight sketch of the extent and capability of these provinces, and hinted at the difficulties that may arise in the working of the Confederation. Canada is now more than threatened with the loss of the advantages which were supposed to depend on the Reciprocity Treaty, and Great Britain is formally warned that she must prepare to meet Federal encroachments on the Lakes. Mr. Galt, in a very elaborate speech, exhaustive of the topics connected with the financial aspect of the future Confederation, lately laid before his hearers a series of calculations which deserve close attention, and which are, we believe, entitled to full confidence. The United States at the end of the year 1865 will either have effected the subjugation of the South by the destruction of all her armies in the field, or she will see an increase to her debt of at least forty millions sterling, or she will have arranged a compromise with the South of which one feature will be the assumption of the Southern debt. In the first case, the North must prepare for a long and costly military occupation. In no case as yet have the trade and commerce of any Southern port or city subjugated and held by Union troops, paid the Federal Government for the cost of holding it. In the second case, increase of taxation must fall with such a crushing weight on the poorer classes, especially in the agricultural States, as to force many of the people to take refuge in Canada, unless deterred by unforeseen obstacles. In the third case, the immediate result will be to throw on the Northern States for some considerable period, a greater amount of debt, and of consequent derangement, than they would have been subjected to by either of the preceding conditions. There can be no just comparison between the United States and the projected Confederation, except in the ratio of taxation *per capita*. And, if we take income, expenditure, and possible debt at the end of 1865, and contrast the financial position of the British Confederate with that of the American Federalist, we will find that the advantage is decidedly on the side of the latter.

According to the Hon. A. T. Galt, the following is a fair statement of the revenue and expenditure of the provinces, of the debts and liabilities, of the trade exports and imports, and of all the assets and demands by which the future Confederation would be influenced, excluding of course the cost of such undertakings as great intercolonial roads or enlargements of canals. Mr. Galt may not be a favourite with some theorists of the Colonial Office; he certainly is not popular at Washington, and he is not more honoured at home than most prophets, but he is an able, clear-headed, trustworthy man :—

CANADA.

THE FINANCIAL POSITION OF THE PROVINCES.

	Debt, 1863.	Income, 1863.	Outlay, 1863.
Nova Scotia	$4,858,547	$1,185,629	$1,072,274
New Brunswick	5,702,991	899,991	884,613
Newfoundland (1862)	946,000	480,000	479,420
Prince Edward Island	240,673	197,384	171,718
Maritime Provinces	$11,748,211	$2,763,004	$2,608,025
Canada	67,263,994	9,760,316	10,742,807
Totals	$79,012,205	$12,523,320	$13,350,832

INCREASED REVENUES IN 1864.

Canada, without the produce of the new taxes	$1,500,000
New Brunswick	100,000
Nova Scotia	100,000
	$1,700,000
Deficit of 1863	$827,512
Surplus of 1864	872,488
	$1,700,000
Total Revenues of all the Colonies, 1864	$14,223,320
Outlay	13,350,832
Estimated Surplus	$872,488

THE POSITION OF THE CONFEDERATION, ESTIMATED ON THE BASIS OF 1864.

	Revenue now produced for General Government.	Local Revenues which would not go into the general Chest.	Subsidy to be paid to each Province.	Difference, available for the purposes of the Genl. Government.
Canada	$11,250,000	$1,297,043	$2,006,121	
Nova Scotia	1,300,000	107,000	264,000	
New Brunswick	1,000,000	89,000	264,000	
Prince Edward Island	200,000	32,000	153,728	
Newfoundland	480,000	5,000	369,000	
	$14,230,000	$1,530,043	$3,056,849	$9,643,108

	Expenditure.	Local Outlay.	Difference payable by the Genl. Government.
Canada	$9,800,000	$2,260,149	
Nova Scotia	1,222,555	667,000	
New Brunswick	834,518	424,047	
Prince Edward Island	171,718	124,016	
Newfoundland	479,000	479,000	
	$12,507,591	$3,954,212	$8,553,379

Surplus at the disposal of the General Government . . . $1,089,729

AVERAGE OF THE PRESENT TARIFFS.

Canada	20 per cent.	Newfoundland	11 per cent.
Nova Scotia	10 ,,	Prince Edward Island	10 ,,
New Brunswick	15½ ,,		

IMPORTS, EXPORTS, AND TONNAGE.

FUTURE POSITION OF THE PROVINCES.

	Local Revenues.	Estimated Outlay for 1864 under present Government.	Estimated Local Outlay under the Union.
Nova Scotia	$107,000	$667,000	$371,000
New Brunswick	89,000	404,047	353,000
Prince Edward Island	32,000	171,718	124,015
Newfoundland	5,000	479,000	250,000
	$233,000	$1,721,765	$1,098,015 ‡
Canada	1,297,043	{ * 2,021,979 { † 238,170	‡
	$1,530,043	$3,981,914	‡

* Average of the last four years.   † Interest on excess of debt.
‡ Not estimated by Mr. Galt, for reasons given in the speech.

THE AUDITOR'S STATEMENT OF THE LIABILITIES OF CANADA.

Debenture Debt, direct and indirect	$65,238,649	21
Miscellaneous liabilities	64,426	14
Common School Fund	1,181,958	85
Indian Fund	1,577,802	46
Banking Accounts	3,396,982	81
Seigniorial Tenure :—		
Capital to Seigniors $2,889,711 09		
Chargeable on Municipalities' Fund . . . 196,719 66		
On account of Jesuits' Estates . . . 140,271 87		
Indemnity to the Townships 891,500 00		
	4,118,202	62
	$75,578,022	09
Less—Sinking Funds $4,883,177 11		
Cash and Bank Accounts 2,248,891 87		
	7,132,068	98
	$68,445,953	11
From which, for reasons given in his speech, Mr. Galt deducted the Common School Fund	1,181,958	85
Leaving as Net Liabilities . .	$67,263,994	26

IMPORTS, EXPORTS, AND TONNAGE OF THE PROVINCES.

	Imports.	Exports.	Sea-going Tonnage. Inward and Outward.
Canada	$45,964,000	$41,831,000	2,133,000
Nova Scotia	10,201,391	8,420,968	1,432,954
New Brunswick	7,764,824	8,964,784	1,386,980
Prince Edward Island	1,428,028	1,627,540	No returns.
Newfoundland	5,242,720	6,002,312	,, ,,
	$70,600,963 66,846,604	$66,846,604	4,952,934 Lake Tonnage 6,907,000
Total Trade	$137,447,567	Total Tons .	11,859,934

A people of more than four millions will owe something over £13,000,000, as compared with a people of thirty millions owing £900,000,000 sterling; and with a trade of £27,000,000 a-year there is no compensating power in any commercial superiority the United States may possess to establish an equation. If the expenses of the local and of the Federal Governments be properly kept in hand, the condition of the British Confederation, in a pecuniary point of view at all events, must be infinitely better than that of the Federal Union either by itself or with the Southern States.

The Confederation which has just been proposed by delegates at Quebec, and which will come before Parliament soon after this volume escapes from the printers, vests the Executive in the Sovereign of Great Britain; a superfluous investiture, unless the delegates meant rebellion; and it provides for its administration according to the British constitution, by the Sovereign or authorised representative. It does not appear very plain how the Sovereign of a mixed monarchy with a limited franchise for the people can administer his quasi-republican and unaristocratic viceroyalty according to the principles of the British constitution; particularly, as the Sovereign or his representative is to be the Commander-in-Chief of the land and naval forces of the Confederation, which are thus expressly removed from the control of the War-Office at home. Difficulties of a merely technical character will no doubt be overcome. But the King of Great Britain and Ireland, in whom the Executive is vested, will have to deal with a Transatlantic House of Commons founded on abstract returns of population, and elected by the provinces according to their local laws; so that some members will represent universal suffrage, and others limited constituencies, which is very different indeed from the House of Commons of Great Britain and Ireland.

In the Upper House a Wensleydale peerage is reproduced. It is to consist of seventy-six members nominated by the Sovereign for life, of whom twenty-four are assigned to Upper Canada, and twenty-four to Lower Canada, ten for Nova Scotia, ten for New Brunswick, four for Newfoundland, and four for Prince Edward Island. The Lower House, far less aristocratic in its relations to Lower and Upper Canada, has eighty-two members from the latter, and sixty-five from the former, nineteen from Nova Scotia, fifteen for New Brunswick, eight for Newfoundland, and five for Prince Edward Island. "Saving the Sovereignty of England," the powers of the Federal Parliament, as enumerated under thirty-seven different heads, are very large, and on such heads as currency and coinage seem to trench on dangerous ground, and in the last head of all are dangerously vague. The appointment of the Lieutenant-Governor by the Federal Government itself is obviously open to exception, because it is anomalous; but as all the principles as well as the details of the measure will receive the most careful consideration, it is not necessary to treat the proposal as an accomplished fact, although it certainly is most desirable to treat every article with respectful attention, and to give every weight to the expressed opinion of the delegates. Among the objects specially indicated for the future action of the Confederate or Federal Government are the completion of the Intercolonial Railway from Rivière du Loup to Truro, in Nova Scotia, through the Province of New Brunswick, and the completion of communication with the North-Western territories, so as to open the trade to the Atlantic seacoast; both to be effected as soon as the Federal finances permit. Here there is the most tangible proposal for the opening up of the great regions to which I have called attention; and the Valley of the Saskatchewan is promised the facility which is alone wanting to make it the seat of a flourishing colony. When the Red River Settlement is once connected with Lake Superior, the way to the sea is open, but the advantages of access to the world will be increased enormously as soon as the railway is pushed on to the shores of Lake Huron from Nova Scotia.

So eager is one to grasp at the benefits which some such Confederation promises to confer, that the perils to the prerogative of the Crown, and to the body so formed, are apt to lie hid from view. But they must be well guarded against; and I for one am persuaded that it would be far better for us to see the Provinces of British America independent than to behold them incorporated with the Northern Republic. The greatest of all these internal perils is in the maintenance of the Local Parliaments, which may come into collision with the Federal Government on local questions impossible to foresee, or define, or adjust; but as the delegates considered the plan of a complete Legislative Union quite incompatible with the reserved rights of a portion of the Confederation, the only way left to escape the mischiefs which threaten the future life of the new body is to bind those Local Parliaments within the most narrow limits, consistent with local utility and existence.

It is not for the sake of our future connection, but

for their own integrity and happiness that such a course is recommended. They have "an awful example" at their doors. The torrents of blood which have deluged the soil of the North American Republics all welled out of the little chink in the corner-stone of the Constitution, on one side of which lay States' Rights, and on the other Federal Authority. Without some justification in law and in argument, such men as Calhoun, and Stephens, and Davis, would never have reasoned, and planned, and fought, and worked a whole people up to make war against the Union. Sad as the spectacle is of a community of freemen waging war against the principles of self-government, it must be admitted that their instinct may be sounder than their reasoning, and that they are engaged in a struggle for self-preservation, in which they have swelled their proportions into that of a gigantic despotism, but have after all attained a giant's port and strength. It is impossible to say whether the corruption which Montesquieu has declared to be the destruction of a democracy, has yet seized upon the tremendous impersonation of brute force, of unconquerable will, of passion, of lust of empire, which now rules in the Capitol, and occupies the throne whereon feebly sat heretofore the mild impuissance of the old Federal Executive; but if the pictures which have been presented to us be true, there is a prophetic meaning in the words of the philosophic Frenchman:—"Les politiques grecs, qui vivaient dans le gouvernement populaire, ne reconnaissaient d'autre force qui pût le soutenir que celle de la vertu. Ceux d'aujourd'hui ne nous parlent que des manufactures, de commerce, de finances, de richesse, et de luxe même." The giant's feet may be of clay, and his body may be of that artificial stiffening which gives to worthless stuffs a temporary substantiality, but behind the giant stand the great American people, with hands dyed in their brothers' gore, and who, having sacrificed friendship, traditions, constitution, and liberty at home, will think but little of adding to the pyre of their angry passions the peace and happiness of others.

THE END.

www.ingramcontent.com/pod-product-compliance
Lightning Source LLC
Chambersburg PA
CBHW020227240426
43672CB00006B/439